WESTERN NEVADA COMMUNITY COLLEGE

3 1439 00068 6587

WITHDRAWN

D1601637

Library & Media Services
Western Nevada Community
2201 West College Parkway
Carson City, NV 89703

Native American Literatures

CONTINUUM STUDIES IN LITERARY GENRE

Also available in this series:

Irish Fiction: An Introduction, by Kersti Tarien Powell
American Gothic Fiction: An Introduction, by Allan Lloyd-Smith

Forthcoming in this series:
Fantasy Fiction: An Introduction, by Lucie Armitt
Horror Fiction: An Introduction, by Gina Wisker
Crime Fiction: An Introduction, by Alistair Wisker
Science Fiction: An Introduction, by Pat Wheeler

WNC
PS
153
I 62
L 86
2004
JUN 14 '08

Native American Literatures: An Introduction

SUZANNE EVERTSEN LUNDQUIST

 continuum
NEW YORK • LONDON

2004

The Continuum International Publishing Group Inc
15 East 26 Street, New York, NY 10010

The Continuum International Publishing Group Ltd
The Tower Building, 11 York Road, London SE1 7NX

www.continuumbooks.com

Copyright © 2004 by Suzanne Evertsen Lundquist

All rights reserved. No part of this publication may be reproduced or
transmitted in any form or by any means, electronic or mechanical, including
photocopying, recording, or any information storage or retrieval system,
without permission in writing from the publishers or their appointed agents.

Printed in the United States of America

Library of Congress Cataloging-in-Publication Data

Lundquist, Suzanne Evertsen.
  Native American literatures : an introduction / Suzanne Evertsen Lundquist.
    p. cm. — (Continuum studies in literary genre)
  Includes bibliographical references and index.
  ISBN 0-8264-1598-9 (hardcover : alk. paper) — ISBN 0-8264-1599-7 (pbk. :
alk. paper)
  1. American literature — Indian authors — History and culture. 2. Indians
of North America — intellectual life. 3. Indians in literature. I. Title. II. Series.
  PS153.I52L86 2004
  813.009'897—dc22

                                    2004014784

Contents

Acknowledgments

This work would not be possible without the influence of Gary Witherspoon (University of Washington), Gerald Vizenor (Chippewa; Berkeley), P. Jane Hafen (Taos Pueblo; University of Nevada at Las Vegas), or Michalyn Steele (Seneca). I am also grateful to numerous Native American students whose support and conversations have informed my work over the past thirty years. Special thanks go to Abby H. P. Werlock for introducing me to David Barker and Continuum Press. From the inception of this project, Gloria Cronin (Executive Coordinator for the American Literature Association) has given me encouragement and professional feedback. As always, her mentoring is appreciated. Professors Gary Bryner and Carol Ward gave invaluable insights into the political and sociological implications of Native American Literatures. And I must confess that all I write is for my children: Jennifer, Emily, Eric, Margaret, Peter, and Jack.

Particular thanks go to Kristina Kugler for her many hours of proficient research, source checking, editing, and manuscript preparation. Thanks also go to the College of Humanities and Department of English at Brigham Young University for their generous funding for research support.

Chapter One

What Are Native American Literatures?

The plural nature of Native American literatures stems from the plurality of Native American cultures and the multiplicity of types of oral and written literature (genres) that comprise the artistic expressions of Native peoples within the United States. As a general awareness of the magnitude and complexity of this project arises, so too will the ethical, political, and aesthetic demands of this study become more obvious. Fergus M. Bordewich aptly explains the origins of this complexity:

> The continent that Christopher Columbus stumbled upon in 1492 was to Europeans, a terra incognita inhabited by a vast congeries of unknown, and virtually unknowable, peoples. There were literally thousands of distinct native societies, each with its own cosmology, each speaking a language that, as often as not, was completely incomprehensible to groups that lived just a few miles away. Few of them were organized in their modern tribal form, and fewer still were known to each other by the names that we associate with them today (33).

Generally speaking, as representatives of Spanish, French, and English governments conquered these peoples, borders and boundaries shifted and whole peoples were moved, forced to assimilate, exterminated, or suffered from warfare, slavery, disease, and uncharitable public policies.

Within North America, there are currently an estimated five hundred distinct Native American nations speaking an estimated three hundred different languages stemming from eight different language families (see Driver for information on language families; 43–44). While tribal and nontribal religious leaders, linguists, and ethnographers have attempted to preserve, promote, or reclaim Native languages and literatures since contact times, such works are traditionally studied in departments of linguistics, history, or anthropology. Post–Civil Rights tendencies have been to organize Native American Studies programs; these programs then deal with Native literatures in broader historical contexts. Yet, many such programs exist in the margins of academia. Seldom do the grand oral or written narratives of tribal people find their way into the mandatory curricula of American Literature departments—even though a vast variety of exemplary texts have been translated into or written in English. Myths, rituals, prayers, songs, oratory, folklore, legends, Trickster tales, or other Native creations aren't easily accommodated into traditional Western or Euroamerican categories of fiction, drama, and poetry.

Such exclusions, however, challenge Western and democratic claims concerning the search for truth, beauty, equality, and representation. When a full assembly of Native texts are studied, notwithstanding, students—both Native and non-Native—discover compelling alternatives to their own views of the world. Assumptions about the ethical foundations of American democracy are simultaneously challenged. Anglos often reluctantly learn that suffering, humiliation, and discrimination toward Native Nations constitutes the alternative history that is not taught against the romantic narratives of Manifest Destiny.

Although a handful of Native novelists are included in contemporary American Literature courses—N. Scott Momaday (Kiowa), Leslie Marmon Silko (Laguna Pueblo), Louise Erdrich (Ojibwa), James Welch (Blackfoot), and Gerald Vizenor (Ojibwa)—often the mythological foundations of their writings are poorly understood. This is especially true in an era when mythological criticism (a critical approach to literature related to religion, structuralism, and psychoanalytic criticism) is out of favor. And yet, one cannot understand Native American Literatures without a clear understanding of mythology. Mythographer John Bierhorst claims:

Mythology does not have the antiquity of geologic ages, but it is nevertheless a very old pattern, woven into the terrain over the course of thousands of years. Each continent—except Antartica—has its own mythological imprint and will probably never receive another, at least not in the foreseeable future. Viewed at a distance, myths create a luxuriant configuration that gradually changes from region to region. At close range, these same myths reflect the desires and fears of distinct peoples, granting them trusteeship of the land with the consent of unseen powers (2).

What Bierhorst is suggesting, then, is that there are distinct mythological maps that have guided cultures from ancient times to the present.

In more familiar terms, this means that Native Americans have their old and new testaments too. Paula Gunn Allen (Laguna Pueblo) tells us that Native mythologies ("mysticisms") are

based on a sense of propriety, an active respect for . . . Natural powers; on a ritual comprehension of universal orderliness and balance; and on a belief that a person's every action, thought, relationship, and feeling contributes to the greater good of the Universe or its suffering. Human beings are required to live in such a way that balance is maintained and furthered, and disorder (also perceived as disease) is kept within bounds (40–41).

Using the term *mythology* to describe the foundation narratives of particular Native Nations is problematic—particularly when mythologies are often thought to be fictions created by unsophisticated cultures to explain the inexplicable. From Allen's vantage point, however, mythologies house immemorial systems of belief concerning human relationships to the environment—natural (science), moral (ethics), emotional (psychology), communal (politics), and physical (including medicine). Gary Witherspoon suggests that the "emergence accounts" in the Southwest are "literal enough to provide a recognizable framework that resonates with contemporary people and are metaphorical enough not to be mistaken as solely literal representations" ("Emergence in Southwestern History" 3).

Nonetheless, mythologies are commonly treated as though they are the primary oral narratives of primitive peoples advancing toward real religion and civilization.

Another problem with traditional conceptions of mythology stems from a misunderstanding of orality. Contemporary educational systems tend to privilege written texts over oral traditions. Both are speech acts: the oral more communal, performance-oriented, and dynamic; the written more individualist, fixed, and preemptive. Numerous Native authors attempt to erase these prejudices. They also attempt a kind of orality in their prose. Gerald Vizenor (Ojibwa) refers to printed texts as *Dead Voices*, Craig Lesley calls them *Talking Leaves*, and Clifford E. Trafzer (Wyndot) introduces the designation of "paper spirits" (in *Blue Dawn, Red Earth* 6).

Will, a character from Choctaw/Cherokee/Irish novelist Louis Owen's *Nightland*, expresses the oral/print dilemma this way: "He came very early in his life to believe that the Cherokee world was made of spoken words, told into being with living breath, while the White world had been formed and imagined on pages that then waited patiently to be spoken into life." Furthermore, to Will's "young mind, it was as if the Indian world was always new, made again and again when his father or Bill's grampa told the stories, but that the White world had been formed long ago and lay there in books ready to assume the same form each and every time the pages were opened. Like the Bible" (24).

Mythologies, then, are sacred, timeless stories considered true, living, and exemplary. They explain the origins of a people—whether they emerged from the earth, descended from the skies, or migrated to their earthly habitats. Such origin narratives position peoples within their environments. For example, emergence "is foremost an experience of birth, or origin and of beginning. Emergence stories from the Southwest proclaim that all life—human, animal and plant life—[is] conceived in and born from the womb of Mother Earth. In many cases the three underworlds prior to this one are metaphorically linked to the trimesters of pregnancy and prenatal development" (Witherspoon 2). The idea of "prenatal development" also suggests that until birth into this world, all sentient beings are evolving. If creation occurs as a result of descending from the skies, such descent often suggests a separation—earth from sky, human from animal, human from the environment—and therefore the need for reconciliation through appropriate rituals and respectful behaviors. Migration narratives—looking-for-a-home stories—often suggest that peoples must struggle to find or be led to their lands of inheritance. Frequently, whole societies migrate to their acquired homelands in order to gain some ecological or psychological advantage; to flee from dangerous circumstances; or to more fully share in human communities.

Often sacred histories explain the struggles of entire peoples in their repeated attempts to overcome their own frailties. Through their journeys, they learn what constitutes exemplary behavior—learned from their own retelling of their misadventures. Frequently such behaviors are exemplified in the character of Trickster who manifests him or her self in various guises—coyote, raven, spider. Often playing the fool, Tricksters inadvertently create order out of chaos. Or Trickster's escapades mock foolish, obsessive behavior—gluttony, sexual avarice, gender arrogance, self-centeredness, ideological addiction. Through the adventures of Trickster, the contingent nature of human experience is established and invitations to appropriate behavior are made. However, because of the comic rather than tragic intention of Trickster discourse, survival in an often hostile world is made possible.

When catastrophes come upon whole peoples through their misbehavior, heroes are raised up, often as twins, to cleanse the earth from chaos. Prophetic figures also continue, through time, to call people to a remembrance of their former follies and admonish them to live the creators' will anew. Covenants are rehearsed annually through the reenactments of particularly significant sacred events. The Sun Dance among the plains Indians, the healing rituals of the Navajo, the Ritual of Condolence of the Iroquois, or the passage of seasonal rituals among the Hopi are examples of ritual reenactments of sacred stories. Maturation rituals also repeat the life-ways of sacred ancestors; naming ceremonies, adolescent rites of passage, induction into secret societies, marriages, and funerals follow instructions given by ancient sacred figures. Often, the actions of characters in contemporary fiction are generated by knowledge of *or* estrangement from sacred narratives, ceremonies, and communities. When mythologies are deemed infantile, pagan, or primitive, disassociation occurs. And despite the best efforts of "experts" from dominant cultures to bring ailing "primitives" into the body of civilized, Christian communities, sickness, sorrow, and social disorder are often the outcome.

While general introductions to singular tribal mythologies are available, much is withheld from the uninitiated. Many contemporary anthropologists respect the fact that such narratives are the property of the cultures who share them. They also recognize the right of members from those cultures to determine what can or cannot be divulged. However, this does not negate the significance of such narratives as foundational to modern Native fictions—particularly the novel. Mythographer Mircea Eliade claims that "the epic and the novel continue mythological narrative[s], though on a different plane and in pursuit of different ends" (190). Indeed, modern Native American novels are individually authored and are primarily produced for consumption by uninitiated readers—including readers from tribes outside particular narrative contexts. However, transformation of being, expanded consciousness, and greater ethical response to the Other are still desired outcomes.

Contemporary Indian poetry, according to Brian Swann, "is the poetry of historic witness" (xvii). Furthermore, claims Swann, "the Native American poet *is* his or her history, with all its ambiguities and complications." Swann likewise uses the notion of continuity in his assessment of the historical nature of Native American poetry: "the weight and consequences of . . . history make up the continuum of the present" (xviii). Native poets seem "to work from a sense of social responsibility to the group as much as from an intense individuality," says Swann. Again, myth and oral tradition are cited as the wellsprings of contemporary Native poetry: "If grandparents are physical links to the past, myth is the eternal contact," says Swann (xxix). And finally, Swann sees in Native poetry: "a desire for wholeness—for balance, reconciliation, and healing—within the individual, the tribe, the community, the nation; one sees an *insistence* on these things, on growth, on rich survival" (xxxi).

Simon J. Ortiz (Acoma Pueblo) defines another traditional Native genre, Indian Oratory. "At Acoma Pueblo meetings, you formally announce your intention to speak, and when you do so respectfully, you are recognized for what you have to offer" (xi); this includes speeches to outsiders. Individual verbal expression about tribal values, political concerns, community squabbles, and the tragic consequences of Euroamerican incursions are typical to many tribal societies. Noted Indian speeches have been collected since contact times. W. C. Vanderwerth compiled speeches by celebrated leaders such as Cornplanter (Seneca), Joseph Brant (Mohawk), Tecumseh (Shawnee), Sequoyah (Cherokee), Chief Joseph (Nez Perce), Sitting Bull (Sioux), and others in his celebrated *Indian Oratory*.

The same verbal skill demonstrated in traditional oratory has been extended to Native American autobiography and essay writing. The imposition of the category *autobiography* to denote individual expressions of life-ways is also problematic. Arnold Krupat claims that in traditional Western autobiographies, "personal accounts are strongly marked by the individual's sense of herself predominantly as different and separate from other distinct individuals." Native self-life writing, however, is "marked by the individual's sense of himself in relation to collective social units or groupings" (*Ethnocriticism* 212). Not only this, but Native autobiographers also seem to intend a kind of orality in print—the one voice sharing with community. Traditionally, Native individuals did "not tell of . . . war honors in private, to one's wives or best friends, but to assembled members of the tribe, an audience that included eyewitnesses to the events narrated who were dutybound to object to or deny any false claims" (216). The same holds true for reporting individual experiences with significant events of all kinds— including visions. Individual experience has tribal consequence. Says Krupat, Native visions aren't just for the individual nor is the vision "usable or functional until it is spoken, even performed publicly. This sense of personal eventfulness and this manner of communicating the personal orally, dramatically, performatively, in public," is extended to Native autobiographies (217).

Numerous nineteenth and early twentieth century Native American "autobiographies" chronicle various responses to the incursion of "the white man." Many autobiographies often extol the strengths of tribal life-ways while criticizing the hypocrisies of "civilized" peoples—even when the authors voluntarily participated in dominant institutions. John G. Neihardt's *Black Elk Speaks* (Sioux),

Charles Eastman's *From the Deep Woods to Civilization* (Sioux), William Apess's *The Experiences of Five Christian Indians of the Pequot Tribe* (Pequot), Gertrude Bonnin's *Impressions of an Indian Childhood* (Sioux), and Luther Standing Bear's *My People, the Sioux* (Sioux), are among the more familiar of such narratives. Arnold Krupat's *Native American Autobiography: An Anthology* and *For Those Who Come After* plus David H. Brumbles's *An Annotated Bibliography of American Indian and Eskimo Autobiographies* (with 600 titles) include famous examples, discussions of historical contexts, and the challenges to authenticity involved when Native voices are filtered through editors, translators, anthropologists, and other enthusiasts (who have their own agendas).

Contemporary Native authors have turned to *creative nonfiction* or *literary autoethnography* to express how tribal affiliation, myth, ancestry, gender, life stages, education, geographical locale, and historical moment impress their consciousness and inform their identity and works. These authors have become anthropologists of their own experience. Notwithstanding, these authors also see themselves "in relation to collective social units or groups" rather than as isolated individuals (Krupat 212). N. Scott Momaday's *The Way to Rainy Mountain* and *Names* (Kiowa), Leslie Marmon Silko's *Storyteller* (Laguna Pueblo), Janet Campbell Hale's *Bloodlines* (Coeur-d'Alene), Gerald Vizenor's *Interior Landscapes* (Ojibwa), Louise Erdrich's *The Blue Jay's Dance* (Ojibwa), Diane Glancy's *Claiming Breath* and *The Cold and Hunger Dance* (Cherokee), Carter Revard's *Family Matters, Tribal Affairs* and *Winning the Dust Bowl* (Osage), Paula Gunn Allen's *Off the Reservation* (Laguna Pueblo), and Louis Owens's *I Hear the Train* (Choctaw) are among this new genre. These works aren't *memoir* ("usually concerned with personalities and actions other than those of the writer") (Harmon and Holman 312–313), nor are they *autobiography* (as discussed above). They are works that attempt to demonstrate that the observer determines what is seen, the storyteller determines what is told, but in a nontotalizing manner. That is, these writers do not attempt to "re-present" their cultures. They are not spokespersons. They are, however, individuals whose lives are lived with enlivened and often reclaimed tribal awareness.

James Treat has identified another growing number of works that don't fit into traditional literary boundaries either within or without tribal traditions. He calls these works *Native Christian Narrative Discourse*. Treat declares:

> Oral cultures typically preserve worldview and tradition in stories, which teach through example rather than by catechism. The prominence and centrality of narrative accounts in contemporary native Christian testimony suggests that native Christians consider personal and collective experience to play a central role in the development of religious insight (13).

Native Christian Narrative Discourse is "experiential and performative; while conventional Christian theology is often dogmatic, native Christian discourse is confessional," Treat states (13). What is so challenging about this new genre is the contention that traditional testaments and gospels are not the sole possession of the Judeo/Christian/Islamic people. Nor do Jews, Christians, or Muslims have the sole authorized versions of sacred truths about a Messiah. Many of these works—by tribal members who are also Christians— show how tribal experiences with the divine can correct conceptions of Christ proffered by other world religions.

Paula Gunn Allen attempts to describe the complexity of this interactive, corrective, mythic/ritual web:

> So many stories; so many voices telling one huge, complex, multitudinous story, a story so long no single novel can encompass it, a story so vast only the concept of cycle begins to hint at its dimension, a story so complex that only the greatest variety of devices, techniques, points of view, styles, and stances can justly reflect its infinite glittering facets, plumb its mysterious multitude of tunnels and hidden corridors—so many stories a teacher of American Literature is hard put to know where to begin or how to proceed in the face of such vastness (146).

Allen concludes that the stories of cultures that act together become part of larger stories—merging, enfolding, and offering a consciousness of the interrelatedness of peoples and places on this planet. And yet, the differences matter, and matter dramatically. It is in their tribal/individual particularity that Native writers contribute to the world's body of artistic expressions. Furthermore, Native genres oftentimes collapse familiar boundaries between history, anthropology, religion, and literature. Such erasures, in the name of beauty, constitute an alternative aesthetic.

Works Cited

Allen, Paula Gunn, *Off the Reservation* (Boston: Beacon Press, 1998).

Bierhorst, John, *The Mythology of North America* (New York: William Morrow, 1985).

Bordewich, Fergus M., *Killing the White Man's Indian* (New York: Anchor Books, 1997).

Driver, Harold E., *Indians of North America* (Chicago: University of Chicago Press, 1972).

Eliade, Mircea, *Myth and Reality* (New York: Harper and Row, 1975).

Harmon, William and C. Hugh Holman, *A Handbook to Literature* (Upper Saddle River, NJ: Prentice Hall, 2000).

Ortiz, Simon J., "Introduction," in *Speaking for the Generations*, Simon J. Ortiz, ed. (Tucson: University of Arizona Press, 1998).

Owens, Louis, *Nightland* (Norman: University of Oklahoma Press, 1996).

Krupat, Arnold, *Ethnocriticism* (Berkeley: University of California Press, 1992).

Swann, Brian, "Introduction: Only the Beginning," *Harper's Anthology of 20th Century Native American Poetry*, Duane Niatum, ed. (San Francisco: HarperSanFrancisco, 1988).

Trafzer, Clifford E., "Introduction," *Earth Song, Sky Spirit*, Clifford Trafzer, ed. (New York: Doubleday, 1993).

Treat, James, *Native and Christian* (New York: Routledge, 1996).

Witherspoon, Gary, "Emergence in Southwestern History," in unpublished manuscript.

Chapter Two

Timeline

This timeline includes only those events and works mentioned in this book.

* = work by a non-Native

1830	**The Indian Removal Act**
1831–1838	**The Trail of Tears**
1833	*The Experiences of Five Christian Indians of the Pequot Tribe*, William Apess (Pequot)
1854	*The Life and Adventures of Joaquin Murietta, the Celebrated California Bandit*, John Rollin Ridge (Cherokee)
1864–1868	**The Long Walk of the Navajo**
1876	**Battle of the Little Bighorn**
1885	**The Major Crimes Act**
1887	**Dawes Act (Allotment)**
1890	**Wounded Knee Massacre**
1890–1925	**Wounded Knee Era**
1891	*Wynema: A Child of the Forest*, S. Alice Callahan (Creek)
1899	*Queen of the Woods*, Simon Pokagon (Potawatomi)
1900	*Impressions of an Indian Childhood*, Gertrude Bonnin (Sioux)
1902	*Indian Boyhood*, Charles Eastman (Sioux)

1911	*The Soul of the Indian*, Charles Eastman (Sioux)
1916	*Deep Woods to Civilization*, Charles Eastman (Sioux)
1918	*American Indian Magazine*
1924	The Indian Citizen Act
1925–1961	Modernism
1927	*Cogewea: The Half-Blood*, Mourning Dove (Okanagon/Colville)
1928	*My People, the Sioux*, Luther Standing Bear (Sioux)
1932	*Black Elk Speaks*, John G. Neihardt*; *Wah'Kon-Tah: The Osage and the White Man's Road*, John Joseph Mathews (Osage)
1934	The Indian Reorganization Act; *Sundown*, John Joseph Mathews (Osage)
1935	*Brothers Three*, John Milton Oskison (Cherokee)
1936	*The Surrounded*, D'Arcy McNickle (Cree/Metis/Salish)
1946	The Indian Claims Commission Act
1953	The Termination Act
1954	*Runner in the Sun: A Story of Indian Maize*, D'Arcy McNickle (Cree/Metis/Salish)
1956	The Relocation Act
1961–1973	Civil Rights Era
1969	Native American Renaissance; *House Made of Dawn*, N. Scott Momaday (Kiowa); *The Way to Rainy Mountain*, N. Scott Momaday (Kiowa); *Custer Died for Your Sins*, Vine Deloria, Jr. (Sioux)
1970	*We Talk, You Listen*, Vine Deloria, Jr. (Sioux)
1973	Wounded Knee II
1973–present	Postmodernism

1974	*Winter in the Blood,* James Welch (Blackfoot); *Behind the Trail of Broken Treaties,* Vine Deloria, Jr. (Sioux); *American Indian Culture and Research Journal; American Indian Quarterly*
1976	*Names,* N. Scott Momaday (Kiowa)
1977	*Ceremony,* Leslie Marmon Silko (Laguna Pueblo)
1978	**The American Indian Religious Freedom Act;** *Wind from the Enemy Sky* (published posthumously), D'Arcy McNickle (Cree/Metis/Salish); *The White Man's Indian,* Robert F. Berkhofer, Jr.*
1979	*The Death of Jim Loney,* James Welch (Blackfoot)
1981	*Storyteller,* Leslie Marmon Silko (Laguna Pueblo); *An Annotated Bibliography of American Indian and Eskimo Autobiographies,* David H. Brumbles (Sioux)
1984	*Love Medicine,* Louise Erdrich (Ojibwa)
1985	*Wicazo Sa Review*
1986	*Fools Crow,* James Welch (Blackfoot); *The Beet Queen,* Louise Erdrich (Ojibwa); *The Sacred Hoop: Recovering the Feminine in American Indian Traditions,* Paula Gunn Allen (Laguna Pueblo)
1987	*The Jailing of Cecelia Capture,* Janet Campbell Hale (Coeur d'Alene); *I Tell You Now,* Brian Swann and Arnold Krupat, eds.*; *Survival This Way,* Joseph Bruchac (Abenaki)
1988	*Indian Givers: How the Indians of the Americas Transformed the World,* Jack Weatherford*; *Harpers Anthology of 20th Century Native American Poetry,* Duane Niatum, ed. (S'Klallam)
1989	*The Voice in the Margin: Native American Literature and the Canon,* Arnold Krupat*; *Spider Woman's Granddaughters: Traditional Tales and Contemporary Writing by Native American Women,* Paula Gunn Allen (Laguna Pueblo)

1990 *Bearheart: The Heirship Chronicles*, Gerald Vizenor (Ojibwa); *Interior Landscapes: Autobiographical Myths and Metaphors*, Gerald Vizenor (Ojibwa); *Indian Lawyer*, James Welch (Blackfoot); *Mean Spirit*, Linda Hogan (Chicksaw); *The Ancient Child*, N. Scott Momaday (Kiowa); *Medicine River*, Thomas King (Cherokee/Greek/German)

1991 *Almanac for the Dead*, Leslie Marmon Silko (Laguna Pueblo); *Wolfsong*, Louis Owens (Choctaw); *Heirs of Columbus*, Gerald Vizenor (Ojibwa); *Talking Leaves*, Craig Lesley*; *Wounds Beneath the Flesh*, Maurice Kenny, ed. (Mohawk); *Grandmothers of Light: A Medicine Woman's Source Book*, Paula Gunn Allen (Laguna Pueblo)

1992 *The Sharpest Sight*, Louis Owens (Choctaw); *Claiming Breath*, Diane Glancy (Cherokee); *Ethnocriticism*, Arnold Krupat*; *Other Destinies: Understanding the American Indian Novel*, Louis Owens (Choctaw)

1993 *Bloodlines*, Janet Campbell Hales (Coeur d'Alene); *Earth Song, Sky Spirit*, Clifford E. Trafzer (Wyndot); *Tracks*, Louise Erdrich (Ojibwa); *God is Red*, Vine Deloria, Jr. (Sioux); *Sáanii Dahataal: The Women Are Singing*, Luci Tapahonso (Navajo) [poetry/prose]; *Green Grass, Running Water*, Thomas King (Cherokee/Greek/German)

1994 *Bone Game*, Louis Owens (Choctaw); *The Bingo Palace*, Louise Erdrich (Ojibwa); *Grand Avenue*, Greg Sarris (Miwok/Pomo); *Native American Autobiography: An Anthology*, Arnold Krupat*; *Coming to Light: Contemporary Translations of the Native Literatures of North America*, Brian Swann*; *Killing Custer: The Battle of the Little Bighorn and the Fate of the Plains Indians*, James Welch (Blackfoot)

1995	*Dwellings,* Linda Hogan (Chicksaw); *Solar Storms,* Linda Hogan (Chicksaw); *The Blue Jay's Dance,* Louise Erdrich (Ojibwa); *Red Earth, White Lies,* Vine Deloria, Jr. (Sioux); *The Book of Medicines,* Linda Hogan (Chicksaw)
1996	*Blue Dawn, Red Earth,* Clifford E. Trafzer (Wyndot); *Nightland,* Louis Owens (Choctaw); *Tales of Burning Love,* Louise Erdrich (Ojibwa); *Reservation Blues,* Sherman Alexie (Spokane/Coeur d'Alene); *For Those Who Come After,* Arnold Krupat*; *The Woman Who Fell From the Sky,* Joy Harjo (Muskogee) [poetry]
1997	*Blue Horses Rush In,* Luci Tapahonso (Navajo) [poetry]
1998	*Antelope Wife,* Louise Erdrich (Ojibwa); *Family Matters, Tribal Affairs,* Carter Revard (Osage); *Indian Killer,* Sherman Alexie (Spokane/Coeur d'Alene); *Power,* Linda Hogan (Chicksaw); *Watermelon Nights,* Greg Sarris (Miwok/Pomo); *The Cold and Hunger Dance,* Diane Glancy (Cherokee); *Bloodlines: Odyssey of a Native Daughter,* Janet Campbell Hale (Coeur d'Alene); *Man Made of Words,* N. Scott Momaday (Kiowa); *Mixedblood Messages: Literature, Film, Family, Place,* Louis Owens (Choctaw); *Natives and Academics,* Paula Gunn Allen (Laguna Pueblo); *Speaking for the Generations,* Simon Ortiz (Acoma Pueblo)
1999	*Dark River,* Louis Owens (Choctaw); *Garden in the Dunes,* Leslie Marmon Silko (Laguna Pueblo); *Truth and Bright Water,* Thomas King (Cherokee/Greek/German); *Postindian Conversations,* Gerald Vizenor (Ojibwa); *Red on Red, Native American Literary Separatism,* Craig Womack (Cherokee); *Between Earth and Sky: Legends of Native American Sacred Places,* Joseph Bruchac (Abenaki) [poetry]; *Men on the Moon,* Simon Ortiz (Acoma Pueblo)

2000
: *The Heartsong of Charging Elk,* James Welch (Blackfoot); *The Toughest Indian in the World,* Sherman Alexie (Spokane/Coeur d'Alene); *All My Sins are Relatives,* W.S. Penn (urban mixed-blood); *Roads of My Relations,* Devon Abbot Mihesuah (Choctaw); *Nothing But the Truth: An Anthology of Native American Literature,* John L. Purdy and James Ruppert, eds.*; *Postethnic America: Beyond Multiculturalism,* David Hollinger*

2001
: *The Last Report on the Miracles at Little No Horse,* Louise Erdrich (Ojibwa); *Winning the Dust Bowl,* Carter Revard (Osage); *Anti-Indianism in Modern America,* Elizabeth Cook-Lynn (Sioux); *I Hear the Train: Reflections, Inventions, Refractions,* Louis Owens (Choctaw); *Winning the Dust Bowl,* Carter Revard (Osage) [poetry]; *From Sand Creek,* Simon Ortiz (Acoma Pueblo) [poetry]; *Sacred Lands of Indian America,* Jake Page, editor*; *Drowning in Fire,* Craig S. Womack (Creek)

2002
: *Skins,* Adrian C. Louis (Paiute); *The Last of the Ofos,* Geary Hobson (Cherokee-Quapa/Chikasaw); *red matters,* Arnold Krupat*; *Out There Somewhere,* Simon Ortiz (Acoma Pueblo)[poetry]

2003
: *The Master Butchers Singing Club,* Louise Erdrich (Ojibwa); *Ten Little Indians,* Sherman Alexie (Spokane/Coeur d'Alene)

Chapter Three

How to Read Native American Literatures

Traditional oral as well as individually authored works of Native American Literature are more profitably read within cultural and/or historical contexts. This means that the *Night Chant* of the Navajo is more clearly understood when positioned within Navajo cosmology. Or that Chickasaw Indian Linda Hogan's Pulitzer Prize-nominated novel *Mean Spirit* is more accessible when read as a literary study of the tragic consequences of the Dawes Act of 1887 (allotting 160 acres of private lands to individual Indians) on Native Americans during the early-twentieth century oil boom in Oklahoma. Discussions of Native works also become more profitable when informed by the centuries-old conflicts between Native Americans and Whites stemming back to contact times. In general, Whites have imposed images, policies, wars, and religious and economic practices on tribal peoples to the advantage of Whites and the disadvantage of Natives. In contemporary literary terms, Whites, Euroamericans, or Anglos *colonized* the Natives.

In his journal dated October 12, 1492, Christopher Columbus suggests that indigenous peoples "should be good servants and of quick intelligence, since I see that they very soon say all that is said to them, and I believe that they would easily be made Christians, for it appeared to me that they had no creed." Columbus believed not only that these people had no creed but also had no language. "Our Lord willing, at the time of my departure I will bring back six of them to Your Highnesses, that they may learn how to talk" (5). Columbus's goal was India, so the peoples on this newly "discovered" continent collectively became known as Indians. Such impressions of indigenous peoples continued in Europe, among serious intellectuals, for many centuries. For example, in his famous essay "Of Cannibals," first published in 1580, Frenchman Michel D. Montaigne uses his discussion of Native cultures to criticize corruptions in European societies. His image of Native peoples divests from them all civilized qualities. For Montaigne, indigenous people lived in "a state of purity," without literature, mathematics, political rivalries, slavery, social classes, or unemployment (1128). These peoples were also without clothes, agriculture, or metallurgy of any kind. While they did practice a pure kind of religion, in Montaigne's estimation, their military practices led to some barbarism: they ate their enemy captives—hence the title of his essay. However, this "barbarity" was innocent and nothing compared to the "barbarity" of Europeans.

Shakespeare's discussion of "discovery politics" found in *The Tempest* (published 1611) is more critically aware than either Columbus or Montaigne. Prospero's control over Caliban, the *native* on the island that Prospero inhabits, is brought into serious question. Incidentally, Caliban's name is an anagram—a transposition of the letters in Montaigne's cannibal. Even though Caliban learns language (his speeches are often the most poetic in the play), he is denied full citizenship in Prospero's enchanted kingdom primarily because Caliban wants to reproduce offspring off of Prospero's daughter. It is only after Prospero mends his own heart that Caliban is given back governance of his own life and lands. And yet, this Caliban is often characterized as a subhuman unable to learn the finer sentiments that lead to forgiveness, repentance, and reconciliation. Even John Milton, in his grand Christian epic *Paradise Lost* (published 1667), casts the *Indians* that Columbus found as living in a condition of innocence found only before the fall of man. In Milton's cosmology, this kind of innocence, regrettably, also has no access to redemption (Book 9). Milton's Natives possess a primitive kind of goodness; they are without a knowledge of good and evil, and, therefore, without ability to reason their way to real goodness. Primitive goodness, then, is often construed as savage, heathen, or limited. Without Christian or Western consciousness, primitive goodness can lead to childlike aggression, licentiousness, or violence —hence the label "noble savage."

Robert F. Berkhofer, Jr. criticizes this kind of thinking in *The White Man's Indian*. Claims Berkhofer:

> Whether describing physical appearance or character, manners or morality, economy or dress, housing or sexual habits, government or religion, Whites overwhelmingly measure the Indian as a general category against those beliefs, values, or institutions they most cherished in themselves at the time. For this reason, many commentators on the history of White Indian imagery see Europeans and Americans as using counterimages of themselves to describe Indians and the counterimages of Indians to describe themselves (27).

In other words, Whites often engage in bipolar thinking with regard to Native Americans. And as Postmodern thinkers have clearly demonstrated, the first word in any binary is often the privileged one or, in other words, reflects the purposes of the creators of those binaries: civilized/uncivilized; Christian/heathen; reason/passion; free/bound; enlightened/ignorant; progressive/regressive; domestic/wild, hardworking/indolent, and so forth, would cast Europeans or Euroamericans in good standing. However, when using Indians as models of natural goodness, binaries might appear in such dualities as pure/defiled; spiritual/carnal; instinctual/political; natural/contrived; and so forth. Such categories are shown to have been used, however, to call "civilized" people to repentance rather than to actually celebrate Indian character.

In describing attitudes of the early Puritans toward the Indians, Berkhofer shows how groups of people in the Americas "used" or produced images of Natives to suit their own purposes.

> In this drama the Puritans saw themselves as the chosen of the Lord for the special purpose of bringing forth a New Zion, and those who fled from England to the shores of North America believed they had founded just such a holy commonwealth as God wished. The Native Americans, therefore, held meaning for Puritans in terms of the larger drama and the vision of their own place in it. . . . When the Indian helped the early settlers in New England, he became an agent of the Lord sent to succor the Puritan devout; when

he fought or frightened the Puritans, he assumed the aspect
of his master Satan and became one of his agents (81).

Berkhofer's book is full of similar examples of images produced by
politicians, scientists, and creative writers. Inevitably, the notion that
Natives were on the first rung of evolutionary processes became a
predominant belief. Says Berkhofer, "Beneath both the good and bad
images used by explorer, settler, missionary, and policy maker alike
lay the idea of Indian deficiency that assumed . . . Whites do something to or for Indians to raise them to European standards" (119).

One of the most damaging binaries to date has been the one that
produced the notion that while the "Old World" was full of worthy
poor people living under social repression, the "New World" was
empty and ready to receive immigrants into a land of promise—a
new Eden. This idea, that the "New World" was virtually uninhab-
ited before contact times, has been persistent. Peter Nabokov
reports that when Ronald Reagan was running for president, someone asked him what famous peoples' lives he would like to have
lived. "Reagan confessed to being 'fascinated by those who saw this
new world—Cortes, Lewis and Clark, Father Serra—when it was
virtually untouched by man'" (405).

Scholars have long debated the numbers of Natives living in this
hemisphere at contact times. In his essay "1491" in the March 2002
edition of *The Atlantic*, Charles C. Mann supplies a compelling
analysis of pre-Columbian populations and cultural productivity
in the Western Hemisphere. Mann demonstrates not only that
"Columbus set foot in a hemisphere thoroughly dominated by
humankind" (42), but that historians have often estimated populations based on political expediency—wanting numbers to be low to
avert the guilt accompanied by behaviors uncharacteristic of true
Christian members of a fledgling democracy. And yet, contemporary scholarship shows undisputedly that populations were very
high.

The most disturbing analysis presented to date is Henry F.
Dobyns's 1966 article in *Current Anthropology*, "Estimating Aboriginal American Population: An Appraisal of Techniques with a New
Hemispheric Estimate." Dobyns's research suggests that there were
between "ninety to 112 million people" living in this hemisphere

before 1491 (43). Dobyns proposes that European diseases—smallpox, typhus, influenza, diphtheria, and measles— spread before explorers, ravaging Native inhabitants of this continent, decimating millions. "Dobyns estimated that in the first 130 years of contact about 95 percent of the people in the Americas died—the worst demographic calamity in recorded history" (Mann 44). Many have challenged Dobyns's numbers, but few dispute the impact of pathogens on human and animal populations in the New World. Mann, in summarizing the research of Elizabeth Fern, says "whether one million or ten million or 100 million died, she believes, the pall of sorrow that engulfed the hemisphere was immeasurable. Languages, prayers, hopes, habits, and dreams—entire ways of life hissed away like steam" (46).

In "The Demography of Native North America: A Question of American Indian Survival," Lenore A. Stiffarm (Gros Ventre) and Phil Lane, Jr. (Yankton Sioux/Chickasaw) also investigate precontact demographics—including Dobyns's speculations. For Stiffarm and Lane:

> it seems appropriate to follow author Kirkpatrick Sale in suggesting that a precontact North American Indian population of fifteen million is perhaps the best and most accurate 'working number' available to us. Of this total, it follows (based upon Dobyns' proportional calculations) about twelve million resided within the present borders of the United States (27–28).

Stiffarm and Lane suggest that decimation by disease has often been "treated by conventional anthropologists and historians as a sort of 'natural disaster,' induced but never intended by Europeans" (32). Stiffarm and Lane, however, provide ample evidence that this was not always the case.

"Biological warfare" was often used against Native populations throughout the early history of North America. The King Philip's War (1675–1676) between "British colonists and the Wampanoag and Narragansett nations . . . appears to have been fought, in part, because the Indians were convinced the colonials had deliberately spread disease among them" (32). Sir Jeffrey Amherst advised one of his subordinates, Bouguet, to send smallpox among Pontiac's confederation of Ottawas. Bouquet responded: "I will try to [contaminate] them with some blankets that may fall into their hands, and take care not to get the disease myself" (Stiffarm and Lane 32). This strategy worked: an estimated 100,000 people "among the Mingo, Delaware, Shawnee, among other nations of the Ohio river" died of disease, "bringing about the collapse of Pontiac's military alliance" (32). According to Russel Thornton, similar strategies were used among the Iroquois, Cherokees, Mandans, Blackfoot, Piegans, Bloods, Pawnee, Airkara, Osage, Crow, Dakota, Assiniboin, Choctaw, Kiowa, Apache, Gros Ventre, Winnebago, Comanche and so forth—often destroying up to half or all of these tribal populations (Stiffarm and Lane 33). Justification for such practices often came under the guise that Natives were a threat to colonization or Western expansion—an idea labeled Manifest Destiny.

Glen T. Morris (Shawnee), director of the Fourth World Center for Study of Indigenous Law and Politics at the University of Colorado at Denver, says that under the philosophy of Manifest Destiny, "Americans believed that through divine ordination and natural superiority of the white race, they had a right (and indeed an obligation) to seize and occupy all of North America." Morris notes an early claim by Senator Thomas Hart Benton (1846) that Euroamericans "had alone received the divine command to subdue and replenish the earth . . . according to the intentions of the Creator." Morris further substantiates the political sanction for this philosophy by quoting a speech made before the United States Congress in 1880:

> Congress must apprise the Indian that he can no longer stand as a breakwater against the constant tide of civilization. . . . An idle and thriftless race of savages cannot be permitted to stand guard at the treasure vaults of the nation which hold our gold and silver. . . . [T]he prospector and miner may enter, and by enriching himself, enrich the nation and bless the world by the result of his toil (Morris 67).

The desire for Indian lands, resources, and complete obedience can be exemplified by numerous political and military efforts to "remove" whole tribes to "Indian Territory" or reservations.

The Indian Removal Act (1830), for example, forced the Five Civilized Tribes—Cherokees, Chickasaws, Choctaws, Creeks, and Seminoles—from their tribal lands in the southeastern part of the United States to Indian Territory (Oklahoma). Although these tribes had education systems, modern housing, and advanced government systems, their lands were desired by Euroamericans. The journeys of these tribes (from 1831 to 1838) were scarred by disease, starvation, and exhaustion; thousands died en route and others after arrival. This "removal" is known as the Trail of Tears. When Indians resisted this removal, they were rounded up into "concentration camps." The Long Walk of the Navajo (1864–1868) occurred when Kit Carson mounted a campaign to destroy Navajo agricultural productivity. Nine thousand Navajos surrendered and were herded together at Fort Defiance in Arizona, then marched to a concentration camp for captive Indians at Bosque Redondo in Santa Fe—a march of three hundred miles. Thirty-five hundred died during captivity (Stiffarm and Lane 34). Because Chief Joseph and many of his people refused to live on reservations outside their traditional lands, the Nez Perce war of 1877 resulted. For four months, Chief Joseph's people eluded the military in their attempt flee to the borders of Canada and freedom. Hunger, winter weather, exhaustion, and death finally allowed military troops to defeat the Nez Perce, just a few miles from the Canadian border. Between 1855 and 1893, the Nez Perce lands were reduced from 7.5 million to 7, 500 acres (Slickpoo 432). Chief Joseph, despite a lengthy and famous campaign, was never able to regain habitation in the Wallowa Valley (Idaho) for himself or his people.

Other famous military campaigns abound in the annals of the United States history against Native Americans: *massacres* abound —at Wounded Knee, Sand Creek, Washita River, Blue River, Sappa Creek, Bear River, and elsewhere. M. Annette Jaimes (Juaneno/ Yaqui) claims that "Although contemporary history holds no shortage of genocidal examples to which the U.S. destruction of its indigenous population might be in some ways compared . . . the closest parallel is that of the campaigns of Nazi Germany against the Slavic peoples to its east, and against the Jews and Gypsies, during the 1940s" (3). Stiffarm and Lane record whole tribes who were brought to extinction (34–39). Is it any wonder that Professor Jack D. Forbes (Powhatan-Renápe/Delaware-Lenape) of the University of California at Davis claims:

> The Indians are a looking-glass into the souls of North Americans. If we want to dissect the Anglo and analyze his character we must find out what he does when no one else cares, when no one is in a position to thwart his will—when he can do as he pleases. And with the Indian the Anglo has done what he pleased, with no one to care, and with the Indian ultimately too weak to resist, except passively (3).

Many Native writers recount such historical realities in their writings.

The relationship between law and literature is intimate: the first generating endless examples for the latter. Among the laws frequently referred to in Native literature are *The Indian Removal Act* (1830), *The Major Crimes Act* (1885), *The General Allotment Act* (1887), *The Indian Citizen Act* (1924), *The Indian Reorganization Act* (1934), *The Indian Claims Commission Act* (1946), *The Termination Act* (1953), *The Relocation Act* (1956), and *The American Indian Religious Freedom Act* (1978). In historical order, these laws relocated Indian tribes from their immemorial lands to "Indian Territory" in Oklahoma; imposed American ideologies onto tribal governments; allotted communal lands to individual members of tribes—making such lands taxable and unallocated lands open to homesteaders; granted U.S. citizenship to Native Americans against the will of many; patterned tribal governments after colonial government systems; terminated numerous Indian nations' sovereignty; and relocated individual tribal members to urban centers in order to assimilate them.

Honorable Anglos have fought against immoral colonial practices. For example, *The Indian Claims Commission Act* and *The American Indian Religious Freedom Act* were instigated to legislate reparations for the illegal seizure of lands and the banning of tribal religions. And yet, monetary compensation for lost lands is not just compensation, nor can legal recognition of Native religious freedoms alone reform the prejudices of the masses.

Literally hundreds of Native writers have gained recognition in Native and national literary circles. And they have written about the above Indian/White relations in a compelling fashion—thus bringing the underbelly of U.S. history into the consciousness of many readers. Nevertheless, Native Americans, in general, cannot be said to have yet gained Postcolonial status. Arnold Krupat explains:

> contemporary Native American literatures cannot quite be classed among the postcolonial literature of the world for the simple reason that there is not yet a 'post-' to the colonial status of native Americans. Call it domestic imperialism or internal colonialism; in either case, a considerable number of Native people exist in conditions of politically sustained subalternity.

Krupat supports his assertions by noting the actual conditions of many tribal peoples:

> Indians experience twelve times the U.S. national rate of malnutrition, nine times the rate of alcoholism, and seven times the rate of infant mortality; as of the early 1990s, the life expectancy of reservation-based men was just over forty-four years, with reservation-based women enjoying, on average, a life-expectancy of under forty-seven years (30).

Numerous questions abound. How can award-winning Native literary works reach larger audiences and, thereby, raise consciousness? Can raised consciousness also raise the standard of living of Native peoples? Can and should there be a relationship between literary theory, art, and life? And what will it take for the general populace to recognize both the worth and contributions of Native cultures?

Native and non-Native linguists, anthropologists, politicians, literary theorists, and other professionals have provided readers with ample information that revises long-held erroneous images of Natives. Felix Cohen, for example, turns the table on the rhetoric of "civilizing the Native" in his essay "Americanizing the White Man." In his article, Cohen asserts that "few Americans, and fewer Europeans, realize that America is not just a pale reflection of

Europe—that what is distinctive about America is Indian, through and through" (316). Cohen begins with the not-so-threatening contributions of Natives to American culture: "chewing gum, rubber balls, popcorn and cornflakes, flapjacks and maple syrup." Then his argument builds. "Four-sevenths of our national farm produce is of plants domesticated or created by Indian botanists of pre-Columbian times . . . corn, tobacco, white and sweet potatoes, beans, peanuts, tomatoes, pumpkins, chocolate, American cotton, and rubber" (317).

Examples of Native American contributions to medicine, law, government, and even sports constitute the major portion of Cohen's essay. But it is in the assertion that "those accustomed to the histories of the conqueror will hardly be convinced, though example be piled on example, that American democracy, freedom, and tolerance are more American than European and have deep aboriginal roots in our land" (322), that Cohen's article is most startling. Yet, Amerigo Vespucci, Benjamin Franklin, and Thomas Jefferson are cited to substantiate Cohen's claims. It is from the Iroquois Confederacy that many fundamental principles of American democracy stem.

Official recognition of the Iroquois contribution to the U.S. Constitution came on October 4, 1988, when the U.S. House of Representatives passed House Congressional Resolution 331: "To acknowledge the contribution of the Iroquois Confederacy of nations to the development of the United States Constitution and to reaffirm the continuing government-to-government relationship between Indian tribes and the United States established in the Constitution" (reprinted in Utter 434–435). Jack Weatherford's *Indian Givers: How the Indians of the Americas Transformed the World* (1988) contains numerous chapters outlining various contributions of Native cultures to mainstream American life. However, he ends with the question: "When Will America Be Discovered?"—a question that he answers, "America has yet to be discovered" (255).

Certainly, many resist the claims that Weatherford makes. Even when noted scholars make breakthroughs with their works, audiences often can't grasp the significance of many assertions. Noted folklorist Barre Toelken suggests: "We must seek to understand the metaphor of the native American, and we must be willing to witness to the validity of its sacred function, or else we should not pretend to be discussing this religion [system of beliefs]." Cultural metaphors shape individual and collective assumptions about the way the world operates. Toelken suggests that in technological cultures "there has been a tremendous stress on lineal patterning and lineal measurements, grid patterns, straight lines." One of the West's controlling metaphors is the line: "We have to put things 'in order.' And so we not only put our filing cases and our books in straight lines and alphabetical 'order,' we also put nature in straight lines and grid patterns—our streets, our houses, our acreage, our lives, our measurement of time and space, our preference for the shortest distance between two points, our extreme interest in being 'on time'" (15–16). What is most revealing about controlling metaphors, however, is that no other way of conceiving the world occurs to us; we believe that our metaphors accurately describe the way things are. But other cultures have different controlling metaphors. The Navajo, for example, "have the tendency to recreate the pattern of the circle at every level of the culture, in religion as well as in social intercourse." The reason for this, Toelken explains, "is the concept that reciprocation is at the heart of everything going on in the world" (17). What exists, exists in relationship, in wholeness—best symbolized by the circle or sphere. While Toelken's essay is about Navajo culture, his assertions apply to other Native cultures. To know a culture "requires the learning of a whole new set of concepts, codes, patterns, and assumptions," says Toelken (23).

What, then, is the value of learning other "concepts, codes, patterns, and assumptions"? Perhaps an example from Hopi culture might serve to illustrate. Linguist Benjamin Lee Whorf studied the Hopi language, among others, and concluded that the language a person speaks determines the world they inhabit—what a person sees, hears, thinks, and believes is primarily shaped by language. The Hopi talk about events in ways that include both space and time—two of the primary coordinates of modern physics. In his forward to Whorf's book, *Language, Thought, and Reality*, Stuart Chase suggests, that "Properly to understand Einstein's relativity, a Westerner must abandon his spoken tongue and take to the language of calculus." But a Hopi, Whorf implies, has "a sort of calculus built into him" (viii). Why, then, one might ask, didn't the Hopi develop quantum physics? Because their myth/history warns them against such endeavors. In their prehistory, progress, development, materialism, overconsumption of goods, pride in advanced weaponry, architecture, and immoral practices led the Hopi people to their destruction. Human responses to progress brought about contention, warfare, loss of family life, and emotional starvation—states of being that traditional Hopis don't want to reexperience.

Gary Witherspoon's *Language and Art in the Navajo Universe*, nominated for a Pulitzer, also demonstrates other ways of seeing. Witherspoon says, "Whereas the major motivation of [his] book is to bring the Navajo world closer and make it more intelligible to non-Navajos, another purpose is to illustrate what Navajo thought and art have to offer philosophy and art in general" (11). Witherspoon's analysis of the key phrase in Navajo ritual and cosmology demonstrates that "Positive health for the Navajo involves a proper relationship to everything in one's environment, not just the correct functioning of one's physiology"(24). Demonstrating how this "proper relationship" can be accomplished and maintained is the achievement of this text. In a society that views individualism as the primary foundation of the pursuit of happiness, Witherspoon's text offers compelling alternatives. Again, Witherspoon explains that "*In the Navajo view of the world, language is not a mirror of reality; reality is a mirror of language*" (34). Witherspoon tells us that ritual language (the language of performed sacred narratives) "commands, compels, organizes, transforms, and restores. It disperses evil, reverses disorder, neutralizes pain, overcomes fear, eliminates illness, relieves anxiety, and restores order, health, and well-being" (34). And such restoration includes the entire environment—not just the individual patient.

Washington Matthews, a Civil War surgeon who worked among the Navajo, took the time to learn Navajo and to speak to Navajo elders. Matthews became an ethnographer of sorts. What he discovered from his study was that the Navajo, once deemed "heathens, pronounced godless and legendless," possess "lengthy myths and traditions—so numerous that one can never hope to collect them all, a pantheon as well stocked with gods and heroes as that of the ancient Greeks, and prayers which, for length and vain repetition, might put a Pharisee to blush" (23).

What the above examples illustrate, then, is that early assessments about indigenous peoples being without languages, literatures, creeds, or governments are groundless.

And so the examples mount. This chapter, "How to Read Native American Literatures," might best be summarized with this statement: Read Native American Literatures open to the possibility that you might find yourself rethinking your view of the world. And maybe even be open to the possibility that this literature might suggest options to many of the dilemmas facing the multiple cultures within the borders of the United States.

Works Cited

Berkhofer, Robert F., Jr., *The White Man's Indian* (New York: Vintage Books, 1978).

Chase, Stuart, "Foreword," in *Language, Thought, & Reality*, Benjamin Whorf, ed. (Cambridge: MIT Press, 1956).

Cohen, Felix, "Americanizing the White Man," in *The Legal Conscience: Selected Papers of Felix S. Cohen*, Lucy Kramer Cohen, ed. (New Haven, CT: Yale University Press, 1960) 315–327.

Columbus, Christopher, "October 12, 1492," repr. in *The Indian and the White Man*, Wilcomb E. Washburn, ed. (New York: Anchor Books, 1964) 3–5.

Forbes, Jack D., "The Indian: Looking Glass into the Souls of White Americans," *Liberator* 6 (August 1966) 3–9.

Jaimes, M. Annette, "Sand Creek the Morning After," in *The State of Native America: Genocide, Colonization, and Resistence*, M. Annette Jaimes, ed. (Boston: South End Press, 1992) 1–12.

Krupat, Arnold, *The Turn to the Native* (Lincoln: University of Nebraska Press, 1996).

Mann, Charles C., "1491," *The Atlantic* 289:3 (March 2002) 41–53.

Matthews, Washington, *Navaho Legends* (Salt Lake City: University of Utah Press, 1994).

Montaigne, Michel De, "Of Cannibals," repr. in *Harper Collins World Reader*, Mary Ann Caws and Christopher Prendergast, eds. (New York: Harper Collins, 1998) 1125–1134.

Morris, Glenn T., "International Law and Politics: Toward a Right to Self-Determination for Indigenous Peoples," in *The State of Native America: Genocide, Colonization, and Resistance*, M. Annette Jaimes, ed. (Boston: South End Press, 1992) 55–86.

Nabokov, Peter, ed., *Native American Testimony* (New York: Viking Penguin, 1991).

Slickpoo, Allen, "Nez Percé," in *Encylopedia of North American Indians,* Frederick E. Hoxie, ed. (New York: Houghton Mifflin, 1996) 431–433.

Stiffarm, Lenore A. with Phil Lane, Jr., "The Demography of Native North America: A Question of American Indian Survival," in *The State of Native America: Genocide, Colonization, and Resistance,* M. Annette Jaimes, ed. (Boston: South End Press, 1992) 23–54.

Toelken, Barre, "Seeing with a Native Eye: How Many Sheep Will It Hold," *Seeing with a Native Eye,* Walter Holden Capps, ed. (New York: Harper and Row, 1976).

Utter, Jack, *American Indians: Answers to Today's Questions* (Norman: University of Oklahoma Press, 1993).

Weatherford, Jack, *Indian Givers: How the Indians of the Americas Transformed the World* (New York: Fawcett Columbine, 1988).

Witherspoon, Gary, *Language and Art in the Navajo Universe* (Ann Arbor: University of Michigan Press, 1977).

Chapter Four

The Best and the Best Known

What Can Be Understood by "the Best"?

Historically, questions of who and what constitute the *best* authors and literary texts have pivoted around discussions about the interaction between *the good* (ethics), *the true* (metaphysics and physics), and *the beautiful* (aesthetics). If an appropriate interaction between the good, the true, and the beautiful is not realized in a work of art, excesses occur. Too close attention to the good, for example, often produces dogmatism. Over attention on the *true* fosters the pedantic. And belief that art exists for its own sake often creates disassociation from social interchange. Elitism frequently results, with the attendant division between high and low culture. Students who adopt an elitist posture are many times led to "polish the monuments." Genre considerations are also bound up in discussions of artistic merit. As E. D. Hirsch reminds us, "All understanding of verbal meaning is necessarily genre bound" (76). This means that the "truth claims" of any text are generally based on an understanding of genre. One approaches a treatise by Albert Einstein, for instance, with different expectations than one does the Bible or the cartoon page in the Sunday news.

Jose Ortega y Gassett asserts that genres "are broad views of the cardinal directions of the human." Furthermore, "Each epoch brings with it a basic interpretation of man. Or better, it does not bring such an interpretation with it as much as it *is* that interpretation. For that reason, each epoch favors a certain genre" (Beebee 272). Often, literary history is the story of such favoritism: from myth (the story of the gods); to epic (the story of culture heroes); to

tragedy (the story of noble characters whose poor choices eventu-
ate in catastrophe); to comedy (a narrative that discloses the follies
of human beings who eventually recognize their frailties and make
positive change); and so forth. Not that any era does not produce a
variety of genre, however, but that each epoch seems to favor a certain genre—often in connection with particular philosophic pre-
sumptions or preoccupations of the times.

The twentieth century, for example, could be called the age of
the novel. Why this is so requires complex historical exegesis. But
general sketches of these ideas are useful. Classic philosopher
Martha C. Nussbaum believes that "The novel is a living form and is
in fact still the central morally serious yet popularly engaging fiction
form of our culture." Nussbaum explains: "The novel is concrete to
an extent generally unparalleled in other narrative genres. It takes as
its theme, we might say, the interaction between general human
aspirations and particular forms of social life that either enable or
impede those aspirations, shaping them powerfully in the process"
(6–7). This "concrete" nature of the novel allows for an exploration
of the contingent nature of human experience—experience that is
impacted by unexpected, unforeseen, unbidden, and often uncontrollable forces that "enable" or "impede" human "aspirations."

However, in discussions of Native American fiction, certain types
of novels hold sway over others, at least for formidable critics like
Gerald Vizenor (Chippewa). Using a Postmodern term, *simulations*,
Vizenor speaks out against those works of art without authentic,
ironic vision. Simulations are poses, inventions, and false images
manufactured to create a market—to sell what audiences expect
and want: images that perpetuate the romance of the noble savage
or vanishing *Indian*. Such simulations are the *absence* of Natives
rather than a *presence*. In a discussion with A. Robert Lee, Vizenor
explains that "Natives, or simulated *Indians*, are presented as an
absence in the curriculum, more as a minority group, a culture of
disadvantage and victimry. Natives, in other words, are seldom presented as a presence of diverse individuals, cultures, and communities. And only recently has there been much attention to the reality,
or obvious presence, of crossblood natives" (173). What Vizenor is
hoping for, then, is that Native fictions will be recognized as *best*

based on their visionary qualities—literary expressions of Native *presence*. Vizenor explains: "many native stories and novels are visionary, a literary dance of ghosts. *House Made of Dawn* by N. Scott Momaday, and *Ceremony* by Leslie Silko, and *Medicine River* by Thomas King, and *Bone Game* by Louis Owens, and many others, are visionary novels" (*Postindian Conversations* 166). The "literary dance of ghosts," for Vizenor, revolves around irony, humor, change, adaptability, and motion rather than tragic, static, or fixed illusions.

Definitions of the good, the true, and the beautiful as well as genre have undergone numerous alterations based on changes in the generative questions of any given literary period.

Certainly, students of American literary history are familiar with labels assigned to literary periods outlined in such texts as William Harmon and C. Hugh Holman's *A Handbook to Literature*. Harmon and Holman trace literary history though several eras: the Colonial Period (1607–1765), the Revolutionary Age (1765–1790), the Early National Period (1790–1830), the Romantic Period (1830–1865), the Realistic Period (1870–1914), the Naturalistic and Symbolistic Period (1900–1930), the Modernist Period (1914–1965), and the Postmodernist Period (1965 to the present) (564–616). The mere labels given these periods, however, reveal the political and philosophical concerns that might have generated the literary productivity and preoccupations of the times. The juncture between the Romantic and the Realist movements can be readily understood, for example, when students note that the Civil War (1861–1865) era brought into question many of the assumptions of the Romantics. Furthermore, the succession of such labels clearly demarcates American literary history as the grand story of the democratic experiment with individual liberty and the pursuit of happiness.

Contemporary critical approaches to this grand narrative often focus on particular attitudes toward those who have either been misrepresented by or left out of the literary canon: Feminism (women), Marxism (various economic classes), and Ethnocriticism (marginalized ethnic groups), for example. Furthermore, Deconstruction, Postmodernism, and Reader Response theories help readers recognize how literary texts have marginalized various groups or how every reader brings his/her unconscious assumptions (biases

housed in cultural metaphors) to their interpretations of texts—
including those who produce the ideas of a canon (the *best* that has
been written). Other overarching narratives emerge from such
critical awareness. African Americans and Native Americans, for
example, might chronicle their his/story in "America" differently.
According to folklorist Richard M. Dorson, while immigrant
America enjoyed a pattern of immigration, colonization, westward
expansion, and settlement by their choice, others did not. Native
Americans, for example, delineate their experience with "America"
through "precontact, contact, reservation, and pan-Indian periods."
African Americans chronicle their American experience through a
"trans-atlantic crossing in slave ships, slavery, quasi-freedom, and
civil rights movement" (3). Such differences alter notions of the *best*.
And differences, rather than bipolarities (us/them; white/black;
male/female; rich/poor; elitist/commoner), are what more nearly
contribute to the human ability to reason in a more nonviolent fashion, according to Postmodern thought.

Furthermore, Postmodern thinker Emmanuel Levinas reveals
that Western history has been the story of the human ego in search
of freedom and the same (self). Levinas demonstrates how dominant historical narratives have been the story of the "reduction of
the other to the same" (48). In other words, dominant narratives
expose the refusal of tellers to recognize the worth of the Otherness
of the Stranger. This means that a Self desires to see the Other as a
reflection of that Self—Anglo, Christian, Male, Western, Democratic. Levinas, therefore, would determine those narratives *best* that
detail a "movement that leaves a world that is intimate and familiar,
even if we have not yet explored it completely, and goes toward the
stranger" (*Collected Papers* 47). For Levinas, consciousness of
Otherness, the movement toward the Stranger, is the beginning of
knowledge, ethics, freedom, and truth. However, this desire for the
Other's stories can never be fully satiated. No story of the Other is
total, complete, or comprehensive. Levinas suggests that "neither
unity of number nor unity of concepts link me to the Stranger, the
Stranger who disturbs the being at home with oneself. . . . Stranger
also means the free one. Over him I have no power" (*Totality and
Infinity* 8). Levinas uncovers the contradictions that underlie the

desire for freedom in the desire also for complete understanding and total control (*totalization*).

Other additions to conceptions of *best* come from the works of anthropologist Victor Turner. If knowledge of the Other is the beginning of truth and freedom, how is such knowledge encountered? Turner believes that cultures always seek to best enounce themselves through their artistic expressions: that cultures "are better compared through their rituals, theaters, tales, ballads, epics, operas than through their habits. For the former are the way in which they try to articulate their meanings—and each culture has a special pan-human contribution for all of our thinking, remembering species" (Bruner 13). Ethnologist Charles David Kleymeyer concurs with Turner with regard to notions of the *best*. He believes in what he calls "cultural expression and grassroots development." Kleymeyer defines "cultural expression" as "the representation in language, symbols, and actions of a particular group's collective heritage—its history, aesthetic values, beliefs, observations, desires, knowledge, wisdom, and opinions" (3). Kleymeyer further asserts:

> Ethnic pluralism contributes to the richness and breadth of choices in a society's repertoire. It may be that each subculture in a society has dominion over one piece or several pieces of the development puzzle but not over all of them. In the quest for development, the questions may be the same, but the answers are different. Cultural expression helps keep diverse technologies and worldviews alive, transmitting and supporting them within a broader cultural webbing. Efforts to produce a monocultural society have often resulted in increased conflict and alienation, and such efforts ultimately impoverish us all (28).

In addition, in *The Voice in the Margin: Native American Literature and the Canon*, Arnold Krupat asserts "that Afro-American and Native American literary production, when we pay attention to it, offers texts equivalently excellent to the traditional Euramerican great books." Krupat cautions, nonetheless, that "It is not only that these texts should be read in the interest of fairness or simply because they are available; nor it is because they provide charming examples of 'primitive' survivals: they should be read because of their abundant capacity to teach and delight" (54).

Krupat is not naïve enough to suggest that the best books are dogmatic (preachy), however. The best books nevertheless do educate. Krupat suggests:

> In terms of its teaching, let me note only the fact that traditional and contemporary Native literatures tend pretty much without exception to derive from an ecosystemic, nonanthropocentric perspective on the world that we may at last be coming to see—as the ozone layer thins, as the polar ice melts, as the nonbiodegradable garbage mounts to the skies—as being centrally rather than marginally important to human survival (55).

In terms of style, tone, and other literary devices, Krupat states that "even the most recent and most complexly composed Native American works are still likely to have roots in or relations to oral traditions that differ considerably in their procedures from those of the dominant, text-based cultures." Nevertheless, "if these works are indeed equivalently excellent, still it must be recognized that they are differently excellent" (55).

Two more of Krupat's contentions are noteworthy. The first has to do with Krupat's discussion of the contributions of Roy Harvey Pearce's works to the field of ethnocriticism. Pearce's work, claims Krupat, "can provide a theoretical base from which to engage . . . American criticism" which must now "include a specific and historical rethinking of individuality in relationship to Native American collective concepts of the self" (83). The second contention comes from Krupat's attempt to answer this question: why "labor to maintain a special category called literature, a category, as I have claimed, that would be constituted precisely by the dominance of its conjunction of the pleasurable and the pedagogical?" In his answer, Krupat might seem to argue against his former claims:

> What answer I can give depends upon an analogy to the canon: just as it is worthwhile to retain the notion of a body of texts centrally significant to a common culture, an approximation to a collective autobiography, the story of our integrated selves as participants in a common society,

so too is it worthwhile to retain the notion of literature as comprised of those texts that provide instances of and occasions for the integrated self. Literature is where the affective and rational coexist and complement each other in language, where fancy and imagination press for freedom beyond the bounds of a material constraint to which proper due is given. Literature is that mode of discourse which foremost seeks to enact and perform its insights, insisting that we understand with affect, feel with comprehension. In this sense, T. S. Eliot was wrong: there is no literature of dissociated sensibilities; in this sense, Roy Harvey Pearce was right: literature is always an instance of the search for wholeness (43).

Krupat acknowledges the demands of difference in his text on canon formation. However, he concurs with Allon White's "formulation" of difference: "A politics of pure difference which refuses to theorise the unity-in-difference of humanity ends by replicating the individualism of the self-sufficient bourgeois ego— a dangerous fiction if ever there was one" (White in Krupat 52). It is in Krupat's insistence that "literature is always an instance of the search for wholeness" that ideas of difference reveal their Postmodern complexity—the inability, even utter irrationality of reducing the Other to the Same or seeing the Self as an autonomous ego. It is in the literary expressions of brokenness, isolation, separation, segregation, utter marginality, victimage, and social upheaval that Modernism leads us to texts which expose different appraisals of what it means to be whole.

Perhaps Nussbaum's assessment of "the literary imagination and public life" in *Poetic Justice* clarifies the truth claims of literature:

Good literature is disturbing in a way that history and social science writing frequently are not. Because it summons powerful emotions, it disconcerts and puzzles. It inspires distrust of conventional pieties and exacts a frequently painful confrontation with one's own thoughts and intentions. One may be told many things about people in one's own society and yet keep that knowledge at a distance. Literary works that promote identification and emotional reaction cut through those self-protective stratagems, requiring us to see and to

respond to many things that may be difficult to confront—
and they make this process palatable by giving us pleasure in
the very act of confrontation (6).

Understanding what constitutes the *best* authors and works in
Native American Literatures, therefore, must rest on an understanding of the above concerns in the history of literary criticism.

The Best and Best Known in Native American Literature Before 1969

The history of Native American Literatures is often divided
between works published before and after N. Scott Momaday's
1969 Pulitzer Prize for *House Made of Dawn*. Momaday's Pulitzer
brought academic and public attention to Native writers. The flood-
gates opened with interest in a host of other contemporary Native
authors because of Momaday's award. Kenneth Lincoln refers to the
period surrounding Momaday's achievement as a *Native American
Renaissance*. This renaissance took three forms: confidence on the
part of contemporary Native authors in reclaiming their heritage in
their own literary expressions; concern with finding and reevaluat-
ing early literary works by Native authors; and renewed interest in
anthologies of translations of traditional artistic expressions—myths,
prayers, ceremonies, rituals, love songs, oratory, etc.

Furthermore, new understandings of solutions to the "Indian
problem" also emerged during this renaissance. As anthropologist
David Maybury-Lewis explains, "A people's expressive culture,
which is at the heart of its folklore, has a profound significance. It is
a powerful statement of what is most deeply felt and of what gives
meaning to people's lives. If it flourishes, so too does their way of
life" (xv). Moreover, Kleymeyer asserts that "Traditional ethnic
groups offer vital practical knowledge in areas of health, sustainable
agriculture and forest management, and even social and political
organization. If the ethnic group dies out, its knowledge goes with
it" (7). In other words, literary expressions—housing the *best* cultural insights—have political, social, practical, and humanitarian

influence. "Being poor does not mean being impoverished culturally," claims Mayberry-Lewis (xv).

Even though Indian autobiographies and oratory are among what
Andrew Wiget calls "The Historical Emergence of Native American
Writing" (vi), fiction—novels and short stories—constitutes the early
and more widely known contributions of American Indian authors
to mainstream arts and letters—especially during those hundred
years between the Civil War and Civil Rights eras. Few novels were
published before Momaday's *House Made of Dawn*. And yet, what
novels were published have merit. Poet, essayist, and newspaperman
John Rollin Ridge (Cherokee) published *The Life and Adventures of
Joaquin Murietta, the Celebrated California Bandit* in 1854. Although
the novel describes "the trials and revenge of a mixed-blood
Mexican," says Scott B. Vickers, the novel is actually "a picaresque
western adventure based on the resistance of California Natives to
the incursion of whites brought on by the gold rush." Ridge's personal history is every bit as interesting as his novel. Vickers tells us
that Ridge "was among those on the Trail of Tears during the
Cherokee Removal from their eastern homeland to the Indian
Territory of Oklahoma." Both Ridge's father and grandfather were
assassinated for their part in "signing away their ancestral lands" without permission of the Cherokee people (130). Volume Six of the
video series *500 Nations* documents events surrounding the Trail of
Tears. And *The Cherokee Removal*, edited by Theda Perdue and
Michael D. Green, gives the cultural context for the removal that
resulted in 4,000 Cherokee deaths.

S. Alice Callahan (Creek) published *Wynema: A Child of the
Forest* in 1891. A. LaVonne Brown Ruoff explains that although
"this novel incorporates explanations of Creek customs," it is a fictional account "of the events that led to the murder of Sitting Bull
and the massacre at Wounded Knee." *Wynema* is also a plea for
"women's rights and suffrage," says Ruoff (148).

The last Native novelist to publish during the nineteenth century was Simon Pokagon (Potawatomi). While his novel is notable,
his life style left much to be desired; he scammed his people in land
claims. Notwithstanding, he did publish *Queen of the Woods* in

1899. Ruoff describes this novel as "a romance that laments the Potawatomi's loss of their Edenic past and warns about how alcohol can destroy Indians and whites" (148).

Cogewea: The Half-Blood (1927) written by Mourning Dove (Okanagon/Colville); *Brothers Three* (1935) written by John Milton Oskison (Cherokee); *Wah'Kon-Tah: The Osage and the White Man's Road* (1932); and *Sundown* (1934) written by John Joseph Mathews (Osage) are among early twentieth century novels by Indians. D'Arcy McNickle (Cree/Metis/Salish) wrote three novels before the Native American Renaissance: *The Surrounded* (1936), *Runner in the Sun: A Story of Indian Maize* (1954), and *Wind from the Enemy Sky* (published in 1978 after McNickle's death). Of these novels, four have continued to receive acclaim: Mourning Dove's *Cogewea*, Mathews' *Sundown*, and McNickle's *The Surrounded* and *Wind from an Enemy Sky*. Indeed, McNickle is garnering increased critical attention as his works become more widely known.

Mourning Dove's *Cogewea* is a tragic/romantic tale of a mixed-blood female who is wooed by a mixedblood suitor—the foreman on the ranch where Cogewea lives—and a two-faced, fortune-hunting White man. Paula Gunn Allen says, "The novel turns on the question of identity—a question peculiarly American. Cogewea's conflict between traditional family values and the siren call of city life and modern values very nearly costs her her life" (79).

Mathews' *Sundown* chronicles the existential dilemma of Challenge Windser, an Osage youth born of a father who believes in the advantages of allotment (and the oil-rich land) and a mother who relies on traditional Osage beliefs. Chal goes to college, joins the air corps, and is so seduced by the White man's world that he becomes conflicted. While he is ashamed of his Indian ways, Chal is also drawn to the spiritual values of his mother. Terry P. Wilson claims that "The last portion of the novel focuses on Chal's inability to develop meaning and direction in his life after the war, wavering between the hedonism and decadence of oil-rich Indians and the hardheaded capitalism of the white men" (247)—two destructive alternatives.

Robert Allen Warrior disagrees. Warrior says that "Instead of a tragic victim [Chal] and a community caught in the battle between an either/or of assimilation or remaining traditional [the Osage in the early 1920s], we see the real problem—a community having severely limited ability to make choices regarding its own future and the effect of that on a typical individual within the community" (82). Chal does spend the major portion of the novel "waiting for something to happen that will allow him to fully express himself," says Warrior. Chal wants to have an "orgasm [climax] of the spirit" and can't because his spirit is dammed up with self-hate (Warrior 82). Warrior suggests that at the end of the novel when Chal considers going to law school, "Mathews has put into his mind one way through which he can reach out in his virility to establish power over some corner of the life force" (83). Warrior believes that Chal has an awakening of "consciousness and affirmation of tradition" brought about by "hearing the words of Roan Horse [a traditional] and seeing the subtle actions of his mother" (85).

McNickle's *The Surrounded* tells the story of Archilde [our child] Leon, another mixed-blood whose forays into the White world leave him disassociated and passive. Louis Owens writes: "Again and again in the novel, understanding fails and something goes inexplicably wrong for the Indians, as if they are in the grip of an incomprehensible fate" (65). McNickle's Natives are "surrounded"—like fenced-in cattle—by powerful alien government officials and representatives of Christianity trying to turn Indians into artifacts or remake them into their own Euroamerican image. Time and again these authorities misunderstand Archilde's character. Time and again, Archilde inadvertently finds himself in the middle of suspicious events. And due to his personal integrity, he often accepts wrongful punishment.

Louis Owens declares that "More than any other Indian writer, D'Arcy McNickle would prove to be a seminal figure in the new American Indian fiction, publishing three novels over a span of forty years while turning himself into one of the nation's most articulate and knowledgeable spokesmen for Indian concerns" (61). Such statements demonstrate the interaction between the *best* works and the *best known* authors—between the dancer (author) and the dance (the text). McNickle attended boarding schools, studied creative writing at the University of Montana, became a distinguished anthropologist, was one of the founders of the National Congress of American Indians, and became one of the leading advocates for Native American rights. These experiences informed his fiction.

Wind from an Enemy Sky, for example, shows an anthropologist's insights into the varied and conflicting personalities whose behaviors result in unexpected, even unpredictable, cross-cultural misunderstandings and violence. Uninformed yet good intentions advanced by both the traditional Little Elk people (an invented Northwestern tribe) and non-Natives (government agents and philanthropists) inadvertently misfire.

The novel pivots around the desire of Henry Jim (a "progressive" yet disaffected member of the Little Elk) to heal ancient quarrels by going to his brother Bull (the leader of the Little Elk) with a scheme to reunite the Little Elk people by seeking the return of their sacred medicine bundle (which exists in a museum owned by Adam Pell—a wealthy do-gooder). Toby Rafferty, Superintendent of the Little Elk Indian Agency and Special Disbursing Agent, wants to facilitate policies which will promote the well-being of the Little Elk people. Rafferty, over time, comes to realize that the Little Elk have "so little left of the world that was once complete," that he seeks to discover the whereabouts of the bundle in hopes that he can have it returned and thereby both heal and gain the confidence of the people he has come to serve (209). So he seeks the help of Pell to accomplish these ends. Pell, a complex character with growing consciousness, is slow to see the significance of the medicine bundle to the survival of the Little Elk. In his lifetime, he has taken up Native peoples as a kind of hobby. Under the sanctions of Congress, a construction company with which Pell was involved built a dam in Little Elk territory to divide the land and the water—a project intended to move the Little Elk into the valley so that they could become farmers. This dam was built, however, with "no knowledge" of the Little Elk people and their concerns.

Two events conspire to bring Pell to an awareness of the consequences of his uninformed acts—the death of his nephew and the decomposition of the medicine bundle through carelessness. Pock Face, an immature member of the Little Elk, kills Pell's beloved nephew—a guiltless engineer who came, on a brief assignment, to simply inspect the dam. To Pock Face, Pell's nephew represents those men who "killed the water." These events force Pell to realize three things. The first is "Very few Indians had taken pieces of land in the open valley when the reservation was divided up. They knew about the hot, dry summers, the treeless, unsheltered flats," and so chose land "in the foothills, in the timber country, along forested streams." As a result, when the dam was built, "their main perennial streams were blocked off and diverted out to the dry valley, only the white homesteaders benefited." Furthermore, "No compensation went to the Indians for this appropriation of their property" (193).

Pell's second awareness is "The Indians had received money for the land which had been taken over by the homesteaders" at a ridiculously low rate per acre and that "this money was used by the government to pay for surveys, soil studies, engineering estimates and all manner of preliminary work that went into the development of the irrigation project, to benefit the government-invited home-steaders." Pell finally recognizes that the tribe's mountain water and thousands of acres have literally been "impounded"—"taken with-out agreement or compensation of any kind, as far as I can deter-mine, and again, without benefit to the Indians" (193). Pell's final realization comes when he searches for the medicine bundle in his museum only to find that it had been carelessly tossed into a basement, where "Mice had eaten their way through the buckskin covering and had bred and reared countless generations, each gen-eration chewing away at hide and inner contents" until all sacred contents were missing—leaving the bundle "devoid of holy mystery" (210). Pell discerns what the return of the medicine bundle would mean to the people—a chance for wholeness and the opportunity to determine their own destiny. "If I could have returned, bringing this bundle with me, we could have talked together. They shot that young man, my nephew, because nobody tried to talk to them, not in their terms," Pell realizes (211).

Communication failure abounds in this novel. Edwards, the agency physician, firmly believes, "The problem is communication . . . These people find it difficult to believe that a white man, any white man, will give them respect, as it is difficult for me to under-stand why they push me away and keep me from coming into their confidence." Edwards thinks the obvious response to the dilemma "is that we do not speak to each other—and language is only a part of it. Perhaps it is intention, or purpose, the map of mind we follow" (125). In other words, other views (maps) of the world collide—diverse mythologies, incompatible laws, and incommensurate social systems. Bull, who can't speak English and must rely on interpreters, continually seeks wisdom, understanding, and a more abundant life for his people. Yet he also discerns the degree of difficulty involved in cross-cultural communication. "An Indian can't tell what's on his mind until he tells a story," Bull tells the agency representatives (125). Perhaps *Wind from an Enemy Sky* is McNickle's attempt to tell what is on his mind through storytelling. The story, for Bull, expands—beginning with a time of bitterness followed by a "time of confusion." During the time of confusion, "the hardest time,"

> Kinship lines were broken. Children went against their own relatives. The people, left to themselves, could have saved themselves, as they had against days of hunger and winter sickness. But the new men, coming from across the mountains, set family against family, telling them to build legal fences, tear up the sod, build little houses. They only scattered the people, like quail rising from the grass (31).

Bull's brother, Jim Henry, split from the family and became the exemplary model of what the agency wanted the Little Elk people to become—thus beginning a quarrel between brothers lasting decades. Bull's grandson was "kidnapped" and sent to boarding school, an act that brought about the madness and eventual death of Celeste, Bull's daughter, who believed her son Antoine would not return to her (200). In order for agency officials to understand such losses, the old people said: "Today talks in yesterday's voice. . . . The white man must hear yesterday's voice" (28). "Yesterday's voice," however, is not spoken in English. Bull, for example, is an English form of Bull's name. "But the words men speak never pass from one language to another without some loss of flavor and ultimate meaning" (2).

"Yesterday's voice," it must be noted, is communal. Voice does not mean one man, one voice, but the voices of the collective, the councils, and the creative visions handed down through the voices of sacred characters—like Feather Boy, the giver of the Medicine Bundle. And the story of Feather Boy is "a holy story." Yet, Bull warns, "But don't try to tell it to a white man. He'll just laugh at you. There are things we don't even talk about among ourselves" (204). And because the people are fragmented, many of these sacred stories have been forgotten or faith in them eroded. Yet, Feather Boy promised the people when he gave them the bundle: "Keep this. . . . 'All the good things of life are inside. Never let it get away from your people. So long as you have this holy bundle, your people will be strong and brave and life will be good to them. My own body is in this forever'" (208). It is no wonder that the return of the medicine bundle would begin to heal kinship separations. Furthermore, Antoine's return from boarding school and his apprenticeship under his grandfather's tutelage gave the people hope that their way of life would be restored and continue.

However, the final meeting between the Little Elk elders and agency representatives results in disaster; Pell's admission that the medicine bundle has been destroyed plus the confession of his ill-informed part in the people's difficulties create a liminal space. This space—an unknown, undefined, unstructured space/time—could not be adequately negotiated, and violence results. This violence, however, is not a them/us violence. All the central characters, in some way, are "good guys." And as John Lloyd Purdy notes, *Wind from an Enemy Sky* "places the problems of [McNickle's] fictional 'Little Elk' people not solely at the door of the whites, but also upon the inadequate early reactions of the people, themselves, to colonial policies. This expansive view permits a more comprehensive inter-pretation of [his] books, without allowing them or the issues they raise to be easily dismissed" (Purdy xiv). Furthermore, Son Child, the tribal policeman in the novel, is a character with a composite mentality—both empathetic to his own people and fully cognizant of the demands of White man's law. In the final moments of the novel, Son Child's response could be construed as either an inexpli-cable act, an act of compassion, or both—especially in terms of any kind of quality future for Bull, the esteemed leader of the Little Elk.

The themes and issues exposed in these early fictional works pose several questions about the past and future of Native peoples. If, as Edward M. Bruner insists, "Stories, as culturally constructed expressions, are among the most universal means of organizing and articulating experience" (15), what do these narratives, collectively, articulate about Native experience? Bruner asserts, "As we can only enter the world in the middle, in the present, then stories serve as meaning-generating interpretive devices which frame the present within a hypothetical past and an anticipated future." With regard to dominant anthropological interpretations of Native American history, Bruner's "claim is that one story—past glory, present disorganization, future assimilation—was dominant in the 1930s and a second story—past oppression, present resistance, future resurgence —in the 1970s." However, says Bruner, these narratives don't necessarily represent actual Indian life (143). Is there a "vision," therefore, of "actual" Native experience that emerges from these early texts? Certainly these works are ambivalent about the future—each novel ending either in the hesitant submission, forced containment, tentative optimism, or termination of Native protagonists.

However, embedded in several of these texts are characters, like Antoine in *Wind from an Enemy Sky*, who have the potential to overcome the more tragic consequences of events that shape the protagonists' lives. What, then, was happening historically during this period that brought the above authors to their conclusions? Were "terminal creeds"—philosophies and policies that terminated Native ways of life—of the dominant society so imposing that few Natives could survive assimilation (Vizenor)? Perhaps education policies were most influential during this period. In his introduction to *Singing Spirit: Early Short Stories by North American Indians*, Bernd C. Peyer reports that "by 1895 some two hundred institutions were providing services to approximately eighteen thousand students." And their curriculums varied from "teaching Christian principles" to teaching "farming and other secular occupations" (x).

One outcome of such "reforming" educational programs, however, was the rise of "an Indian intellectual elite, which greatly enriched literary production," Peyer explains (x). Numerous Native students used their boarding school experiences as springboards for further education. Or they took advantage of private schools rather than attend Indian missionary institutions. John Joseph Mathews attended the University of Oklahoma, a stint interrupted by WWI. He later was offered a Rhodes scholarship to Oxford, which he declined; however, he did attend Oxford where he studied natural sciences and earned a B.A. Mathews also attended the University of Geneva where he studied International Relations. D'Arcy McNickle attended boarding school in Chewmawa, Oregon, high schools in Washington State and Montana, and the University of Montana where he studied history, literature, and served as a staff member of *The Frontier*, a literary journal. During his time at the university, McNickle published several short stories. McNickle sold his allotment on the Flathead Reservation to get sufficient funds to attend Oxford. However, his finances ran out and he wasn't able to complete his degree.

Similar academic profiles mark the careers of other pre-1970 writers: Pauline Johnson (Iroquois), William Jones (Sac and Fox), Francis La Fleshe (Omaha), Gertrude Bonnin (Sioux), Alexander Posey (Creek), and Charles A. Eastman (Sioux) among others. Careers varied among these writers—from anthropology, education, and politics to medicine. And yet, their enduring fame has come through their literary productivity. A sampling of these authors' short stories, accompanied by brief biographical sketches, appears in *Singing Spirit*. Paula Gunn Allen also edited *Voice of the Turtle: American Indian Literature 1900–1970*—a fine collection of excerpts from major works, short stories, and brief autobiographical essays. What is most remarkable about these authors, however, is their status as acculturated rather than assimilated Natives. Acculturated Indians often live and work in the White world while maintaining or promoting Indian life-ways and rights.

Any study of "the best" works produced before 1970 would be flawed without particular attention to the contributions of two Sioux gentlemen—Charles A. Eastman and Nicholas Black Elk. While the primary works of these men are not fiction, their literary merit, academic regard, and immense popular appeal still find them among assigned texts on numerous university course syllabi. Of the eighteen or so works published by Eastman, three are among the most studied: *Indian Boyhood* (1902), *The Soul of the Indian* (1911), and *Deep Woods to Civilization* (1916). David Reed Miller asserts, "Whether he was an ethnographer is dubious." And yet, Eastman "attempted to define ideals, moral codes, sex roles, mythology and cosmology; and finally, he attempted to influence White civilization by his version of the contribution of his Indian heritage." Furthermore, "By teaching and even helping to invent a new conception of the American Indian, Eastman wanted American society to learn about itself using the mirror provided by the first Americans" (82). James Treat observes that "Eastman struggled throughout his life to reconcile two seemingly contradictory allegiances: native and Christian" (5). In *From Deep Woods to Civilization*, Eastman affirms: "I am an Indian, and while I have learned much from civilization, for which I am grateful, I have never lost my Indian sense of right and justice. I am for development and progress along social and spiritual lines, rather than those of commerce, nationalism, or material efficiency" (194).

Eastman's career as a medical doctor was troubled and sporadic, at best. Eastman's uneasy career as a physician began when he was assigned to the Pine Ridge reservation days before the massacre at Wounded Knee. Needless to say, this and other agonizing events brought Eastman into continual conflict with agency officials. Nevertheless, because Eastman was a graduate from Dartmouth, Boston University School of Medicine, and a Christian convert, government officials often sought his genius. Eastman "became one of the leading public figures in Indian affairs and worked with a variety of organizations including the Society of American Indians, the Young Men's Christian Association, the Boy Scouts and the Camp Fire Girls, and the Bureau of Indian Affairs," Treat recounts (4).

However, Eastman's continual disappointment with mainstream Christianity often brought him to point out hypocrisies and to reflect fondly on his own Native upbringing. In *From Deep Woods to Civilization*, for example, Eastman writes:

> From the time I first accepted the Christ ideal it has grown upon me steadily, but I also see more and more plainly our modern divergence from that ideal. I confess I have wondered much that Christianity is not practiced by the very people who vouch for that wonderful conception of exemplary living. It appears that they are anxious to pass on their religion to all races of men, but keep very little of it themselves (193–194).

When Eastman was fifty-one, his disillusionment with "civilization" became more penetrating. He decided to retire to the north woods of Minnesota to regain the vision of life he had as a boy. His experiences in the untrammeled wilds brought Eastman to a more meditative contemplation of his own Indian ideals. In the fall of 1910,

Eastman composed his most philosophical work, *The Soul of the Indian*. Typical of the thoughts expressed in this text are:

> Long before I ever heard of Christ, or saw a white man, I had learned from an untutored woman the essence of morality. With the help of dear Nature herself, she taught me things simple but of mighty import. I knew God. I perceived what goodness is. I saw and loved what is really beautiful. Civilization has not taught me anything better (87).

Some critics feel that Eastman's works romanticize his Indianness—especially by ignoring problematic Sioux cultural practices. However, if Treat is correct in his assessment of works like Eastman's, Eastman might be one of the forerunners of the genre Treat calls Native Christian Narrative Discourse.

Genre designations create many of the critical concerns with both Eastman's and Black Elk's narratives. The issues lie firmly in the desire on the part of many academics that Native works be "accurate," "authentic," and "pure" texts—texts uncontaminated by "outside" or romantic influences. Native Christian Narrative Discourse is a designation given to texts that "employ autobiographical narratives as primary methodological techniques for making (and not merely illustrating) theological points, and many of them also make use of stories drawn from a more general collective, cultural context," claims Treat. He further explains, "Oral cultures typically preserve worldview and tradition in stories, which teach through example rather than by catechism." Treat suggests that "native Christian reflection is experiential and performative; while conventional Christian theology is often dogmatic, native Christian discourse is confessional." He also claims: "This new genre of native literature resists the interpretive boundaries implied by literary categorization" (13).

Current discussions of *Black Elk Speaks* (first published in 1932) also hinge on what critics construe this text to be—ethnography, autobiography, mythology, or literature. Julian Rice declares, "Until Raymond J. Demallie edited the complete transcripts of John G. Neihardt's 1931 and 1944 interviews with Black Elk for the University of Nebraska Press (*The Sixth Grandfather*, 1984), *Black*

Elk Speaks was received by most readers as a sacrosanct revelation" (ix). *Black Elk Speaks* was the outcome of interviews Neihardt conducted with Black Elk in 1931. These interviews were complicated by the fact that Black Elk knew little English. Black Elk's son Ben translated his father's words for Neihardt. And Neihardt's daughter, Enid, transcribed the interviews. This exchange was not a simple linear retelling of Black Elk's life which then appeared as an unedited text. DeMallie explains that "Neihardt perceived Black Elk's religion in terms of art; Black Elk perceived Neihardt's art in terms of religion. Both tried to use their special skills to enrich human life by merging it into something greater than the individual" (37). Both men were Christian; however, one was an epic poet and university professor; the other was a Lakota Holy Man and beloved leader of his people. This was no ethnographer and informant transaction. This is not to say that important ethnographic and historical information was not shared. Gretchen M. Bataille reminds:

> In the narrative account of Black Elk's life the reader receives American history from a Sioux or Lakota perspective. The book includes accounts of the Custer battle and the Wounded Knee incident given by a participant in both events, the Indian reaction to being rounded up by the Army and placed on reservations, and the Indian rationale for participating in Buffalo Bill's Wild West shows. The reader is also introduced to both ceremonial and everyday Oglala life during the last decades of the nineteenth century and into the twentieth century (135–136).

More importantly, however, the book is organized around what Neihardt believed to be the thesis of his interviews. The book was to be, according to Black Elk, "not the tale of a great hunter or of a great warrior, or of a great traveler, although I have made much meat in my time and fought for my people both as boy and man, and have gone far and seen strange lands and men. So also have many others done, and better than I" (*Black Elk Speaks* 1). The text was to be "the story of a mighty vision" that Black Elk believed "was true and mighty yet" (2).

Furthermore, the whole interview experience was entered into through the ritual process of "The Offering of the Pipe." In other

words, Black Elk inducted Neihardt into a sacred storytelling enter-
prise by sending "a voice to the Spirit of the World" that would
"help" Black Elk "be true" (2). This offering was accompanied by the
story of the origins of the pipe as a gift from Buffalo Calf Woman.
This narrative warns Neihardt and readers not to engage in the
sacred without proper respect, through recounting how two young
men received the coming of Buffalo Calf Woman: one received her
with esteem, the other with lustful thoughts. The second man was
destroyed. Experience with the sacred, then, is not a warm, fuzzy
moment; it is an engagement with the powers of the universe—
what Black Elk calls the Six Grandfathers. In addition, Neihardt and
his daughters were adopted into Black Elk's family and tribe as
preparation for Neihardt to recognize his sacred obligations as a relative to "save [Black Elk's] great vision for men" (xi).

Critical opinions of the success of *Black Elk Speaks* vary. Arnold
Krupat, for example, believes that this as-told-to narrative was trans-
posed into a "presumptive transcendental . . . religious romance"
which follows Northrop Frye's stages of a romance: "the *agon* or conflict, the *pathos* or death-struggle, and the *anagnorisis* or discovery,
the recognition of the hero, who has clearly proved himself to be a
hero even if he does not survive the conflict" (*For Those Who Come
After* 134). Krupat believes Lakota scholar Vine Deloria's assessment
denies the imperfections in the text. Deloria, in his introduction to
Black Elk Speaks, calls the work "a North American bible of all
tribes." Deloria contends that Black Elk "shared his visions with John
Neihardt because he wished to pass along to future generations
some of the reality of Oglala life and, one suspects, to share the burden of visions that remained unfulfilled with a compatible spirit"
(xiii). Furthermore, Deloria professes that "the Black Elk theological
tradition" will become "the central core of a North American Indian
theological canon which will someday challenge the Eastern and
Western traditions as a way of looking at the world" (xiv).

So many of the critical debates surrounding this book hinge on
genre expectations. Lucy Looks Twice, Black Elk's daughter, wanted
this work to be a complete biography of her father including his
long life as a Catholic catechist (Steltenkamp 25). Lucy felt the
public needed to know that there was a clear demarcation between
her father's life as a Sioux Holy Man and his life as a Christian. And

yet in *Black Elk Lives*, Benjamin Black Elk, who was the interpreter for what his father told Neihardt, calls *Black Elk Speaks* his father's book (8). Furthermore, Ben Black Elk says he ceased to live two lives—one grounded in Indian religion and the other in Christianity. He believes that he lives "one life now" with the two religions merging into "our modern religion" (5). Few critics challenge the validity of Black Elk's great vision. Perhaps Ben's understanding of the relationship between religious systems stems from part of his father's vision:

> Then I was standing on the highest mountain of them all, and round about beneath me was the whole hoop of the world. And while I stood there I saw more than I can tell and I understood more than I saw; for I was seeing in a sacred manner the shapes of all things in the spirit, and the shape of all shapes as they must live together like one being. And I saw that the sacred hoop of my people was one of many hoops that made one circle, wide as daylight and as starlight, and in the center grew one mighty flowering tree to shelter all the children of one mother and one father. And I saw that it was holy (43).

Black Elk clearly understood the difficulty of surrendering visions into language. "It was as I grew older that the meanings came clearer and clearer out of the pictures and the words; and even now I know that more was shown to me than I can tell" (49).

N. Scott Momaday says that *Black Elk Speaks* "is now deservedly recognized as a classic in literature. . . . We know this without knowing what the book is, exactly, without knowing precisely where to place it in our traditional categories of learning." Momaday believes "we need not concern ourselves with labels here, any more than we need concern ourselves with the question of authorship or the quality of translation or transcription. It is sufficient that *Black Elk Speaks* is an extraordinarily human document—and beyond that, the record of a profoundly spiritual journey, the pilgrimage of a people towards their historical fulfillment and culmination, towards the accomplishment of a worthy destiny." What is more, Momaday claims that this book "exerts its prominence" in various contextual frames—as "Literature, Anthropology, Folklore, and Religious Studies, not to mention American Studies, and Native American Studies" ("To Save a Great Vision" 31).

Without question, *Black Elk Speaks* has been the gateway into the study of Native American religions and literatures for countless thousands of people in many countries. The questions such a text raises for academics are worthy of study because they can make us all more careful and cautious readers. However, such challenges should not deflect from what Paula Gunn Allen calls "one of the stranger of the many collaborations that have shaped Native literature in this century, the old holy man and the old poet" working together: "the one recounting [in Lakota], the other writing [in English]" so that such a vision could become accessible to those beyond the borders of the Sioux reservation (*Voice of the Turtle* 163).

The Best and Best Known Native Writers from 1969 to the Present

In 1997, when Kenneth M. Roemer edited *Native American Writers of the United States* for the 175th volume of *Dictionary of Literary Biography*, he was hard pressed to determine which "thirty-five to forty-five authors would best illustrate the complex issues and literary diversity of Native American writing." Roemer felt impressed to explain that "more than half of the authors treated in [that] volume are still living" (xi). Since Roemer's volume, numerous Native writers have risen to local and national acclaim. Readers need to understand, therefore, that any work that discusses Native authors must, of necessity, be selective. This present study, therefore, will focus on those contemporary authors whose works are continually taught in university courses throughout the United States. Roemer rightly explains that the reasons for his own emphasis on modern authors stems from the fact that "it was the work of a few of them during the late 1960s and the 1970s—notably the Standing Rock Sioux Vine Deloria Jr.; the Kiowa/Cherokee N. Scott Momaday, who won the 1969 Pulitzer Prize for Fiction for *House Made of Dawn* (1968); the Laguna Leslie Marmon Silko; the Acoma Simon J. Ortiz; and the Blackfeet/Gross Ventre James Welch—that first gained widespread and sustained recognition for Indian oral and written literatures" (xi). The time was ripe for the recognition of such authors who began publishing, as they did, during the rift between Modernism and Postmodernism brought about by the recognized failures of the grand narratives of the Enlightenment.

In *The Postmodern Explained*, Jean-François Lyotard says: "The thought and action of the nineteenth and twentieth centuries are governed by . . . the Idea of emancipation." Philosophers, theologians, historians, and political scientists have attempted to organize the "mass" of historical events around grand emancipation narratives:

> The Christian narrative of the redemption of original sin through love; the *Aufklärer* narrative of emancipation from ignorance and servitude through knowledge and egalitarianism; the speculative narrative of the realization of the universal Idea through the dialectic of the concrete; the Marxist narrative of the emancipation from exploitation and alienation through the socialization of work; and the capitalist narrative of emancipation from poverty through technoindustrial development (25).

What theorists have since realized are the dichotomies between theory and practice; universal ideas and particular agency; representation (in words) and corporeality (actual people and events); and homogenization (desire for consensus) and difference (diversity of peoples and world views). Certainly, the causes and aftermaths of World War I, World War II, the Korean and Vietnam wars; the growing loss of dispositions to romanticize war; and the consciousness raised by the Civil Rights Movement brought about a space for alternative, corrective literatures. War and the language often used to represent struggles between opposing forces seldom particularize the anguish of individuals and peoples caught up in global politics. Holocaust literatures only begin to suggest the absolute horror Jewish individuals suffered at the hands of Nazis, for example. Certainly, the Civil Rights Movement brought attention to the various failures of the democratic narrative of emancipation. During this era, Kiowa Indian N. Scott Momaday's *House Made of Dawn* won the Pulitzer (1969).

N. Scott Momaday (b. 1934)

The year Momaday won the Pulitzer, he also began his position as associate professor of English and Comparative Literature at Berkeley, published his masterwork *The Way to Rainy Mountain*, and was inducted into the Kiowa Gourd Dance Society. Such recognition, prominence, and ability to combine favorable Native and dominant cultural reception thrust Momaday into his role as the dean of the Native American Renaissance. Even so, Momaday's training at Stanford in Western paradigms, alongside his reclamation of Native life-ways, lay the groundwork for Momaday as an artist who could reimagine human epistemologies through recombinations of mythical/psychological narratives. Furthermore, says Baine Kerr, Momaday endeavored to "transliterate Indian culture, myth, and sensibility into an alien art form without loss." Kerr, in fact, believes that in writing *House Made of Dawn*, Momaday was "seeking to make the modern Anglo novel a vehicle for a sacred text" (205). Sacred texts, in this circumstance, are those texts which deal with ultimate human concerns: time, suffering, loss, the power of language, the human ability to imagine, and the reorienting intent of ritual. Indeed, Momaday's seminal works—*House Made of Dawn*, *The Way to Rainy Mountain*, and *Names*—are continually taught at major universities because of their capacity to help students reconsider. Such rethinking frequently causes students to overcome ignorance or come to consciousness, especially with regard to those elements of human genealogy that shape human identity. For these reasons, close examination of Momaday as an originative author seems appropriate.

Raised an only child, Momaday traveled with his parents from Oklahoma to the Southwest where they held positions as teachers of art and literature among the Navajo and Jemez. Momaday became a keen observer of the people and landscapes among whom he lived during his formative years. In two separate interviews, Momaday explained the genesis of his first novel to Laura Coltelli and Kay Bonetti. Momaday told Coltelli that Abel, the central character,

> represents a great many people of his generation, the Indian who returns from the war, the Second World War. He is an important figure in the whole history of the American experience in this country. It represents such a dislocation

of the psyche in our time. Almost no Indian of my generation or of Abel's generation escaped that dislocation, that
sense of having to deal immediately, not only with the traditional world, but with the other world which was placed
over the traditional world so abruptly and with great violence (162).

To Bonetti, Momaday recounted that he "knew a lot of young men"
at Jemez "who had been in the Navy or the Army, and they had
come back from WWII. And they were a sad lot of people in that
they had been disoriented in a way that Abel is. Terrible things happened to them; they murdered each other. And they drank themselves to death. . . . And they died violent deaths" (141). *House
Made of Dawn*, then, is Momaday's attempt to not only define the
causes of this behavior, but to imagine what it would take to heal
from such estrangement or illness.

   In his work, *Navaho Symbols of Healing*, medical doctor, psychiatrist, and anthropologist Donald Sandner addresses the issues of
"inescapable suffering." Sandner suggests that humans "can accept a
tremendous amount of legitimate suffering; what [they] cannot
accept is suffering that has no purpose. To be endured and accepted,
suffering must be given a meaning." Sandner further explains that
"the heart of all cultural-psychological methods of healing . . . is a
symbolic structure that explains, or at least provides a context for,
the sufferings of its members" (11). What makes Momaday's novel
so splendid, then, is his ability to provide not only a context for formidable suffering but to offer avenues for healing such suffering—
especially when this suffering is unparalleled in the annals of traditional mythologies. This means that traditional life-ways didn't have,
as yet, reasonable or ritual solutions for the kind of dislocation suffered by members like Abel. In Sandner's terms, Abel experiences
an "apocalyptic appearance of illness and misfortune" as well as the
painful consequences of human "ignorance and malice" (12).

   What Momaday offers, then, is an artistic experiment with radical suffering within a regenerative cosmos. Paula Gunn Allen
claims, "As the mythic structure of *Moby Dick* is the Bible, so the
mythic structure of *House Made of Dawn* is [the Navajo] Beautyway
and the Night Chant" ("Bringing Home the Fact: Tradition and
Continuity in the Imagination" 573). This is a significant claim;

however, Gunn Allen does not note that Momaday plays with recombinations of mythic paradigms: Navajo, Kiowa, Jemez, and Christian. Abel is a tentative member of the pueblo community, even before going to war. "His father was a Navajo, they said, or a Sia, or an Isleta, an outsider anyway, which made him and his mother and Vidal somehow foreign and strange" (*House Made of Dawn* 15). Furthermore, Abel's grandfather, Francisco, was rumored to be the offspring of Nicolás *teah-whau*—a pueblo witch, and Fráy Nicolás—an old consumptive priest. And the long complex history of incursions of both other Native peoples and Spanish missionaries onto the pueblo make this village an already complex locale. "Out of the doorways he passed came the queer, halting talk of old fellowship, Tanoan and Athapascan, broken English and Spanish," the narrator reports (71–72). Even so, such complex genealogies must be acknowledged and attended to.

The title of the novel, *House Made of Dawn*, is a line taken from the Night Chant—a restoration ritual given both to Dreamer and the Stricken Twins by the *Diyin Dine'é* (holy people) during the Navajo genesis. Paul Zolbrod explains that Navajo cosmology is replete with tales of "errant and persecuted heroes and heroines thrust into alien situations where they are pushed, abused, or injured, sometimes fatally. Ultimately, those protagonists are saved or restored by the gods and eventually return to their kinship groups with valuable information about how others might be cured of the same afflictions" (13). The Stricken Twins—one blind, the other lame—are of particular significance in relationship to Momaday's plot. Susan Scarberry-Garcia fully examines the commonalities between Abel's dilemma and the Stricken Twins' saga in her *Landmarks of Healing: A Study of* House Made of Dawn. Of singular importance, however, are the lengths to which these characters go to find relief. Furthermore, the dialogue across cultural paradigms through various conceptions of space and time adds significantly to the power of this novel.

Conceptions of space and time are of particular relevance in a post-Einsteinian time frame. Indeed, conceptions of linear time and three-dimensional space have been simultaneously brought into radical question by modern physics. Momaday's novel speaks to these reconceptions as they resonate with Native cosmology.

Certainly, seasonal time is still apparent, as is the cycle of life through various stages—the four seasons, birth/death, etc. And yet Momaday thrusts his novel into contention between linear time (chronological time—past, present, future), sacred time (synchronic time—mythological interventions into history), and memory (fragmented and nonsequential or syncretic time—or meaning begetting thought that can imagine connections).

Preceded by a prologue that addresses mythic time, *House Made of Dawn* is divided into four sections. Four is a sacred number among many Native tribes, representing the seasons, stages of life, four directions, and wholeness (symbolized by the cycle or circle). These meanings attend this novel as well. However, the four sections of *House Made of Dawn* also represent four diverse perspectives regarding Abel's malady and its prognosis; four conceptions of the sacred—Jemez, Kiowa, Navajo, and Christian; as well as four conceptions of the power of language: deracinating effects of language loss as well as Kiowa, Navajo, and Christian theologies about the power of the word. Each section is named after the pivotal roles played by Native characters (and their various conceptions of language) in relationship to Abel. "The Longhair" is Francisco, Abel's grandfather and a Jemez Indian traditional; this chapter begins on July 20, 1945, in Wallatowa Valley upon Abel's return from the war. "The Priest of the Son," is a Kiowa Indian and preacher, Tosamah; this chapter takes place on January 26, 1952, after Abel has been relocated to Los Angeles following a six-year prison term. During his sermons at the Native American Church, Tosamah introduces Abel to Native conceptions of the power of the word in comparison with the Gospel of John. Tosamah also rehearses the recovery of his Kiowa roots and the oral tradition. "The Night Chanter" is a Navajo Indian and traditional, Benally; this chapter also takes place in Los Angeles a month following the preceding chapter, on February 20, 1952. Benally reports on Abel's beating and hospitalization as well as the plans that he and Abel make to return home. Benally introduces Abel to the Night Chant. And "The Dawn Runner" is Francisco and subsequently Abel. The story has come full circle and back to Wallatowa. The dates given are February 27–28, 1952. And yet, on Abel's return, his grandfather is dying and rallies at dawn to remember the various passage rites he has undergone in his own journey toward death/rebirth. Although each section is given a date and place name, each section includes a complex of fragmented memories that transcend such delineations, and the reader must imagine how those fragments cohere.

When Abel returns from WWII, he is suffering from what is now known as Post-Traumatic Stress Disorder (PTSD), a psychological inability to reconnect with one's environment. This disorder is caused by repeated exposure to violence (the war), loss (the pre-war deaths of his mother and brother as well as the deprivation of his father's identity), and repeated victimization (maltreatment at the hands of an albino at the feast of Santiago on his return, as well as scapegoating by various Natives, followed by a near-fatal beating by Martinez, a Chicano policeman). Symptoms of this disorder include the incapacity for self-reflection as well as a vulnerability to exploitation. Abel attracts exploitation, generally in the behaviors and attitudes he dreads most: brutality, pity, humiliation, and disrespect. Bernard A. Hirsch further suggests that the "strong responses Abel generates," in particular male characters—the albino, Martinez, Tosamah, and even Benally—come because "In his suffering Abel is both a sorry example and stinging rebuke to them, a warning and a goad, someone both to fear and reverence, for he reminds them of who and what they are—of what they find most contemptible in themselves and most holy" (307). Two female characters recognize Abel's spiritual core: married and pregnant Angela Grace Martin St. John (who cohabits with Abel on retreat to the pueblo), and Abel's social worker in Los Angeles, Millie (who also cohabits with Abel—a major violation of ethical protocols for social workers). Sexual episodes with these women are drawn out to demonstrate Abel's aggressive sexual prowess as well as his appeal.

Further discussion of Abel's malady suggests the depth of PTSD in conjunction with Native wisdom:

> Had he been able to say it, anything of his own language—even the commonplace formula or greeting "Where are you going"—which had no being beyond sound, no visible substance, would once again have shown him whole to himself; but he was dumb. Not dumb—silence was the older and better part of custom still—but *inarticulate* (57).

In Native psychogenic paradigms, this *inarticulateness* is an illness of enormous consequence. Momaday explains his "unconditional belief in the efficacy of language" that he feels abides "at the heart of American Indian oral tradition" in this way:

> Words are intrinsically powerful. . . . By means of words can one bring about physical change in the universe. By means of words can one quiet the raging weather, bring forth the harvest, ward off evil, rid the body of sickness and pain, subdue an enemy, capture the heart of a lover, live in the proper way, venture beyond death. Indeed, there is nothing more powerful. When one ventures to speak, when he utters a prayer or tells a story, he is dealing with forces that are supernatural and irresistible ("The Native Voice in American Literature" 16).

Oral and written language, social and sacred speech, journals and questionnaires, sermons and ceremonial lyrics are all discussed within this narrative.

Indeed, in this novel Momaday warns, through Tosamah, that "The white man takes such things as words and literatures for granted, as indeed he must, for nothing in his world is so commonplace. On every side of him there are words by the millions, an unending succession of pamphlets and papers, letters and books, bills and bulletins, commentaries and conversations." For dominant, long literature cultures, "the Word itself—as an instrument of creation—has diminished nearly to the point of no return." Whereas in oral traditions, like those handed down through Tosamah's grandmother, "words were medicine; they were magic and invisible. They came from nothing into sound and meaning. They were beyond price; they could neither be bought nor sold. And she [Tosamah's grandmother] never threw words away" (89). These oral narratives represent, for Tosamah, "a very rich literature, which, because it was never written down, was always but one generation from extinction. But for the same reason it was cherished and revered" (90).

Another particular worry with regard to Abel's malady is his tendency to perpetuate his own victimage through retreating from life or acting out. When the albino defiles the feast of Santiago by beating Abel with a rooster, Abel responds with violence. He revenges this humiliation by killing the albino—an act that the narrator, during Abel's trial, characterizes as a necessary act. As attorneys and witnesses discuss terms like *homicide, murder,* and so forth, "word by word these men were disposing of him in language, *their* language," the narrator explains. Abel knew what the albino, the White man, signified: "and he would kill him if he could. A man kills such an enemy if he can" (95). However, as a result of his own aggression and its consequences, Abel is confined to "a desperate loneliness" (97). The narrator tells us that Abel has "no real insight into his own situation." Abel's lack of insight pertains to numerous situations, and as a result, Abel invariably turns to drink. In fact, the duration of Abel's stay in Los Angeles is plagued with drunkenness; Abel becomes the "drunken Indian" who fails to adapt to the American Dream and the intent of relocation. Abel, to further Vizenor's wisdom, is an *absence* to himself and not a *presence.*

Abel, however, becomes one who is *able* to achieve insight—and this through the power of the imagination and ritual language: "restore my voice for me" is the injunction of the Night Chant (134). Such an injunction *wills* the environment to return to an ongoing, re-creative, interactive cosmos where one "walks in beauty" and well-being (135). Abel is able to locate himself, once more, at the center, and he does so because he is present during his grandfather's last days; his grandfather's voice speaks "six times in the dawn, and the voice of his memory was whole and clear and growing like the dawn." In the presence of death, natural and seasonal, Abel remembers his world. He remembers, through his grandfather's voice, that he knew/knows "the long journey of the sun on the black mesa, how it rode in the seasons and the years, and they must live according to the sun appearing, for only then could they reckon where they were, where all things were, in time" (177). The house made of dawn, then, is that substantive moment of re-creation—both for Francisco and Abel, the dawn runners, and through Navajo ritual.

Because rituals are central to many contemporary Native American masterworks, a discussion of their sacred/psychological import is warranted. There are many kinds of rituals—reenactments of sacred narratives. There are rites that move an individual from the state of an initiate into the calling of a holy man. There are communal rituals—like the Sundance or the feast of Santiago—where entire communities are renewed and rededicated to living lives in harmony with the earth. There are healing ceremonies—like the Night Chant. And there are individual rites that move a person from one state of being to another—through maturation processes —like the vision quest for Plains youth or the rites for becoming a woman, man, warrior, healer, and so forth in other tribes.

To understand such moments of becoming or renewal, several concepts need explanation. First, symbolic recreation or healing ought to be addressed. In such instances, like those involving Abel, individuals are moved from passive or reactive onlookers to active participants in their own futurity, and therefore, the active renewal of entire communities. Sandner explains that "Life symbols make of a culture what it is specifically, and govern the thoughts and feelings of the people who are part of it. By means of origin myths and cosmogonic myths, a picture is built up of what the world is, how it came to be, and how it may be expected to function in the future" (13). These ideas are not archaic. For, as Sandner reminds us, using the words of Leslie White, "All human behavior originates in the use of symbols." Furthermore, "All civilizations have been generated, and are perpetuated, only by the use of symbols" (13). Words, paintings, musical notations, mathematic equations, dreams, and so forth are symbols/symbolic—one sign used to represent something else, to create images, sounds, structures, and meaning. Clifford Geertz reports that the effects of a sign (like the Night Chant) rest "ultimately on its ability to give the stricken patient a vocabulary in terms of which to grasp the nature of his distress and relate it to the wider world." Such signs are "concerned with the presentation of a specific and concrete image of truly human, and so endurable, suffering powerful enough to resist the challenge of emotional meaninglessness raised by the existence of intense and unremovable brute pain," Geertz explains (Sandner 14).

Symbols act powerfully, according to Sandner, to "change the psyche by converting energy into a different form, a form that can heal" (14). Carl Jung, in his analysis of numerous cultures, came to the conclusion that "Symbols act as transformers, their function being to convert libido from a 'lower' into a 'higher' form. This function is so important that feeling accords it the highest value"

(Sandner 14–15). This kind of psycho/social/spiritual healing is cultural, intuitive, and relies on the patient's willing participation and desire to gather in and act upon large amounts of information (the recombining of symbolic elements into new wholes). Such healing processes, however, thrust patients into liminal space—a space where the sick person is willing to leave one mode of being (a death) and enter into another (a rebirth). Such a state is not without grievous alternatives. Like atomic energy, the power to create or to destroy originates from a common source. When Abel assumes his grandfather's place as a dawn runner, he is both chasing away evil (the night) and running toward re-creation (a new day).

And such running exhausts—thrusts Abel into another dimension: "All of his being was concentrated in the sheer motion of running on, and he was past caring about the pain. Pure exhaustion laid hold of his mind, and he could see at last without having to think. He could see the canyon and the mountains and the sky." The novel concludes: "He was running, and under his breath he began to sing. There was no sound, and he had no voice; he had only the words of a song. And he went running on the rise of the song. *House made of pollen, house made of dawn. Qtsedaba*" (191). In that ending/ beginning, Abel is a pueblo dawn runner with the words of a Navajo healing ritual in his possession. And "Qtsedaba" is the Jemez formal marker indicating the end of a story. This moment is preempted (the end is told; but not the "thereafter"). Does Abel live or does it matter if he lives? If he can imagine—re-image his own being at the center, at the moment of creation, is that enough?

Pollen often symbolizes a creative potential. Renowned anthropologist, Victor W. Turner outlines several ritual processes. This complex of cultural expressions deserves thorough study. However, Turner's definition of liminality is pertinent and useful to a discussion of life-crisis narratives like Abel's. Turner claims that "Liminality can perhaps be described as a fructile chaos, a storehouse of possibilities, not a random assemblage but a striving after new forms and structures, a gestation process, a fetation of modes appropriate to postliminal existence" (42). Momaday's point is this: what is the postliminal existence for a character such as Abel? Can he find a center? Ritual, like theater, like the novel, is expectant. In this past-pain moment, does Abel experience a "sense of harmony with the universe" (Turner 42)? Is this moment synchronic, a time when Abel feels the whole planet in community with him? Is ritual transformation at hand? Can Abel, a man who has inherited so many cultural paradigms, be "at home" in this complex Postmodern moment? The story ends without clarification of the possibility of an anterior space where Pueblo, Kiowa, Navajo, and Christian symbolic systems meet to create new mythic potentials. And yet, Abel is running on . . . toward the dawn. Certainly, in the dawn, the regenerative potential is evident.

This power of the imagination, the ability of language to put ideas together (to gather disparate ideas into relationship) is a special function of creative memory for Momaday. And such imaginative processes are especially hard worked. While Momaday is a published poet, playright, painter, and has written numerous other works, two other works by Momaday have become classics—*The Way to Rainy Mountain* and *Names*. Both works deserve ample exploration. And yet, these works continue the topics explored in *House Made of Dawn*. And perhaps together, they continue to demonstrate Momaday's experiments with curative mythic models. However, these works aren't fiction. They are what is now being called creative nonfiction or literary autoethnography.

In *The Way to Rainy Mountain*, Momaday has assembled mythological and ancestral sketches, anthropological and historical fragments, and personal recollections of his Kiowa heritage. *The Way to Rainy Mountain* is the first work by a Native American to be recognized as a masterwork by the Modern Language Association. Indeed, in *Approaches to Teaching Momaday's* The Way to Rainy Mountain (1988), editor Kenneth M. Roemer draws on the insights of eighteen scholars who, in their essays, explore the power of this often anthologized work. The epistemology represented in this work mark it as singular in literary annals. In his essay "Tribal Identity and the Imagination," Matthias Schubnell explains the origins of this text. While Momaday was attending Stanford, his mentor Ivor Winters told him that "unless we understand the history which produced us, we are determined by that history; we may be determined in any event, but the understanding gives us a chance" (Schubnell 26). In his thirties, then, Momaday says he "suddenly realized that my father had grown up speaking a language that I didn't grow up speaking, that my forebears on his side had made a migration from Canada along with . . . Athapaskan peoples I knew nothing about, and so I determined to find out something about these things, and in the process I acquired an identity: it is an Indian identity as far as I am concerned" (Schubnell 26).

Momaday became an ethnographer, an autoethnographer in his attempt to reclaim his identity. Schubnell tells us that "As Momaday focused his attention on retrieving the remnants of Kiowa oral tradition, he realized how much American Indian poetry and mythology had already deteriorated and that speedy research was imperative to salvage what was still within reach" (29). Momaday had to rely on materials in archives and libraries alongside the fragmented recollections of Kiowa tribal elders to formulate his work. And in so doing, he conceived of an epistemology that is at once mythological/genealogical (the mythos), historical/anthropological (the logos), and personal (the ethos). In other words, Momaday is the knowing subject who collects, sorts through, and gives meaning to fragmented artifacts.

Edward M. Bruner explains this kind of self-referential epistemology in this way: "Every telling is an arbitrary imposition of meaning on the flow of memory, in that we highlight some causes and discount others; that is, every telling is interpretive. The concept of an experience, then, has an explicit temporal dimension in that we go through or live through an experience, which then becomes self-referential in the telling" (7). What Bruner suggests is that there is a reality, our experience or consciousness of that reality, and then our interpretation of that reality through verbal expression. *The Way to Rainy Mountain*, then, is Momaday's coming to consciousness with several realities. On a chronological level, the narrative is a record of the rise and fall of the Kiowa people and is retold in three sections: "The Setting Out," "The Going On," and "The Closing In"—contained within a prologue, introduction, and epilogue framed by two poems: "Headwaters" and "Rainy Mountain Cemetery." Momaday took the journey to Rainy Mountain intellectually (through his research) and personally. Rainy Mountain is a symbol of the journey toward the sacred center of Kiowa being. Momaday's grandmother is also buried in the Rainy Mountain cemetery, so Rainy Mountain is both the beginning and end of

Momaday's genealogical quest as well as the custodian of his grand-mother's grave.

In the prologue, Momaday writes:

> In one sense . . . the way to Rainy Mountain is preemi-nently the history of an idea, man's idea of himself, and it has old and essential being in language. The verbal tradition by which it has been preserved has suffered a deterioration in time. What remains is fragmentary: mythology, legend, lore, and hearsay—and of course the idea itself, as crucial and complete as it ever was. That is the miracle (4).

Note Momaday's interpretation of this journey—he gives value and meaning to his Kiowa heritage. Furthermore, Momaday claims that this journey is an "evocation of three things in particular: a land-scape that is incomparable, a time that is gone forever, and the human spirit, which endures." Momaday is not claiming the right to speak for the Kiowa people. Issues of authenticity, tribal sovereignty, and intellectual property taken into account, Momaday is orienting himself in relationship to tribal reality with particular characters drawn from his own ancestry—an ancestry which includes the sacred family of the Kiowa.

In the three major sections of this work, Momaday has organized materials into twenty-four triads (units of three paragraphs each). Each triad concerns a particular Kiowa reality organized into three different genres: myth, history, and personal witness. Therefore, while the entire work proceeds chronologically, each unit is organ-ized vertically or synchronically, thus demonstrating the timeless-ness of mythic events and their interaction with or influence on particular moments of life as lived by tribal members—on Momaday in particular. For example, when Momaday includes the sacred narrative of the coming of Tai-me (a holy being) to the Kiowa, he also includes anthropologist James Mooney's 1889 description of Tai-me as an artifact. These paragraphs are then fol-lowed by a third, which records Momaday's reaction to being in the presence of the Tai-me bundle. And each paragraph is rendered in a different font to draw attention to the relative ontological density or genre identification of each assertion. The mythological para-graph is rendered as story (the *mythos*); the anthropological paragraph as scientific or factual description (the *logos*—size, shape, color, use); and the third, as Momaday's personal evaluation of the meaning/value (the *ethos*) of the topic. In the *ethos* paragraph, for example, Momaday says:

> Once I went with my father and grandmother to see the Tai-me bundle. It was suspended by means of a strip of ticking from the fork of a small ceremonial tree. I made an offering of bright red cloth, and my grandmother prayed aloud. It seemed a long time that we were there. I had never come into the presence of Tai-me before—nor have I since. There was a great holiness all about in the room, as if an old person had died there or a child had been born (37).

When the holiness of the Tai-me is compared to the moment of birth and death, Momaday assigns a depth of meaning to his personal experience with this fragment of Kiowa mythology.

Two important concerns derive from Momaday's epistemology. First, as Bruner suggests, "the anthropology of experience sees people as active agents in the historical process who construct their own world." And second, Momaday confirms Bruner's assertion that "Culture is alive, context sensitive, and emergent" (Bruner 12). What this means, finally, is that while Momaday's main narrative demonstrates the catastrophic implications for the Kiowa of such events as the last Kiowa Sun Dance, the Kiowa culture lives on in Momaday's imaginative reassembling of Kiowa history. Momaday's admission that his life is consciously, directly, and continually influenced by his autoethnographic project also draws attention to the metaphoric implications of the idea of "the way." The *way* to Rainy Mountain, then, is paradigmatic of how other personal journeys can be undertaken to recover cultural identity. And such journeys do draw attention to particular landscapes, individual genealogies, collective mythologies, research, and the contemplation of various constructions of time.

The Names: A Memoir further explores Momaday's theories on language and identity: this time the focus is on the power of naming, memory, and the imagination. In his essay "Man Made of Words," Momaday claims: "we are what we imagine. Our very existence consists in our imagination of ourselves. Our best destiny is to imagine, at last, completely, who and what and that we are. The greatest tragedy that can befall us is to go unimagined" (200). This imaginative endeavor is not an experiment with fantasy; quite the contrary. Momaday, in contemplating his Anglo and Native names, rehearses his own genealogy back five generations. In truth, the meaning of Momaday's names can only be ascertained at his naming ceremony when complex genealogical histories are taken into account. In an italicized, three-paragraph, set-apart segment establishing the theme of the book (following Momaday's genealogical tree and preceding the "Prologue"), Momaday tells us that *"The storyteller Pohd-lohk gave me the name Tsoai-talee. He believed that a man's life proceeds from his name, in the way that a river proceeds from its source"* (*The Names* ii). The "Prologue" tells the origins of the Kiowa people *"through a hollow log,"* why they were a small tribe in number (a pregnant woman clogged the passage of further ancestors from the underworld), and why they called themselves *Kwuda,* *"coming out."* Such naming requires recognition of an "order of things . . . from the beginning." And this "order" acknowledges the "unfinished" nature of "emergence" from "primordial darkness . . . into the light" (1).

Again, the major sections of *The Names* are four in number—each section marked by a passage from one kind of consciousness to another, more expanded consciousness. In section one, for example, Momaday names his ancestors, names and describes various originary landscapes and singular events, and arrives at his naming ceremony —a ceremony where he is given the name of a character in Kiowa mythology:

> Pohd-lohk spoke, as if telling a story, of the coming-out people, of their long journey. He spoke of how it was that everything began, of Tsoai, and of the stars falling or holding fast in strange patterns on the sky. And in this, at last, Pohd-lohk affirmed the whole life of the child in a name, saying: Now you are, Tsoi-talee (57).

Section two tells about Momaday's travels from "Oklahoma to the Navajo reservation in New Mexico and Arizona and back again" (59). Books and places inform these formative years as do Momaday's beloved parents. Again in this section, Momaday underscores imaginative powers. He explains that "Memory begins to qualify the imagination, to give it another formation, one that is peculiar to the self. I remember isolated, yet fragmented and confused, images—and images, shifting, enlarging, is the word, rather than moments or events—which are mine alone and which are especially vivid to me." Even though Momaday admits that the memories in section two are the "disintegrated impressions of a young child," he also claims that these images "are not stories" but "they are storylike, mythic, never evolved but evolving ever" (61). In other words, childhood memories take on multiple meanings when recalled in various contexts over the duration of one's life.

Furthermore, Momaday underscores the power to delineate—to name—experiences. He asks: "Of all that must have happened to and about me in those my earliest days, why should these odd particulars alone be fixed in my mind?" The answer is: "If I were to remember other things, I should be someone else." In other words, we are what we remember. And there are hints of memory that remain "shapeless," says Momaday. But he has "no voice" with which to articulate them. And then he remembers the line from the Night Chant: "*Restore my voice for me*," followed by another insight into the importance of naming:

> How many times has this memory been nearly recovered, the definition almost realized! Again and I have come to that awful edge, that one word, perhaps, that I cannot bring from my mouth. I sometimes think that it is surely a name, the name of someone or something, that if only I could utter it, the terrific mass would snap away into focus, and I should see and recognize what it is at once; I should have it then, once and for all, in my possession (63).

The Names is constantly shifting from fragments of remembered people, events, and places to philosophical conjecture.

Of time, for example, Momaday at one point says: "Notions of the past and future are essentially notions of the present. In the same way an idea of one's ancestry and posterity is really an idea of the self" (97). And so, when Momaday tells his readers about his grandparents, parents, and their role in his life, he is shaping his own idea of himself in the process. And Momaday's ideas about place are

equally significant—geography and genealogy are inseparably connected. Momaday says, "The events of one's life take place, *take*
place. How often have I used this expression, and how often have I
stopped to think what it means? Events do indeed take place; they
have meaning in relation to the things around them" (142). As geography and genealogy become relatives in Momaday's estimation, so
too does time. Following a rehearsal of the ceremonial calendar of
the Jemez people that Momaday witnessed while he and his parents
lived at Jemez, Momaday notes:

> There was at Jemez a climate of the mind in which we, my
> parents and I, realized ourselves, understood who we were,
> not perfectly, it may be, but well enough. It was not our
> native world, but we appropriated it, as it were, to our-
> selves; we invested much of our lives in it, and in the end it
> was the remembered place of our hopes, our dreams, and
> our deep love (152).

Jemez is particularly important to Momaday. He says: "At Jemez I
came to the end of my childhood" (160).

Much can be said about the elegant and profound nature of *The*
Names and the themes found therein. After a near fall to his death,
Momaday concludes that he had been "within an eyelash of eternity.
That was a strange thing in my life, and I think of it as the end of an
age. I should never again see the world as I saw it on the other side
of that moment, in the bright reflection of time lost. There are such
reflections, and for some of them I have names" (161). This "eyelash
of eternity" is a time reference that permeates *The Names*. And
Momaday continually breaks the barriers between such dimensions.
The epilogue, for example, recounts a spiritual experience Momaday
had with his ancestors—*Mammedaty, Aho, Pohd-lohk, Keahdinekeah,*
Kau-au-ointy and his grandmother's close friend Ko-sahn—in the
arbor at Rainy Mountain. To be sure, this experience was imaginary,
but then, as Momaday suggests, what can be imagined is the better
part of reality still. Although Momaday is Kiowa, his primary texts
deal primarily with Pueblo cultures, particularly the Jemez Pueblo.
The Pueblo people are considered descendants of the ancient
Anasazi people. Leslie Marmon Silko is from the Laguna Pueblo and
will, therefore, be considered next.

Leslie Marmon Silko (b. 1948)

In his 2002 biographical essay on Silko, Dennis Cutchins explains: "Despite that her most successful work is an early one, Leslie Marmon Silko remains a central voice in Native American literature. Her first novel, *Ceremony* (1977), is taught in colleges and universities around the world" (271). The volume of scholarly articles that have been produced on Silko and her works is indicative of the quality of her work. In 1997, the *American Indian Culture and Research Journal* published William Dinome's "Laguna Woman: An Annotated Leslie Silko Bibliography." In his introductory essay about "The Author and Her Works," Dinome notes that "critical attention to [Silko's] work has seen no abatement" (208). As a matter of fact, Dinome includes eighty-five titles in his bibliography.

Silko was born of mixedblood heritage. Silko's father was mixedblood Laguna Pueblo and her mother was mixedblood Cherokee. Silko was raised on or near the Laguna Pueblo in New Mexico where her family participated in clan activities to the extent allowed for mixed bloods. Much of Silko's most famous novel, therefore, stems from Silko's experiences as a mixedblood Laguna Indian. Indeed, a great deal of the mythic content of the novel comes from ancient clan creation narratives. In *Other Destinies*, Louis Owens says of *Ceremony*: "Within her story of Tayo's journey toward wholeness and health, Silko—as did Momaday in *House Made of Dawn*—conducts a healing ceremony for all of us, for the world at large" (170). Other similarities abound between Silko's and Momaday's seminal works. Their theories on mythology, language, storytelling, ritual, landscape, ancestry, and healing are informed by similar contexts—Pueblo, Navajo, Chicano, and Southwestern histories. And their intent on dealing with radical evil in a modern context in curative ways makes a discussion of them, side by side, more fruitful.

Tayo, the central character in *Ceremony*, is also emotionally ill from experiences he has suffered during WWII. Tayo is an orphan: his mother was a prostitute, his father is unknown, and he is raised by his aunt, Thelma, and uncle, Robert. His aunt is a Christian who holds Tayo in contempt—especially for his "illegitimate" origins. And so raising and caring for Tayo, "her dead sister's half-breed child" (30), becomes her Christian burden. Tayo is a mixed-blood but traditional; his cousin Rocky is full blood but assimilationist. Again, like the similarities between Abel, his brother, and the Navajo Stricken Twins, Tayo and Rocky also continue mythic twin concerns. Tayo promises to bring Rocky back safe from war; Rocky dies in Tayo's arms. While away at war, Josiah, Tayo's beloved uncle and surrogate father, dies, and his cattle—a special breed bought to survive harsh Southwest weather—are scattered South, into Mexico. Furthermore, Tayo cannot comprehend killing Japanese people who resemble his own. And the putrid killing fields of jungle terrains make Tayo pray against rain—a request that appears to be answered with drought at home. When Tayo comes home from war, he is hospitalized with "battle fatigue"—an illness that is a "mystery" to Army doctors (31). Owens furthers Tayo's diagnosis by asserting that "Tayo also suffers from survivor's guilt" (174), a severe emotional illness that is often experienced by Jewish survivors of the Holocaust.

Once home, Tayo wretches daily, convulses with pains in his stomach, doesn't "have energy to move his lips, to even form . . . words," and dreams in fragmented memories (29). Typical of his response to his death in life is this passage:

> He woke up crying. He had dreamed Josiah had been hugging him close the way he had when Tayo was a child, and in the dream he smelled Josiah's smell—horses, woodsmoke, and sweat—the smell he had forgotten until the dream; and he was overcome with all the love there was. He cried because he had to wake up to what was left: the dim room, empty beds, and a March dust storm rattling the tin on the roof. He lay there with the feeling that there was no place left for him; he would find no peace in that house where the silence and the emptiness echoed the loss. He wanted to go back to the hospital . . . where he could merge with the walls and the ceiling, shimmering white, remote from everything (32).

His grandmother's response to his condition is this: "That boy needs a medicine man. Otherwise, he will have to go away" (33).

Readers are told from the poems in the beginning of the text that this story is being told by "Ts'its'tsi'nako, Thought-Woman," the spider woman who spun the world into existence. And through the power of the word, Thought Woman "named things and / as she named them / they appeared" (1). Again, like Momaday, Silko draws on mythology to formulate her narrative, a narrative that asserts the power of words and the necessity of storytelling. Silko's poem "Ceremony" prefaces the novel and announces her assertions about storytelling:

> I will tell you something about stories
> [he said]
> They aren't just entertainment.
> Don't be fooled.
> They are all we have, you see,
> All we have to fight off
> illness and death (2).

In the same poem, Silko also speaks of evil, but in this manner: "Their evil is mighty / but it can't stand up to our stories" (2).

And evil abounds in this novel on local and global planes. Tayo's worst enemies are his war buddies, also Indians—Harley, Emo, and Leroy—who want Tayo to remain desolate. Globally, evil is perpetuated by "the destroyers" who don't want wholeness. These destroyers are "white skin people / like the belly of a fish / covered with hair." And they constantly look for victims to "grow" them "away from the earth," "away from the sun," "away from the plants and animals." And they want their victims to become like them, humans who "fear the world" and so attempt to "destroy what they fear" (135). The destroyers "bring terrible diseases / the people have never known. / Entire tribes . . . die out / covered with festered sores / shitting blood / vomiting blood" (137). And this witchery desires destruction, suffering, torment, deformation, and sterility. However, this is not a Native/Anglo split. For the real "trickery of the witchcraft," says Betonie, the Navajo healer, is that the destroyers "want us to believe all evil resides with white people. Then we will look no further to see what is really happening" (132). This is an albino, mutant kind of whiteness—a colorless, degenerate, sick humanity. However, the novel informs readers that this evil was generated by Indian contests involving negative power or witchery.

Witcheries' destructive powers are formidable—especially in the Southwest. As Tayo completes his journey, he realizes that he has been moving around the space known as Trinity Site. Trinity Site,

> where they exploded the first atomic bomb, was only three hundred miles to the southeast, at White Sands. And the top-secret laboratories where the bomb had been created were deep in Jemez Mountains, on land the Government took from Cochiti Pueblo. Los Alamos, only a hundred miles northeast of him now, still surrounded by high electric fences and the ponderosa pine and tawny sandrock of the Jemez mountain canyon where the shrine of the twin mountain lions had always been. There was no end to it; it knew no boundaries; and he had arrived at the point of convergence where the fate of all living things, and even the earth, had been laid (245–246).

Indeed, Silko writes that such destructive power unites people in "the fate the destroyers planned for all of them, for all living things; united by a circle of death that devoured people in cities twelve thousand miles away, victims who had never known these mesas, who had never seen the delicate colors of the rocks which boiled up their slaughter" (246).

Tayo finally sees a pattern, "the way all stories fit together—the old stories, the war stories, their stories—to become the story that was still being told. He was not crazy; he had never been crazy. He had only seen and heard the world as it always was: no boundaries, only transitions through all distances and time" (246). In other words, Tayo's journey to consciousness is panhuman—a story others throughout the world are called to also live. And the power of Silko's narrative is in her theory of healing and, thereby, escaping the destroyers' net.

A third poem in the beginning of the novel explains: "*What She Said*: / The only cure / I know / is a good ceremony / that's what she said" (3). Indeed the entire novel is curative—diagnosing the causes of this sickness and prescribing the cure. The novel begins and ends with words from a Pueblo prayer: "Sunrise" "accept this offering"

(4, 262)—in the creative house made of dawn. What lies in between is complex, intricate, and of enormous consequence. And this is why *Ceremony* has been translated into so many languages and has remained popular in so many academic circles. However, while Silko and Momaday both address the causes of radical illness in the modern world and attempt to find a path to a regenerative ceremony, Silko's novel evinces that Momaday didn't get it quite right —especially in his conception of ritual and in his failure to recognize that he had written a novel about masculine transformation and ascendancy. Certainly, as Paul Zolbrod so rightly explains about Navajo cosmology: "the basic theme of the Navajo creation story is that solidarity must be maintained between male and female if there is to be harmony in the world" (14). The women in *House Made of Dawn* are useful to Abel only so far as they provide sexual release or advance his healing. Silko, however, recognizes the need for male and female regenerative powers to unite in harmony if true healing is going to occur. In the "he said" "what she said" location of the voices in Silko's introductory poems, Silko establishes mythic, or timeless, gendered, congruent, and coequal truth claims. Owens explains, "The male-female dialogue here emphasizes the inextricable interrelatedness of story, ceremony and cure while also pointing toward the male-female balance that is the desired state in Pueblo ritual" (170–71).

However, Silko contends that traditional ceremonies are not adequate for healing someone who has been contaminated by modern, radical evil. As Owens suggests, "The unmistakable message is that though Silko, like a traditional storyteller, is remaking the story, reforming it, molding it to fit new situations and times, she is not inventing it" (170). The same can be said of Silko's ceremonial creations. Constant attention is paid to traditional mythology in connection to the contemporaneous story of Tayo—each narrative in dialogue with the other. However, the ancient healing methods need revision. When Ku'oosh, one of the Pueblo healers, attends to Tayo, he first tries to comprehend the enormity of his injury. And then he explains: "There are some things we can't cure like we used to . . . not since the white people came" (38). What Tayo comes to realize from this exchange is something he "feared all along." Ku'oosh only helped him understand that "It took only one person to tear away the delicate strands of the web, spilling the rays of sun into the sand, and the fragile world would be injured" (38). In other words, within mythic/historical/global vistas, each individual counts—one person's singular actions, like a pebble in a pond, ripple to the edges and back of their environs.

Tayo is finally led to Betonie, a mixedblood Navajo healer, who figures out how Tayo can heal. Betonie introduces Tayo to the ideas of ceremonial mutability and transitions. "After the white people came, elements in this world began to shift; and it became necessary to create new ceremonies. I have made changes in the rituals." Furthermore, "when the people were given these ceremonies, the changing began, if only in the aging of the yellow gourd rattle or the shrinking of the skin around the eagle's claw, if only in different voices from generation to generation, singing the chants." Betonie proposes: "In many ways, the ceremonies have always been changing" (126). If a people attempt to cling to ancient ceremonial practices within a changing world, the destroyers can find a toehold into their rigid patterns. Betonie warns: "don't be so quick to call something good or bad. There are balances and harmonies always shifting, always necessary to maintain. . . . It is a matter of transitions, you see; the changing, the becoming must be cared for closely. You would do as much for the seedlings as they become plants in the field" (130).

Another similarity between Momaday and Silko is their contention that if you can name something, you have power over it. Kenneth Lincoln explains, for example, that the central scene with Betonie "implies that healing involves the right triggering of memory, a health within things, natural to body and mind. And, similarly, to name things right is to make medicine through memory, to heal and give strength." Furthermore, says Lincoln, "This right naming connects inner and outer forms, the *ianyi* ('breath') or spirit with matter, by way of living words" (242). This naming includes understanding the interconnectedness of all stories, centuries of plotting by destroyers, the mutability of ceremonies, and the individual power to find particular or personal healing and, thereafter, to return to one's people with knowledge to share so that others might also be cured. Lincoln says, "Betonie would have Tayo take responsibility for what is: his own life mediating several cultures, races, tongues, and times. The ceremonies of the stars and mountains and woman and rain, even rounding up the speckled wild cattle, account for everything without dehumanizing or denaturalizing any one part." What is significant here, is the idea of not "displacing one's own pain on others, 'me' against 'them,' castigating, warring, killing, dividing the people," Lincoln concludes (243).

What this kind of accountability requires constitutes the major portions of *Ceremony*. Tayo travels to the four quarters of his world: he travels south to reclaim Josiah's cattle; west to Gallup, where he was born and where he and his mother lived in a shanty as well as where he finds old Betonie; east to Albuquerque and the direction of the atomic testing site—with the attendant war ramifications; and finally north where he finds the sacred woman, Ts'eh Montano, whose name translates from Pueblo and Spanish words into *water mountain*. He also finds a center place—at Laguna and within himself—which constitutes two more directions or a sphere: the symbol of wholeness. Sacred colors, directions, psychologies, and seasons—integral yet always in transition, like the many phases of daylight and darkness, attend each segment of this novel. This material world mediates human existence—contextualizes and supports all existence. "According to Pueblo cosmology," Owens explains, "everything in the universe—whether animate or inanimate—is significant and has its ordered place and is knowable and therefore controllable. Such knowledge and control, however, require extreme vigilance and attention to detail coupled with proper action." And such action requires guides, helpers, and community participation. In the Pueblo world, Owens continues, "the individual has little significance alone; an individual such as Tayo has identity and a coherent self only insofar as he is an integral part of the larger community" (172).

What ultimately heals Tayo, therefore, is his visit to the north, to Ts'eh Montano. Ts'eh is a sacred woman. And Tayo's experience with her is like the intervention of the divine into human affairs. Together, Tayo and Ts'eh relive an ancient myth. Ts'eh is married to hunter or Mountain Lion. And they both come to the aid of Tayo. Owens explains that in this story, the hunter represents Winter, and he lives, in Keres tradition, on North Mountain. Tayo, in this context, represents Summer. "Tayo is reenacting a role in a story from

Pueblo mythology in which Yellow Woman, Winter's wife, meets Summer one day and invites him to sleep with her while her husband is out hunting deer." Tensions, logically, occur between the rival desires for Ts'eh. However, in mythic fashion, both men agree that this holy woman "will spend part of the year with Winter and part with Summer" (187). Thus the realignment of the world begins to take place. Eventually, Tayo is led to a moment, "in the sunrise," where "it was all so beautiful, everything, from all directions, evenly, perfectly, balancing dawn with night, summer months with winter. The valley was enclosing this totality, like the mind holding all thoughts together in a single moment" (237). Tayo, at this moment, is at the center.

And yet, Tayo's love for Ts'eh makes his multiple healing decisions possible. His momentary encounter with her leads him to realize "He had lost nothing." There were enduring realities beyond the power of the destroyers:

> The mountain outdistanced their destruction, just as love had outdistanced death. The mountain could not be lost to them, because it was in their bones; Josiah and Rocky were not far away. They were close; they had always been close. And he loved them then as he had always loved them, the feeling pulsing over him as strong as it had ever been. They loved him that way; he could still feel the love they had for him. The damage that had been done had never reached this feeling. This feeling was their life, vitality locked deep in blood memory, and the people were strong, and the fifth world endured, and nothing was ever lost as long as the loved remained (219–220).

Tayo acknowledges that "The breaking and crushing were gone, and the love pushed inside his chest, and when he cried now, it was because she loved him so much" (227). However, this intimacy expands. Especially because Ts'eh warns Tayo that the destroyers don't want their story to continue. "They want it to end here," she tells him, "the way all their stories end, encircling slowly to choke life away." Yes, many narratives end when lovers find one another; the thereafter often goes untold. Tayo has retreated to the hills to evade being returned to the hospital as a crazy person. It would suit the world (the destroyers) to isolate Tayo—either in the hills with his lover or in a hospital, consigned to the status of the terminally ill. "They have their stories about us—Indian people who are only marking time and waiting for the end" (232).

Emo has informed the Bureau of Indian Affairs (BIA) police and doctors from the hospital of Tayo's location. None of them can decide who Tayo is, can define him. In one last violent evening, Tayo is almost seduced into participating in the violence of the destroyers. Tayo is the intended victim, and when they can't retrieve him, Leroy, Emo, and Pinkie turn on Harley. However, their attempt to draw Tayo from his hiding place in order to rescue Harley fails. Tayo moves "back into the boulders":

> The witchery had almost ended the story according to its plan; Tayo had almost jammed the screwdriver into Emo's skull the way the witchery had wanted, savoring the yielding bone and membrane as the steel ruptured the brain. Their deadly ritual for the autumn solstice would have been completed by him. He would have been another victim, a drunk Indian war veteran settling an old feud; and the Army doctors would say that the indications of this end had been there all along, since his release from the mental ward at the Veteran's Hospital in Los Angeles (253).

Tayo returns to the center of the Laguna kiva and reports on his entire adventure. In the two final mythic poems, Silko writes: "Every evil / which entangled him / was cut / to pieces" (258). And the "witchery / has returned upon it" (261)—upon itself. The Laguna people now have a new ceremonial pattern to release them from the evils concomitant with the modern world. And it is Tayo the orphan, the mixed-blood from multiple racial and contextual identities, Tayo the wounded healer, that knows the way. Indeed, Tayo's name "may amalgamate from a kashare song when the sprits came out of . . . the Place of Emergence . . . to live in the house of the sun." His name reintegrates "a split Laguna personality and cultural schism," Lincoln conjectures (235).

Other Silko works have gained wide spread critical acclaim at conferences and among academic circles. *Storyteller* (1981) is Silko's exemplary autoethnography. *Almanac for the Dead* (1991) is an epic work dealing with the prophecy that the conquering races in the Americas will so pollute the continent that the Native people will rise up to reclaim her. And *Garden in the Dunes* (1999) is Silko's magnificent foray into the many uses of the vegetative universe assumed by her characters from the "old" and "new" worlds.

James Welch (b. 1940)

In 1982, Alan R. Velie published *Four American Indian Literary Masters*—a work identifying Momaday, Silko, Vizenor, and Welch as *the* four consummate authors writing from Native perspectives. While the number of accomplished authors has increased over the years, Welch still maintains his master's status. Welch (Blackfoot and Gros Ventre) is a poet, novelist, essayist, and history buff. His works have been translated into numerous foreign languages and his plaudits are international. Welch has garnered acclaim both for his literary works and for his contributions to Native American Studies. *Fools Crow,* Welch's third novel, for example, received three prestigious awards: an American Book Award, the Pacific Northwest Book Award, and a *Los Angeles Times* Book Prize. In 1997, the Native Writer's Circle presented Welch with their Life Time Achievement Award. In 1994, Welch also published a historical work, *Killing Custer: The Battle of the Little Bighorn and the Fate of the Plains Indians* with Paul Stekler—a work made into a documentary film. While Welch's poetry is first rate, his fiction is more widely taught and, therefore, will be emphasized here. Indeed, four of his novels are continually taught in university classrooms across America: *Winter in the Blood* (1974), *The Death of Jim Loney* (1979), *Fools Crow* (1986), and, with growing frequency, the epic, *The Heartsong of Charging Elk* (2000). Welch's first four novels, including *Indian Lawyer* (1990), deal with Blackfoot protagonists, and his fifth, *The Heartsong of Charging Elk*, deals with an ailing Sioux Indian abandoned in France by Buffalo Bill's Wild West Show.

An important dialogue exists between Welch's Blackfoot novels. *Winter in the Blood* and *The Death of Jim Loney* are about estranged, emasculated, and demoralized men, while *The Indian Lawyer* is about a successful Indian, at least by White standards (Yellow Calf is an athlete, scholar, and Stanford University graduate with a bright future in politics). However, the unnamed protagonist in *Winter* and Jim Loney and Yellow Calf have something in common; they are without cultural moorings. Each, with varying outcomes and to varying degrees, is initially without life-transforming access to Blackfoot mythology, ancestry, community, or satisfactory connections to landscape. This lack impacts characters' lives. "Unnamed" experiences a tentative transformation as he acquires some ancestral knowledge; Loney causes his own and another's violent death; and Yellow Calf appears to yearn for escape from political life back to the reservation.

Fools Crow, on the other hand, explores the daily lives of the Lone Eaters band of traditional Blackfeet during a crucial moment in their history. Action in the novel pivots around three principal families. First, there is Rides at the Door; his wives—Double Strikes Woman, Striped Face, and Kills Close to the Lake; and their children—White Man's Dog and Running Fisher. The second family is headed by Yellow Kidney and his spouse Heavy Shield Woman; their children are Red Paint, Good Young Man, and One Spot. And the third family is the widowed Boss Ribs and his son Fast Horse. Although he is a singular man, having lost his family, Mik-api is also central to the unfolding of this novel.

Welch writes that *Fools Crow* is "an account of the Blackfeet (Pikuni) people of that era that culminates in the Massacre on the Marias" (*Killing Custer* 39). "That era" was marked by several hard events. The Blackfoot were experiencing a third decimating epidemic of small pox. Welch reports that a third to a half of the people died of white scabs disease during 1869 through 1870 (44). Owl Child, a Pikuni youth, and his small band of rebel Indians brought inordinate U.S. government attention onto the Blackfeet—especially with their raid on the ranch of trader Malcolm Clarke in the fall of 1869. As a result of Owl Child's many exploits, Major Eugene M. Baker's troops massacred 173 helpless Blackfoot men, women, and children on the Marias River in January of 1870. General Sheridan was told that Owl Child's gang was living with Mountain Chief's band. "So when Sheridan's order came down that 'if the lives and property of the citizens of Montana can best be protected by striking Mountain Chief's band, I want them struck,' it didn't matter a whit to the army and to the citizens of Montana that the wrong band, a band led by a peace chief, had been struck," Welch explains (*Killing Custer* 45). Welch believes that, "The Massacre on the Marias River was more representative of what happened to Indian people who resisted the white invasion than Custer's Last Stand. I tell it not only because it happened to my own people, but because it needs to be . . . known if one is to understand this nation's treatment of the first Americans" (22–23). Furthermore, "When the soldiers could not find the 'hostiles,' they simply punished the available 'friendlies' by massacring them" (*Killing Custer* 53). During this difficult period, Blackfoot lands were being seized by the American government at an alarming rate. No wonder, then, that in *Fools Crow*, government representatives are called "seizers."

Despite these appalling intrusions into the Blackfoot world, the male protagonist of *Fools Crow* is still able to experience the rites of passage into manhood offered to males living within a dynamic communal context; he moves from being called Sinopa, to White Man's Dog, and finally to Fools Crow—each name representing a life-stage or certain status Fools Crow attains among his people. Welch researched historical archives, tribal records, and family histories in order to write *Fools Crow*. "Although an old woman, who refused to learn even grocery-store English, [my great-grandmother Red Paint Woman] remembered everything that had happened to her and her people. It was her stories, related to me by my father, that informed many stories I told in *Fools Crow*," says Welch (*Killing Custer* 39). Names of historical figures are given to characters throughout this novel—Yellow Kidney, Eagle Ribs, Mik-api, Heavy Runner, Little Dog, Mountain Chief, Joe Kipp, Owl Child and more. Welch gave Fools Crow's beloved wife his great-grandmothers's name, Red Paint. Louis Owens suggests that "By re-imagining, or remembering the traditional Blackfoot world, Welch attempts to recover the center—to revitalize the 'myths of identity and authenticity'—and thus reclaim the possibility of a coherent identity for himself and all contemporary Blackfoot people" (157). This historical novel, then, provides readers with ample insights into the life-ways that traditionally provided spiritual and emotional integrity to the lives of Blackfoot people. In other words, *Fools Crow* supplies insight into what the characters in Welch's other Blackfoot novels lack.

In order to fully access this novel, readers need to understand that Welch does not dichotomize between the sacred and profane.

As Vine Deloria explains, for traditionals, "If there were other dimensions to life—the religious experiences and dreams certainly indicated the presence of other ways of living, even other places— they were regarded as part of an organic whole and not as distinct from other experiences, times, and places in the same way that Western thinkers have always believed" (39). Throughout *Fools Crow*, dreams, visions, animal helpers, and spirits within natural phenomena continually inform the characters. When Fast Horse does not carry out the wishes of Cold Maker sent to him in a dream, a raid on the Crows goes badly for him and for Yellow Kidney. Fools Crow also has warning dreams but cannot interpret them until he hears Yellow Kidney describe his misadventures among the Crows, then he realizes he could have prevented the catastrophe had he known the meaning of his dream. Deloria proposes: "The funda-mental premise [in these episodes] is that we cannot 'misexperi-ence' anything; we can only misinterpret what we experience" (45–46). As a young man who continually accepts more responsi-bility for the well-being of his people, Fools Crow is finally sent by Dream Maker to dwell with Feather Woman—a sacred female fig-ure from Blackfoot mythology. Feather Woman gives Fools Crow visions of the future of the Pikuni so he can help people endure ensuing tragedies.

"We are, in the truest sense possible, creators or co-creators with the higher powers, and what we do has immediate importance for the rest of the universe," Deloria declares (47). Such theology informs the vision quests and Sun Dance ritual in *Fools Crow*. Furthermore, *Fools Crow* describes what Deloria calls an essentially moral universe: "In the moral universe, all activities, events, and enti-ties are related, and consequently, it does not matter what kind of existence an entity enjoys, for the responsibility is always there for it to participate in the continuing creation of reality" (47). This not only applies to people but also to the entire sentient world. Raven, for example, leads Fools Crow to the aid of his animal helper Wolverine. Raven can "speak the language of the two-leggeds. It's easy, for I have lived among you many times in my travels. I speak many languages," Raven tells Fools Crow. "I converse with the black-horns and the real-bears and the wood-biters" (*Fools Crow* 54). It is Raven who explains the gifts given to Fools Crow through his animal helper. "You will fear nothing, and you will have many horses and wives. But you must not abuse this power, and you must listen to Mik-api, for I speak through him, that good many-faces man who shares his smoke" (*Fools Crow* 58).

In Native American Spirituality, Lee Irwin defines spirituality as "that connectedness to core values and deep beliefs"—

> a pervasive quality of life that develops out of an authentic participation in values and real-life practices meant to connect members of a community with the deepest foundations of personal affirmation and identity. In this sense, spirituality is inseparable from any sphere of activity as long as it really connects with deeply held affirmative values and sources of authentic commitment, empowerment, and genuineness of shared concern (3).

The life experiences of numerous characters in this novel are measured against their ability to make decisions with "shared concerns" in mind. Owl Child and his rebels choose a life of rebellion and vengeance against the Whites and thereby bring suffering into the lives of their people. Fast Horse, the son of Boss Ribs (a healer), goes against his own dreams and arrogantly puts himself forward at the expense of others—especially Yellow Kidney, one of the chief warriors among the Pikunis. And Yellow Kidney sexually violates women in an enemy camp—young women about to die from small pox. Although he confesses his crimes, his actions result in physical, emotional, and social scarring—especially in Yellow Kidney's life and the lives of his wife and children. Even Running Fisher, Fools Crow's brother, in the rashness of his juvenile mentality, breaks sexual taboos and has an affair with his father's third wife, a woman Fools Crow also covets.

Welch establishes these many violations of social protocols as a means of introducing the culture's methods for addressing ruptures in the social fabric. *Fools Crow* examines traditional responses for dealing with the imbalances brought about by anti-social behavior: councils, the aid of medicine men, the annual sun dance, and the elders' compassionate, yet decisive, discipline dispensed for crimes against communal solidarity. Indeed, an examination of language patterns, life cycle paradigms, and how disparate tribal details converge reveal how Welch's Pikunis continually regenerate tribal cohesion. For example, despite the fact that Welch writes in English, he is able to thrust readers into Blackfoot ways of naming experience. Within the first few paragraphs of the novel, for instance, Welch immerses readers into the cosmology of the three tribes of the Blackfeet—the Pikunis, Kainahs, and Siksikas. "Now that the weather had changed, the moon of the falling leaves turned white in the blackening sky and White Man's Dog was restless. He chewed the stick of dry meat and watched Cold Maker gather his forces," the novel begins (3). Seasons of the year are described in terms of what occurs in the natural world. A close-by river is Two Medicine River; the mountain range near by is the Backbone of the World; winter is Cold Maker; the big dipper is Seven Persons; the sun is Sun Chief; the moon is Night Red Light; and the thunder is Thunder Chief. Each aspect of the Pikuni world, however, is named without reference to familiar English equivalents. Whites are called *Napikwans*—a Blackfoot term meaning Old Man Person (Owens 268). The root of *Napikwans* is *Napi* the name for the Blackfeet Creator and Trickster figure; therefore, calling Whites *Napikwans* is recognition of their collective and relentless power.

Readers are likewise quickly introduced into Blackfoot life-cycle patterns. White Man's Dog, we are told, has failed his first vision quest—an important passage rite for Blackfoot males. His animal helper did come, explains White Man's Dog, "and I smelled his sour breath, I saw his yellow eyes, but he didn't speak to me. He gave me no song, no vision" (7). Although the protagonist is introduced as White Man's Dog, throughout the novel he goes through several life-changing events which cause him to earn his man's name: Fools Crow. Everything within the Pikuni environment is described in terms of kinship and function. And cultural metaphors determine the way humans interact with their environments. For example, if one lives in a Newtonian universe—a universe whose functions are equated with machines—one is invariably caught up in a world of work. The machine metaphor generates conceptions of a world that can run down. Members of a society become cogs in the machine who produce commodities. Medicine is seen as repair. The mind accumulates information or data. Communication is achieved through mechanical extensions of the eyes, ears, and mouth:

telescopes, telephones, recorders. Storytellers are replaced by radio and television. Humans, therefore, often experience the world through tacit means. The problem is that they believe what they experience is actual, real, and nonmediated.

The universe seen in terms of kinship and life cycles is not static; it is full of birthing, mating, dying, seasons, growth and decline, and dependencies. One depends on the seasons, on animal and plant life, on family members, on tribal operations, and on personal contributions to the whole. In such an interactive world, individuals learn how to control their environment through right action. This includes gender relationships. For example, when Yellow Kidney does not return home from a raid on a Crow camp, his wife Heavy Shield Woman asks if she can become the Sacred Vow Woman at the next Sun Dance in order to secure his return. Barry M. Pritzker tells us, "Unlike most Plains tribes, women participated in the Blackfeet Sun Dance" (304). Welch underscores the central role women played among the Blackfoot through his meticulous attention to details concerning the Sacred Vow Woman's role in the Sun Dance—especially in identifying the connection between the Sacred Vow Woman and Feather Woman.

"Only the most virtuous of women" can "accomplish" such a task, explains Three Bears. Heavy Shield Woman must gain approval for such a role from Three Bears, the chief of the Lone Eaters, as well as the leaders of the other bands. "I wish my man back. My children need their father. I have assisted twice as a coming-forward-to-the-tongues woman. With the help of my sisters and the older ones, I will carry out my duties correctly," Heavy Shield Woman tells Three Bears (42–43). The role of Sacred Vow Woman is heavy with expectations. She and her helpers must "build a lodge for the Sun Chief," a place where they could "honor him with sacred ceremonies, songs and dances." She must purchase the "Medicine Woman bundle from her predecessor" as well as procure "sacred bull blackhorn tongues" for sacrifice and to feed the poor and the faithful there assembled. She must be instructed "in her duties" by the previous Sacred Vow Woman. She must fast and be purified. She must gain confirmation from Sun Chief regarding her virtue. She must travel in the four directions surrounding the sacred lodge. She must pray "to the Above Ones, to the Below Ones and to the four directions for strength and courage." And she must be instructed with regard to the origins of the sacred clothing she must wear as the Sacred Vow Woman—clothing which once belonged to Feather Woman. In hearing the story of the origins of the Sun Dance, Heavy Shield Woman realizes the gravity of her sacred obligations. It is through the heroic deeds of Feather Woman's son, Star Boy, that the Sun Dance was given to the Blackfoot. If the Blackfeet will honor Star Boy every summer, says Sun Chief, he will "restore their sick to health and cause the growing things and those that [feed] upon them to grow abundantly" (108–113). When all of this is accomplished, Feather Woman can break her fast.

Before Sacred Vow Woman carries out her vows, Yellow Kidney returns maimed and disgraced. Yellow Kidney confesses to the council, "I . . . copulated with one who was dying of the white-scabs disease" (75). And, "In fornicating with the dying girl, I had taken her honor, her opportunity to die virtuously" (81). Yellow Kidney has always been an honorable person, except for his actions during the Crow raid. And the dream shared by Fast Horse before the raid had warned Yellow Kidney not to proceed, but his desires for glory got the better of him. When caught, Crow warriors severed Yellow Kidney's fingers from his hands. "Oh, I cried bitterly, for I had lost my ability to draw a bow, to fire a musket, to skin the blackhorns. I would be as useless as an old dog, and I not yet thirty-nine winters!" (79). Despite Yellow Kidney's circumstances, Heavy Shield Woman keeps her vow.

White Man's Dog has intentions of becoming a warrior; however, the incursion of diseases and threats to tribal integrity from within and without move White Man's Dog into the company of healers: Mik-api (a many faces man) and Boss Ribs (a heavy singer for the sick). Without intending to, Fools Crow becomes Mik-api's apprentice. Natural curiosity, innate ability, and continual revelatory dreams further Fools Crow's journey toward becoming a visionary. Fools Crow learns to depend on Mik-api's kindness and wisdom. In fact, Mik-api helps Fools Crow become a pledger in the Sun Dance—a role that Fools Crow accomplishes with distinction. Each time Fools Crow must endure new challenges, Mik-api performs appropriate ceremonies or instructs Fools Crow in appropriate procedures.

However, Fools Crow's most daunting ordeal is the journey he must go on to meet Feather Woman (So-at-sa-ki). Feather Woman is the wife of Morning Star who is the son of Sun Chief and Night Red Light. In Blackfoot mythology, she is a mortal who lives in the sky with her husband and son. She grows homesick. While digging turnips, she digs up the sacred turnip—an act which creates a hole in the sky through which Feather Woman can see her people on earth. Because she was told not to dig up the sacred turnip, she is exiled from her home in the sky. At home among her own people on earth, Feather Woman grows despondent and lonely. Each morning she begs her husband to take her back; he will not. Eventually she dies of a broken heart (111). Interspersed with events back in camp, the journey to Feather Woman comprises the latter portion of the novel and resembles the journey of many heroes in world mythologies: He is called to go on an arduous journey; he suffers during this journey from fatigue, hunger, and other deprivations. He goes as a beggar to receive enlightenment. "I myself do not understand, but if my journey is successful, perhaps it will help the Lone Eaters find a direction," Fools Crow tells Red Paint (316).

Perhaps this portion of the novel is most Postmodern in intent and impact. That is, Fools Crow questions his own meta-narrative (sacred stories). He questions the justice of Feather Woman's ongoing suffering and exile; "her only sin was one of loneliness, then and now and forever," thinks Fools Crow.

> She had been punished, and the people were being punished for a reason that Fools Crow could not understand. The people had always lived in harmony with their sacred beings. Always they had performed the ceremonies to the best of their ability. They sacrificed often and without stinginess. And yet they were being punished (360).

While gazing on what he believes to be a hide with a traditional winter count recorded on it, Fools Crow sees the images begin to move; he does not want to see what is on the robe, but can not avert his eyes. He sees the dead and dying of his people in their lodges. He sees the loss of massive numbers of kindred and friends. He sees disease, warfare, and isolation. He sees the loss of the blackhorns (buffalo). He also sees the starvation of survivors and their growing

THE BEST AND THE BEST KNOWN   89

poverty. And he sees Blackfoot children discriminated against (353–358). "And for the first time, he came to think of them, the Above Ones, as cruel spirits to allow Feather Woman to suffer so. And to allow what he had seen" (359).

Fools Crow is angry with what he sees on the skins. "Anger can sometimes do a man good, but now it is futile," explains Feather Woman. "There is much good you can do for your people." And yet the alternatives that Feather Woman offers are dire. "You can prepare them for the times to come. If they make peace within themselves, they will live a good life in the Sand Hills. There they will go on to live as they always have. Things will not change." In other words, in death, the people will find release and peace. "But I grieve for our children and their children, who will not know the life their people once lived. I see them on the yellow skin and they are dressed like the Napikwans, they watch the Napikwans and learn much from them, but they are not happy. They lose their own way," Fools Crow responds. "But they will know the way it was. The stories will be handed down, and they will see that their people were proud and lived in accordance with the Below Ones, the Under-water People—and the Above Ones," is Feather Woman's reply (359–360).

The last chapter of the novel records a ceremony the surviving Pikuni celebrate. Mik-api directs them in prayers, drumming, and singing. Fools Crow attends with Red Paint and their son—the next generation. "For even though he was, like Feather Woman, burdened with the knowledge of his people, their lives and the lives of their children, he knew they would survive, for they were the chosen ones." That night, the people feasted. . . . And they did so with hope in their survival. Critics have been confused by Welch's ending—the return of the buffalo and "all around, it was as it should be" (391). Is this a flight into the Sand Hills? Is this the Ghost Dance vision? Or is Welch projecting his own vision of what might be possible beyond the parameters of the closing decades of the nineteenth century? Certainly Welch has given meaning to the suffering of his people. He has also written a novel whose central generating forces are female: Heavy Shield Woman, Feather Woman, and Red Paint. Indeed, Fools Crow's forays into the spirit world find sustenance from Red Paint's love. And the power, wisdom, and justice of Fool's

Crow's mentors—his father, Mik-api, and Boss Ribs—demonstrate positive, though humanly flawed, male models. For these reasons, among others, William Bevis believes that Welch has written a "unique American Novel" whose historical "design," "stark realism, clear prose, and pure imagery" establishes *Fools Crow* as a literary masterwork (605).

Gerald Vizenor (b. 1934)

The geographical move from the Blackfeet and James Welch's birth-place in Montana to the Anishinaabe and the birthplace of Gerald Vizenor in Minnesota maintains imposed boundary lines between the United States and Canada. Anishinaabe is the traditional name for the Ojibwa or Chippewa people—a people whose homelands straddle numerous boundaries, from southern Ontario to the north-ern parts of Montana, North Dakota, Minnesota, Wisconsin, and Michigan. Boundary straddling is myth, metaphor, and discourse strategy for Vizenor. Kimberly M. Blaeser, in her biographical essay on Vizenor, claims, "Throughout his life Vizenor found ways to thrive in circumstances that might have destroyed a less hardy indi-vidual" (299). In fact, any discussion of Vizenor's status among Native American writers generally pivots around three themes: Vizenor's remarkable personal odyssey; his enormous productivity; and his theoretical and creative genius.

Vizenor and his immediate ancestors are *Metis*: mixedblood Anishinaabe and French Canadian. Vizenor's father, Clement William Vizenor, was a member of the White Earth Reservation. In order to secure employment, Clement moved to Minneapolis, where he was married, had a child, and was murdered; Vizenor was just eighteen months old when his father was found in an alley with his throat slit. Vizenor's Anglo mother, Laverne, was unstable and often abandoned Vizenor to the care of his grandmother or foster parents. In his autoethnography, *Interior Landscapes*, Vizenor writes, "My fosterage was for money, not for parental love, salvation, or my moral restoration" (40). The only stable parent Vizenor had was his mother's third husband, Elmer Petesch, who formed a bond with Vizenor only after they were both abandoned by Laverne. Unfortunately, Petesch fell from an elevator shaft and died on

Christmas Eve, 1951—just five months into his surrogate father/son experiment with Vizenor. When Vizenor was informed of Petesch's death, he recalls: "I was calm at first, the relatives were notified, and then the loss of my best friend was too much to bear. I was overcome for hours, and hours, and the loss overcomes me now in these words about his death" (93). In order to survive such events, Vizenor escaped into an inner world. Of his youth, Vizenor says: "My interior landscapes were never secure, but my silence was solace, a bold mixedblood reservation at the word line. I created new trinities, benign demons, little people and tricksters from the woodland, in my head" (46). In other words, Vizenor retreated into his creative imagination where he learned how to re-imagine his sundry encounters with social poverty. Such re-imaging included recuperation of his tribal heritage as a survival technique.

Vizenor has developed ever-expanding theories of *survivance*—a term coined by Vizenor to describe survival and endurance in a comic mode. Tragedy is terminal; comedy is not. What is more, Vizenor's Anishinaabe progenitors were members of the Crane Clan, a clan noted for skill in oratory. Clan identity places individuals within systems of privileges and obligations—obligations to know clan and tribal histories, genealogies, landscapes, mythologies, and to evaluate and share such knowledge in dialogue with others. In addition, one of the most influential characters from Ojibwa mythology is Trickster—a symbolic figure who brings all established ideologies concerning human behavior into radical questioning through antic humor. In his biographical essay on Vizenor in *American Novelists Since World War II* (2000), Alan R. Velie insists that "Since adolescence Vizenor has considered himself a living avatar [incarnation] of Nanabozho, the Chippewa Trickster" (326). Vizenor's status as Trickster is doubly subversive, however, due to his ability to combine traditional Native American approaches to human folly with Postmodern thought; both are methods of challenging what Vizenor calls "terminal creeds." Terminal creeds are those *fixed* religious, cultural, anthropological, scientific, and government constructions of human society, including interactions with the natural world, which result in misunderstanding, misappropriation, violence, and death.

Postmodern/Trickster insights are founded on the instability of *signs*: words, symbols, acts, or creeds used to convey meaning. Such

instability draws attention to the fact that the *signifier* (a word, gesture, action, or thing as symbol) is not the *signified* (those realities
that words, gestures, actions [like rituals], or things refer to). In
Interior Landscapes, Vizenor explains:

> Tribal tricksters arise in imagination, create the earth,
> chance, praise, impermanence, humourous encounters, and
> totems, and liberate the mind in their stories. The cranes
> endure these creations, these interior landscapes, and turn
> their voices to the seasons, the remembered seasons . . . My
> tricksters are tender on the wild rise in dreams, memories,
> myths, and metaphors now, and hold their chances over the
> wicked seams in ecclesiae. The best stories are survival
> trickeries on the borders, marcescent blues on the margins,
> on the colonial curbs; the rest would be simulations [imi-
> tations, poses, imposed images] (73).

This location at the "seams," in the "margins" on "curbs," and in
"dreams, memories, myths, and metaphors" locates Vizenor's discourse *between* memory (including histories) and imagination in a
game with words, a language game intended to liberate students and
readers from their inherited terminal creeds.

There is a close connection in Vizenor's words between Trickster
discourse and Shamanic occupation. A Shaman is a combination
priest and doctor—in Vizenor's case, a doctor for the culturally
estranged and emotionally, psychologically, or *terminally* ill.
Shamanic wisdom is derived in numerous ways: through genetic
inheritance; through a calling; through dramatic encounters with the
sacred; through training; or through protracted and often inchoate
(un-storyable) or inconceivable experiences with the traumatic
incongruities of human experience. Vizenor's wisdom is derived
genetically as well as through confrontations with agonizing incon-
gruity. Throughout his various vocational and avocational pursuits,
Vizenor has encountered absurd incongruities. For example, Vizenor
served in the military, first as a soldier and then as an entertainment
director. Vizenor was also a student at New York University and the
University of Minnesota. At the University of Minnesota, Vizenor
double majored in unrelated fields—Asian Studies and Child
Development. After his education, Vizenor obtained a series of jobs:

as a social worker for the Minnesota Department of Corrections; as director of the American Indian Employment and Guidance Center in Minneapolis; as a journalist for the *Minneapolis Tribune*; and as an instructor at numerous colleges and universities, including such prestigious institutions as the University of Minnesota, the University of California at Santa Cruz, the University of Oklahoma, and the University of California at Berkeley. Somewhere in his teaching career, Vizenor also taught in China. Ironies abound in Vizenor's educational pursuits. For example, he earned his high school equivalency while serving in the military—a fact that annoyed the administrators at New York University.

Traditionally, the shamanic task has been to reestablish order out of chaos. The kind of "order," however, that Vizenor seeks is a playful, healing, reviving, moving, or nonstatic moral consciousness. Vizenor explains the connections between shaman and writer: "The shaman returns with a vision and must earn the trust of a community. Similarly, the creative writer must earn a presence in literature and the politics of the time. Shamans earn respect as healers, and so writers must earn their readers, but not as mere consumers" (*Postindian Conversations* 62). Furthermore, "the visionary literature that transforms what we once thought of as a native presence becomes a literature that heals, and a literature that liberates" (63). Writing liberating fiction is not without risk, however. Vizenor affirms that "creative literature of this kind, stories that have a sense of shamanic visions are dangerous" (62). Vizenor admits being "scared" into "creation" of his first novel. Such fear promotes a separation between writer, reality, and alternative states of consciousness (63). "Late at night, on my walks after writing [*Bearheart*] most of the day, scenes of the novel came alive at every turn, and some of the characters, the most evil, lurked in the alleys, at the darkest intersections," Vizenor remembers. "I walked faster and hummed over the menace. I even tried to overcome my fear of the novel by lurking, by pausing in alleys, by courting the unknown to beat the temptations of victimry" (63).

Vizenor's refusal to succumb to the "temptations of victimry" is the response to colonial violence that Vizenor advocates throughout his writing. Rather than retreat into despair, poverty, passivity, or debilitating addictive behaviors, Vizenor recommends proactive pursuits. In fact, many of his works are guides out of the morass of self-deprecating reactions to life's degrading circumstances. Who would want to emulate the more ridiculous antics of Trickster—sporting a fifty-foot penis ready for brachydactylous activity at every turn? Trickster is constantly tripping over his enormous organ: a phallic symbol of male aggression, dominance, and avarice ready to erupt at the slightest provocation. Because Vizenor points out, metaphorically, that most humans walk around with their flies open or their skirts up, his works are controversial. And Vizenor has produced many works that often incite offense from those who like their violence and perversity in simulations (in media fictions) rather than up close, real, and historically verifiable. Velie contends that "Gerald Vizenor is often called the most prolific and controversial writer of the American Indian literary renaissance that began in 1968" ("Gerald Vizenor" 326). By the close of the year 2000, for example, Vizenor had published thirty books; a play (*Ishi and the Wood Ducks: Postindian Trickster Comedies*); written and produced a film (*Harold of Orange*); edited six books; and published numerous essays in scholarly journals. Many of his works have been translated into Italian, French, and German. His collected news articles appear in *Tribal Scenes and Ceremonies* (1976) and *Crossbloods: Bone Courts, Bingo, and Other Reports* (1990). Poetry, prose, fiction, plays, film scripts, scholarly essays, and news articles are among the genres produced by Vizenor. And so many of his works are interactive; characters, themes, and motifs often reappear—weaving a web of interrelationships familiar to the dynamics of oral narratives.

Of necessity, only Vizenor's most-often-taught novel, *Bearheart: The Heirship Chronicles*, will be discussed. *Bearheart* is a novel within a novel. Ostensibly, the major portion of the text is a work written by Saint Louis Bearheart, a Native who works for the Bureau of Indian Affairs in Washington. During a raid on his office, Bearheart asks a young female radical to search through the BIA's file cabinets to find and then read a novel he has written called *The Heirship Chronicles*. Bearheart's novel chronicles the journey of a mangy miscellany of mixedblood pilgrims who travel from Minnesota to New Mexico in search of an escape window into the fourth world (the existence after this world) at Pueblo Benito. In traditional Southwestern mythologies, survivors have already gained the fourth world as a result of their ingenuity and desire to escape the degeneracy of the third. In Bearheart's narrative, humans replicate the former apocalypse; Indians, Whites, and Mixed-bloods alike are trapped in a third world—ensnared and despoiled by the consequences of living in a chemical, drive-through, consumer, greed-driven, sexually obsessed, and racist civilization whose supplies of gas have been exhausted. Without any economic motivations for cooperation, humans exist in isolated pockets of chaos.

After introducing the history and genealogy of the major character in his novel, Bearheart says: "Fourth Proude Cedarfair, the last leader of the Cedar nation, avoided word wars and terminal creeds. He convinced himself that through political and religious interdependence he could protect the sovereign Cedar nation as well as did his diplomatic father who abhorred human violence." Proude believed his nation existed "in the minds and hearts of the living, he did not feel he needed to prove the endurance of sovereignties" (15). And yet treekillers wanted his Cedar Circus (reservation) as a lumber resource, and pantribal peoples flocked to Proude Cedar "less drawn to visions than to ceremonial entertainment" (16). Bearheart writes that, "Economic power had become the religion of the nation; when it failed, people turned to their own violence and bizarre terminal creeds for comfort and meaning" (23).

Realizing that he and his wife would suffer death if they did not comply with the wishes of Jordan Coward, Proude plans their escape—taking only what sacred objects might sustain them in their journey to the Fourth World. Jordan Coward, it must be noted, was a "federal humanoid." Bearheart writes, "Coward, possessed by evil revenge, dreamed of the Cedar nation being cut into little sticks and burned in the federal offices of the bureau of public remorse" (23). Along their way to New Mexico, Proude and his wife Rosina Parent Cedarfair accumulate eleven other pilgrims: Benito Saint Plumero, Zebulon Matchi Makwa, Belladonna Darwin-Winter Catcher, Inawa Biwide, Sun Bear Sun, Lilith Mae Farrier, Little Big Mouse, Bishop Omax Parasismo, Pio Wissakodewinini, Justice Pardone Cozener, and Doctor Wilde Coxwain (114). Each character shares his/her story as they travel along, often revealing historical contingencies for their bizarre character—rape, incest, sex changes, bestiality, erotic desire, and naive ideologies. Only Inawa Biwide and Proude Cedarfair make it to the escape window.

Perhaps a brief discussion of a few of the females in the novel will demonstrate the difficulty readers have had with this novel. Proude and Rosina's first encounter in their travels is with Benito Saint Plumero—a clownish fop "dressed in this finest blue satin ribbon shirt and suede leather trousers" (35). Plumero is Trickster in his sexually obsessive guise. He is also the doorkeeper to the "scapehouse of weirds and sensitives"—"organized and founded during the first national energy crisis when the price of gasoline and heating fuels soared and people were building wood burners in their houses in the cities. Thirteen women poets from the cities obtained state and federal funds to develop a survival center in a rural area" (936). Their survival center is on the Red Cedar Indian Reservation. In actuality, these women are victims of violence, and their only solace in their community is Plumero's "president jackson." "The women of the scapehouse speak of the male organs of copulation with the names of presidents," Bearheart explains (39). Outside their compound, the women are known as cannibals because they eat their pets—birds, dogs, cats. Inside, they enjoy the sexual pleasures of "president jackson" (the president who legalized the forced removal of the Five Civilized Tribes from their eastern homelands to Oklahoma).

The primary concerns of the women in the scapehouse are revealed in their various conversations with Rosina, whom they call "sister." "The women asked her questions about identities, her dependencies, her sexual and political responses to men, and her rituals as a person, to which she did not have abstract answers." And Rosina's character is revealed in Bearheart's casual assessments: Rosina's "lie was visual and personal. She did not see herself in the abstract as a series of changing ideologies" (39). Indeed, although Rosina has grown children, her passive yet empathetic personality causes her to absorb the advances of those around her—without consciousness of the consequences of using her body as an instrument, a receptacle.

Vizenor's female characters are caricatures—burlesques of types of women who can't survive. Lilith Mae Farrier is the wounded healer. An incest survivor, Lilith Mae channels her female energies into the care of school children on a reservation. On the reservation, the Native women call her a dog woman—a cruel put-down indicating their disgust with the White do-gooder. Lilith Mae believes their nickname to be an indication of her love of animals, when in actuality the Native women are accusing her of making love with dogs. Lilith Mae eventually leaves the reservation, further damaged by loss of any positive sexual identity. Her companions become two boxers—with whom she frequently copulates. Lilith Mae, in her attempts to get five gallons of gas for the pilgrims, eventually loses a game with the "evil gambler." And rather than face his violent terms for her death, she burns herself along with her dogs.

Little Big Mouse is an innocent. When she views an assortment of cancer victims (victims of a chemical civilization) along the road, she attempts to give them some kind of relief from their infirmities by dancing for them. Little Big Mouse's physical beauty and perfection, her innocence, arouses desire and envy in those cancer victims whose various body parts are deformed or missing. In a frenzy, these cancerous people rip apart Little Big Mouse's body.

Belladonna Darwin-Winter Catcher is the consummate ideologue caught up in romantic notions without any ability to actually perceive the complex demands of surviving in a world where actual evil exists. She wants admiration for her beliefs. And yet, she is guilty of "collective generalizations" (196), "narcissistic revisionism," and romanticized, terminal tribal creeds (198). For example, in her conversations with the "breeders and hunters" who live in Orion (a constellation of arrogant male stars) behind a "framed wall of earthen bricks," (189) she says:

> The tribal past, our religion and dreams and the concept of mother earth, is precious to me . . . Living is not good for me if a shaman does not sign for shadows in my dreams. Living is not important if it is turned into competition and material gain . . . Living is hearing the wind and speaking the language of animals and soaring with eagles in magical flight (196).

Belladonna (a drug), Darwin (the evolutionist of "survival of the fittest" fame), and Winter Catcher . . . believes her "tribal blood is timeless" and gives her "strength to live and deal with evil" (196). Belladonna is accused of making "Truth in beautiful words." And for this, she receives her just desserts—a poisoned sugar cookie. While Belladonna assumes she is among kindred souls or lovers of life, she is actually among insulated Native men who challenge the ideas of visitors. Their mission (another thrust of male arrogance) is "against terminal creeds wherever and whenever" they find them (193).

Similar narratives are told about the male pilgrims—all symbols of various failed approaches to the gamble that life is. In "Real Stories: Memory, Violence, and Enjoyment in Gerald Vizenor's *Bearheart*," John Hauss explains Vizenor's insights into the several ideologies which create "cultures of death."

Vizenor's *Bearheart* studies the deadlocks of enjoyment possible at moments of history

> when desire's metonymic movements and transformations are weakened or deadened, and enjoyment is overbalancingly channeled into superegoic functions of the objectification, judgement, and punishment of bodies. What such moments demand, what they in fact are inevitably destined for, regardless of interventionist intention, is renewed eruptions of enjoyment—the eruptive laugh of the bear in *Bearheart*—making possible new articulations of the sociosymbolic order (*Real Stories* 3).

In other words, violent federalist histories have engendered obscenity and any chance for gendered wholeness. 'The visibly phallic character of federal violence," in many passages in *Bearheart*, "the obscene foregrounding of the phallus in acts of mutilation and destruction—registers expansionist America's proclamation that it acts as bearer of sacred totem—the final term of history as 'Progress,'" explains Hauss (3). Furthermore, "Violent traumas survived are revisited." In other words, victims of violence perpetuate their victimage. Moreover, "'Instincts for survival' are at stake here because the self-protective anxieties they induce mitigate against psychic encounters with traumatic memory," Hauss explains (5). This means that most of the female and male characters in this text can't become critically self-aware, can't heal. They bury rather than confront their violent histories.

These ideas are difficult, and many readers are untrained in analysis of issues regarding the psychological and political relationships between sex and violence. In the "Afterword" of *Bearheart*, Louis Owens explains that several publishers refused to consider this novel for publication—too much sex and violence and unexpected criticism of Natives. "Indians in the novel were capable of cowardice as well as courage, of greed and lust as well as generosity and stoicism" (247–248). Three of Owens's mixedblood students complained to his department chair when he assigned this novel. Owens believes "not the violence or bestiality, not the transsexual shapeshifting . . . upset" his students, but the "novel's outrageous challenge to all preconceived definitions" of Indians (248). At the heart of *Bearheart* is the episode where the pilgrims meet up with Sir Cecil Staples, the evil gambler—a figure right out of Chippewa mythology. Vizenor's novel, in many respects, is a gamble with the evil gambler—it is Vizenor's attempt to outwit evil. But you can't outwit evil unless you keep an eye on the game. And the game, when lost, exacts limbs, loves, and lives.

Studies in American Indian Literatures (SAIL), devoted their Spring 1997 issue to the works of Gerald Vizenor. Louis Owens was the guest editor.

(Karen) Louise Erdrich (b. 1954)

The works of Louise Erdrich and Gerald Vizenor are similar in several ways: Erdrich is Chippewa and engaged in Trickster discourse; one of her central characters, Nanapush, is a version of the mythic Nanabozho; other of her characters recapitulate or challenge mythic patterns—both tribal and Christian; Erdrich uses gambling and gamblers as a way of addressing the possibility of change; Erdrich is interested in redefining place in a Postmodern era; and Erdrich is interested in healing through humor. But unlike Vizenor's characters, Erdrich's characters practice a unique kind of religion to promote this healing: "love medicine." Kate McCafferty explains Erdrich's use of the term *medicine* as a central controlling metaphor in her novels: "Rather than discuss their traditional 'religion,' many contemporary Chippewa [including Erdrich] speak in terms of medicine." McCafferty further explains that "Native American 'medicine' is really an interdisciplinary network of religion, philosophy, spirituality, health care, psychology, ecology, natural history, and more. In the indigenous context, medicine is a way of life" (730). Using "love" as an adjective preceding "medicine" denotes passion/compassion as the central motivating, integrating, or healing force in an otherwise chaotic environment. Erdrich was born in Little Falls, Minnesota. Her parents, Ralph and Rita (Gourneau) Erdrich, raised her in Wahpeton, North Dakota, where they taught at an Indian Boarding School. Through her mother's line, Erdrich is an enrolled member of the North Dakota Turtle Mountain band of Chippewa. Erdrich's grandfather, Pat Gourneau, served as tribal chair of the Turtle Mountain Chippewa. Gourneau is a French name inherited from marriages between early French Canadian trappers and the Chippewa. Erdrich's father's ancestors come from Germany. Thus Erdrich, like Vizenor, is also *Metis*—a mixed-blood of Chippewa, French, and German birthright.

Erdrich received her B.A. from Dartmouth and her M.A. from Johns Hopkins. While attending Dartmouth, Erdrich met anthropology professor Michael Dorris (Modoc) whom she later married. Many of Erdrich's works are dedicated to her husband. For example, in her dedication in *Tracks*, she writes: "Michael / The story comes up different / every time and has no ending / but always begins with you." Dorris often collaborated with his wife—as editor, critic, and creative resource. Dorris was also an author in his own right, publishing novels, literary criticism, and nonfiction works— including the National Book Critics Circle award-winning *The Broken Cord: A Family's Ongoing Struggle with Fetal Alcohol Syndrome* (1989). Dorris brought three adopted children into the marriage, and together Erdrich and Dorris had three daughters. Shortly before the publication of *The Antelope Wife*, acute clinical depression and inordinate stress from raising children with Fetal Alcohol Syndrome caused Dorris to commit suicide, leaving Erdrich to mourn the loss of her mentor, lover, and muse.

Singling out any one of her works as best or best known would undermine Erdrich's accomplishments. Helen Jaskoski likens Erdrich's complex of stories and attention to place to the works of William Faulkner: "Like the sagas of the Compsons and the Snopeses," Erdrich's narrative organization "aims at a complex rendering of the intricate and far-reaching minglings and conflicts and interlocking fates among people of differing races and culture groups, all of whom feel a deep sense of their ties to the land and to their history upon it" (33). Indeed, in her complex of novels, Erdrich continually draws on numerous genealogical lines and particular characters to indicate the complicated social field besieging Chippewa peoples on and off the reservation. In *The Bingo Palace*, Lipsha Morrissey explains: "But us Indians, we're so used to inner plot twists that we just laugh. We're born heavier, but scales don't weigh us. From day one, we're loaded down. History, personal politics, tangled bloodlines. We're too preoccupied with setting things right around us to get rich" (17). In a humorous attempt to explain his relationship to Lyman Lamertine, for example, Lipsha says: "The truth is, our relationship is complicated by some factors over which we have no control. His real father was my stepfather. His mother is my grandmother. His half brother is my father. I have an instant crush upon his girl" (16).

Erdrich's North Dakota novels include *Love Medicine* (1984; republished with revisions and additions in 1993), *The Beet Queen* (1986), *Tracks* (1993), *The Bingo Palace* (1994), *Tales of Burning Love* (1996), *The Last Report on the Miracles at Little No Horse* (2001), and *Four Souls* (2004). *Antelope Wife* (1998) is about urban Ojibwe in Minneapolis, and *The Master Butchers Singing Club* (2003) chronicles the lives of Fidelis and Eva, immigrants from Germany to Argus, North Dakota. Argus is also the site for Native off-the-reservation experiences in *Tracks*, *Bingo Palace*, and *Tales of Burning Love*. Erdrich has likewise published books of poetry, an autoethnographic work focusing on childbearing (*The Blue Jay's Dance* 1995), a novel coauthored with Dorris (*The Crown of Columbus* 1992), as well as juvenile fiction (*Grandmother's Pigeon* 1996).

Erdrich says of place in her novels: "*Ozhibi'iganan*: the reservation depicted . . . in all of my novels is an imagined place consisting of landscapes and features similar to many Ojibwe reservations. It is an emotional collection of places dear to me, as is the town called Argus. It is not the Turtle Mountain Reservation, of course, although that is where I am proud to be enrolled" (*The Last Report on the Miracles at Little No Horse* 357). In her essay, "We Anishinaabeg are the Keepers of the Names of the Earth," P. Jane Hafen (Taos Pueblo) outlines and discusses "Place Names," "The Power of the Land," "Reservation Border Towns," and "Story and Place" in Erdrich's novels. Hafen concludes: "Her writing presents a 'tribal view' of complicated human interactions and histories. As a master storyteller, she renders language and art gracefully across the Great Plains. Like the antelope, she pursues the elusive horizon, the infinity of the world's edge and its brand of light through narratives of indigenous survival" (331). Indeed, the life-stories of Erdrich's characters are inextricably tied to place. Place supports, informs, mediates, and alters human experience in Erdrich's works. Erdrich says:

> In our own beginnings, we are formed out of the body's interior landscape. For a short while, our mothers' bodies are the boundaries and personal geography which are all that we know of the world. Once we emerge we have no natural limit, no assurance, no grandmotherly guidance . . . for technology allows us to reach even beyond the layers of air that blanket earth. We can escape gravity itself, and every semblance of geography, by moving into sheer space, and yet we cannot abandon our need for reference, identity, or our pull to landscapes that mirror our most intense feelings ("Where I Ought to Be" 49).

Narrating, numbering, and naming are reciprocal (between earth and earth born) endeavors in Erdrich's works. She explains this reciprocity mythologically:

> Every feature of land around us spoke its name to an ancestor. Perhaps, in the end, that is all that we are. We Anishinaabeg are the keepers of the names of the earth. And unless the earth is called by the names it gave us humans, won't it cease to love us? And isn't it true that if the earth stops loving us, everyone, not just the Anishinaabeg, will cease to exist? (*The Last Report on the Miracles at Little No Horse* 361)

Because of this ontology—the being of the earth and her beings —numerous characters in Erdrich's novels endeavor to win back lost territories, primarily through trickery and gambling. Fleur Pilliger, for example, gambles for lost homelands in *Tracks, Bingo Palace,* and *Four Souls.* Part of her power as a Pilliger shaman resides in her craftiness as a gambler. Fleur gambles for land and lives. She gambles for the life of her stillborn daughter in the land of the dead in *Tracks*, and she bargains for her great grandson's life in *Bingo Palace*. In fact, *Bingo Palace* is a wild romp into the various aspects of tribal gaming —mythic, ritual, and casino gambling. It should be noted that poker games for Fleur are played for high stakes. Kristan Sarvé-Gorham writes that Fleur engages in Western profane gambling to *cheat* the entire colonial project: the "commodification of land"; the false legit-imacy of treaties; the allotment system; tax assessments; any method "the government employed to wrest Anishinaabe land away from her people" (287). Fleur, we are told in *Bingo Palace*, "was never one to answer injustice with fair exchange" (145). Sarvé-Gorham writes that Erdrich "tacitly [and comically] suggests that Indians receive a fairer chance at positive resolution to land disputes through gam-bling than they do through the Euro-American legal system" (287).

Principal family lines in Erdrich's North Dakota saga include the Nanapushes, the Pillagers, the Kashpaws, the Lazarres, the Lamartines, and the Morrisseys—names bespeaking the complex combinations of genetic and ethnic inheritances existent among the Ojibwe. Erdrich writes, "Everything is all knotted up in a tangle. Pull one string of this family and the whole web will tremble" (*Antelope Wife* 239). Inside the cover of *The Last Report on the Miracles at Little No Horse*, Erdrich includes a genealogy chart of the families included in that novel with a legend of symbols to help readers untangle love relationships between characters who are connected through traditional Ojibwe or Catholic marriage rites as well as through sexual affairs or liaisons. Children issue from these cou-plings; other children are adopted into families. Many critics have tried to create complete genealogy charts for the intertwining blood lines in Erdrich's novels—including time lines outlining what hap-pened and when. Erdrich's narrative technique also contests chronological time as a factor in creating meaning. Time enfolds. Memory and connection are complexes of causes and effects—bits and pieces of information reaching into mythic time and space as well as throughout generations. The space/time continuum, as in quantum physics, can never be fully grasped or measured but only analyzed for properties of light: as a particle (singular character) or wave (characters in motion) whose ripples bump up against multi-ple shore (blood) lines.

Kathleen M. Sands comments on Erdrich's narrative technique. Sands says that the "anecdotal form of storytelling may well derive from the episodic nature of traditional tales, that are elliptical because the audience is already familiar with the characters, their cultural context, and the values they adhere to." In addition, Sands suggests, "The gossip tradition within Indian communities is even more elliptical, relying on each member's knowledge of every individual in the group and the doings of each family (there are no strangers). Moreover, such anecdotal narration is notoriously biased and fragmented, with no individual [storyteller] being privy to the whole story." Such technique also "preserves the multiplicity of individual voices and the tensions that generate gossip." Hence, there is "no identifiable right version, no right tone, no right interpretation." As a result, the "audience members [readers] are intimately involved in the fleshing out of the narrative and the supplying of the connections between related stories" (37). This is also a Postmodern approach to *Truth*. The storyteller or observer determines what is seen or told. There is no transcendental knower or teller. In actuality, truth can only be referred to with a lower case 't': *truth*—especially about people—is fragmented, partial, dynamic, and continually revisable.

These narrative strategies are also influenced by Erdrich's theories concerning family dynamics. Gary Storhoof points out that one of Erdrich's "persistent" concerns is "how one's family shapes, patterns, or even determines life choices in the future. The 'lines,' symbolizing patterns of choices and actions the child learns intergenerationally through family conduct, become, in Erdrich's novels, fundamentally directional" (341). In addition, Storhoof says "the self's identity is an unstable product of interactions between entire generations, always subject to the formations of new and different systems at any particular time" (342). Orphaned, abandoned, neglected, or abused children in Erdrich's novels unconsciously or consciously yearn for a position within bloodlines where they matter. Often, adult characters—Nanapush, Marie (Sister Leopolda's "illegitimate" daughter), Zelda, and others—attempt to secure a space for such children within healing kinship patterns. Kinship matters. The ontology of kinship is crucial in Erdrich's works. In her foreword to *The Sons of the Wind* (the Sioux creation story), D. M. Dooling explains that the Creator Inyan's "longing for relationship" is the cause of all creation—the heavens, earth, and all living things (xi). Such ontology exists in Erdrich's novels as well. However, the interdependence of all things in creation—ecosystems and family systems—is illusive. That is, life is a gamble, a struggle, to come to an understanding of such interrelationship. This *longing for relationship*, however, generates opposition: love/envy, good/evil, and, therefore, ethics. What does this mean, then, for *survivors* of undeserved, unimaginable, or uncontrollable loss or estrangement from kinship, from relationship?

In "Where I Ought to Be," Erdrich posits: "Contemporary Native American writers have . . . a task quite different from that of other writers. . . . In the light of enormous loss, they must tell the stories of contemporary survivors while protecting and celebrating the cores of cultures left in the wake of the catastrophe" (48). Nanapush, in *Tracks*, describes the catastrophe in these terms:

> We started dying before the snow, and like the snow, we continued to fall. It was surprising there were so many of us left to die. For those who survived the spotted sickness from the south, our long fight west to Nadouissioux land where we signed the treaty, and then a wind from the east, bringing exile in a storm of government papers, what descended from the north in 1912 seemed impossible.
>
> By then, we thought disaster must surely have spent its force, that disease must have claimed all of the Anishinaabe that the earth could hold and bury (1).

In using the term "catastrophe" and "disaster" to describe the losses and devastation experienced by Native Americans as a consequence of colonization, Erdrich also enters into the Postmodern discussion of ethics. And the scope of her concern is given in her metaphor of the four directions—devastation coming from the south, west, east, and north. Erdrich's ethics, however, are especially addressed by her ongoing concerns with kinship obligations: in the face of the child. These obligations are not theological prescriptions, however. They are emotional attachments arising out of an aboriginal need for relatives—being: before myth and after metaphor. Storytelling best reveals the complexities of that need because storytelling particularizes.

In *Against Ethics*, John D. Caputo attempts to expose the failures of Western discourse concerning ethics. He traces the "jewgreek" origins of ethics in connection with the *word* of God. Multiple grand narratives have connected god figures with the origins of ethics. However, says Caputo, "We cannot tell when we are dealing with the word of God and when we are not, which would resolve the issue, since no one has seen God or given us a reliable report of what words are God's and of what language game God prefers." Indeed, most contemporary wars are mythologically justified—wars between Catholics and Protestants, Jews and Palestinians, Christians and Muslims, all contending Truth from *the* Divine Source. Caputo says, "We cannot get at it 'ethically,' from the beginning, as if we inhabited the *principium*, but only *poetice*, by imagining its effect on the receiving end, from the standpoint of the one who is obligated." In other words, abstract principles have not resulted in an ethics that prevents radical violence. Only *poetice* can get at a more satisfactory understanding of ethical obligations in a postcolonial, postholocaust era. Caputo further explains that "Perhaps the way to adjudicate, poetically, among conflicting obligations is to tell as many competing stories as possible in order to see which, under the circumstance, is most obliging, or which obligation produces the lesser evil, that is to say, is less disastrous" (26).

By *disaster*, Caputo means "events of surpassing or irretrievable loss. By irretrievable loss, I mean a wasting of life, something that cannot be repaired, recompensed, redeemed, as disaster is a loss that cannot be incorporated into a 'result,' that cannot be led back into a gain." Furthermore, "Disasters throw all reckoning and cost-accounting, every *logos* and *ratio*, into chaos" (29). Of particular note: "The suffering of a child is not part of the progress of the Spirit or the History of Being. I cannot be led to a 'result'" (30). Caputo claims that "Evil is highly unimaginative and uninventive: it keeps producing the same sort of bloodied, emaciated, or lifeless bodies, ruined, hopeless, desperate, damaged lives; with or without technology"—"with or without religion." Caputo further suggests that "the claim of victims, who are usually victims of somebody's Good, is singular, compelling, claiming" (34). And, finally, "Let us take the case—let us 'begin with' the case—of a disaster, of a damaged life, of an irretrievable loss, of innocent, avoidable suffering, a case where we cannot easily blame the victim for his or her destitute condition, say, of a child born with AIDS" (36). Caputo's discussion of innocent victims, expressly the suffering child, is crucial to an understanding of Erdrich's novels. Her works are compelling because they enunciate, in a radically understated ethics, how damaged individuals respond to what should be, by all accounts, irretrievable loss.

Erdrich's novels are full of innocent victims of others' actions or goods; however, those others are often also victims of others' actions or goods. Children—fatherless, motherless, abandoned, orphaned because of violence or even necessity—abound in Erdrich's novels. And the response of various characters to such loss constitutes the movement, on Erdrich's part, toward a Postmodern ethics. Such responses often focus on gender relationships—on erotic desire. In her essay, "Making Babies," Erdrich writes:

> We conceive our children in deepest night, in blazing sun, outdoors, in barns and alleys and minivans. We have no rules, no ceremonies, we don't even need a driver's license. Conception is often something of a by-product of sex, a candle in a one-room studio, pure brute chance, a wonder. To make love with the desire for a child is to move the act out of its singularity, to make the need of the moment an eternal wish. But of all passing notions, that of a human being for a child is perhaps the purest in the abstract, and the most complicated in reality (*The Blue Jay's Dance* 3).

Erdrich's "complicated . . . reality," her ethics, her narrative strategies, can be exemplified by a study of singular characters.

June (Morrissey) Kashpaw's death is the first story told in Erdrich's North Dakota novels (*Love Medicine*). Sands says: "[June] is the catalyst for the narrations that follow, stories that trace the intricate and often antagonistic relationships in the two families from which she came." Continuing on, Sands comments: "One life —and not a very special life at that, just a life of a woman on the fringes of her tribe and community, a woman living on the margins of society, living on the hard edge of survival and failing, but a woman whose death brings the family together briefly, violently, and generates a multitude of memories and stories that slowly develop into a whole" (38). On her way to catch a bus back to the reservation, June meets a man (who calls himself Andy) in a bar. They hook up, travel to the outskirts of town, have a failed attempt at casual sex (Andy passes out in a drunken stupor)—all in a few pages. June leaves the truck with the heater running and heads home—only to freeze to death, Easter 1981.

In *Tales of Burning Love*, readers find out that Andy is really Jack Mauser, and he married June. June's marriages and liaisons often produce children. She has a son, King, by her husband Gordie Kashpaw, and a son Lipsha Morrissey, by a lover Gerry Nanapush (Son of Lulu and a Pilliger). June's mother, Lucille Lazaree, dies when June is very young. June's father is known only as No-Good Morrissey. June is taken to Lucille's sister Marie (married to Nector Kashpaw, who is also in love with Lulu Nanapush); Marie then raises June, until June decides to live with Eli, Nector's brother. Both Marie and Eli love June, but she is a "wild" child. Lipsha finds out, late in his teens, that June is his mother; he has known all along that his mother threw him into a lake after he was born. Marie retrieves Lipsha and takes him in too (Marie "in-gathers" children).

At the end of *Bingo Palace*, Lipsha tries to help his father, Gerry, escape from the police into Canada—in another blizzard. They steal a car that they discover has a sleeping baby in the back seat (a baby identified as Jack Mauser's in *Tales of Burning Love*). Unable to see, they focus on any vehicle ahead of them whose lights they can follow. June's car, with June driving (she is dead, remember), comes to view. Gerry "wants her so hard that the desire takes me over too," says Lipsha, "and I can't catch him back because I'm caught up in the anxious necessity" (257). Gerry leaves the stolen car to follow June. And Lipsha is abandoned again. Lipsha wants to follow the cold into oblivion, but he cannot—because of the child. Lipsha explains:

> Come what might when we are found, I stay curled around
> this baby. . . . I rummage in the seat for whatever I can find
> to keep us warm and find small blankets, baby size. I know
> it will be a long night that maybe will not end. But at least

I can say, as I drift, as the cold begins to take me, as I pull
the baby closer to me, zipping him inside of my jacket, here
is one child who was never left behind (259).

Child, grandchild, great-grandchild. . . . One child. This moment,
when Lipsha faces death, is the moment that his great-grandmother,
Fleur Pillager, leaves her cabin and "only" takes with her "those
things she carried with her all her life." "Outdoors, into a day of deep
cold and brilliance that often succeeds a long disruptive blizzard,
she went, thinking of the boy out there. Annoyed, she took his
place" (272).

Fleur Pillager is an enormous spiritual force in Erdrich's novels.
Erdrich never gives Fleur a narrative voice; readers only learn about
her from the tales others tell. Fleur is feared, envied, sought after,
and loved. She is the main topic of *Tracks*. And we learn of her
through Nanapush, who saves her from smallpox, and through
Pauline—the crazed Chippewa Christian who becomes Sister
Leopolda. Nanapush knows the various rumors about Fleur. He says
some people "have ideas. You know how old chickens scratch and
gabble. That's how the tales started, all the gossip, the wondering, all
the things people said without knowing and then believed, since they
heard it with their own ears, from their own lips, each word" (9).
Again, Fleur's image can only be taken by collecting the various narratives about her: her animal lust; her rape; her love of her children
—one born of rape, the other from love; her gambling for land and
her power over it; her wisdom and knowledge of Chippewa medicines; and her ability to see the coexistent planes of reality—the
spiritual and physical landscapes. At her death, when she exchanges
her life for Lipsha's, "Her grandmother, Four Soul, who had given
Fleur the burdensome gift of outliving nearly all of those whom she
loved, sang quietly with her thin arms open, waiting. Nanapush was
there to smooth her face . . . rubbing his clever hands with pollen,
and talking without cease." Stories of Fleur are like "tracks" that can
be followed in and outside mortality. And Lipsha is related to Fleur
through his grandmother, Lulu—the daughter born out of Fleur's
gang rape. Lulu, another *one* child.

When Father Damien assesses Lulu's life, he claims "'She is good
. . . one day you will understand this. She is goodness itself'" (*The

Last Report on the Miracles at Little No Horse 337). However, it is from a series of stories in various novels that such an assessment emerges. Lulu has eight children by different men (*Love Medicine*). She has an affair with Nector, the husband of Marie (*Love Medicine*). She is drawn by sexual desire, yet she soon tires of male attention (*Bingo Palace*). She is the daughter sent to boarding school by her mother Fleur as a consequence of Fleur's desire that her daughter survive. She is the one who won't forgive her mother for sending her away. She is adopted by Nanapush who gives her his name on government records. She is rescued from freezing to death by Nanapush while her mother Fleur flees to the land of the dead to gamble for her second daughter's life (*Tracks*). Father Damien also gives Lulu his name as "father" on her birth certificate (*The Last Report on the Miracles at Little No Horse*). Lulu's stories are complex and interwoven. How could they not be? She is the mother of eight sons by different fathers.

And yet there is still more to understand about Erdrich's kinship patterns as they reveal her ethics. In *Tracks*, Nanapush says:

> Many times in my life, as my children were born, I wondered what it was like to be a woman, able to invent a human from the extra materials of her own body. In the terrible times, the evils I do not speak of, when the earth swallowed back all it had given me to love, I gave birth in loss. I was like a woman in my suffering, but my children were all delivered into death. It was contrary, backward, but now I had a chance to put things into a proper order (167).

Somehow, Erdrich's ethics involve that "proper order." In various novels, Nanapush blesses the lives of other characters through his storytelling, his humor, and his constant attempts to live in and create appropriate relationships between relatives—to give birth.

At the end of *Tales of Burning Love*, the narrator asserts:

> *We are conjured voiceless out of nothing and must return to an unknowing state. What happens in between is an uncontrolled dance, and what we ask for in love is no more than a momentary chance to get the steps right, to move in harmony until the music stops* (Erdrich's emphasis; 452).

Getting the "steps right" means stumbling, yet continually attempting to overcome scatterbrained and ludicrous mistakes. Jack Mauser has had five wives! He fakes his death to solve his many personal and financial dilemmas. After his funeral, four of his wives find themselves trapped in Jack's van in a snow storm. In order to survive the freezing weather, the women tell stories of "burning love." Roberta Rosenburg suggests that these stories formulate a ceremony of healing for the women involved (122). Early in the novel, Mauser describes himself as a creative man—a builder of

> banks, half the hospital complex, the highway, Vistawood Views, the nursing home, most of the mall, house upon house—you'll see it's set up and hooked in and put there to stay by Jack Mauser. I do things from plans. I make them real. I could do it for myself if I could get a guy that could design me. But since that's not possible, I've always relied on women. Somewhere inside I think—they're women, they should know (158).

And yet the women Jack chooses are often as messed up, emotionally, as he is. Their "tales of burning love" reveal the reasons for each failed marriage. Eleanor comes to realize "Jack probably showed a separate facet of himself to each one of us. Or we brought it out in him. Made him as different as we are different from one another. In fact, it isn't entirely far-fetched to say that we each married a different man." These once quarreling women "shift from antagonism to tentative sisterhood" and arrive at new comprehensions of intimacy through storytelling (Rosenburg 125).

However, even then, these four wives of Jack Mauser can't take the full measure of him. They don't know, for example, about Jack's yearning for his own mother, Mary Stamper. His memories of her are vague. He thinks:

> she came of some wandering people who joined right in with Ojibwas but might have been created out of a lot of different other tribes—Crees, Menominees, even some secretive Winnebago knowledge might well have been hers. Who knew? She was listed as a full-blood on the tribal rolls but from somewhere in her background French blood paled her skin to the warmth of brown hen eggs and also freckled

her face with childish dots of deep brown. . . . She loved
him with the secret, wild, despairing love that mothers bear
their boy children, an ardor bound up in loss and foreign-
ness and fur (184).

Nor do his four storytelling wives know that Jack's son is also lost
in the same blizzard, wrapped in the arms of Lipsha. Nor do they
know that Jack, following the image of June, is led to Lipsha and the
baby, John Joseph Mauser (384–387). In other words, these various
characters are each trying to "get the steps right" (452)—to rescue,
to love, to help one another. Sister Leopolda even gets into the mix.

Through the character of Sister Leopolda, many of Erdrich's
concerns with Catholicism get addressed. Erdrich was raised
Catholic. In an interview with Joseph Bruchac, Erdrich admits, "I
don't deal much with religion except Catholicism. Although
Ojibway traditional religion is flourishing, I don't feel comfortable
discussing it. I guess I have my beefs about Catholicism. Although
you never change once you're raised a Catholic—you've got that.
You've got that symbolism, that guilt, you've got the whole works
and you can't really change that" (159). And yet, Erdrich constantly
arrives at complex religious insights through composing characters
whose actions reveal fruitful tensions between Chippewa and
Christian practices. In *Love Medicine*, Sister Leopolda is an obsessed
nun who sees the devil in the face of Marie. And she tries to exor-
cize that evil with prostituted symbols of Christ's passion. In *Tracks*,
readers learn that Pauline Puyat became Sister Leopolda to escape
her own perverse envy of Fleur as well as to mask her aggressive sexual desire and murderous heart. She practices an excessive *Pauline*
type of Catholicism—denigrating her body, practicing severe acts of
penance, and plotting salvation through immolation. And the symbol of her own perversity exists in the body of her daughter, Marie
Lazarre, the product of her sexual obsession for Napoleon
Morrissey. Leopolda strangles Morrissey with a rosary in a desperate attempt to rid the world of evil, of the devil incarnated in the
form of Napoleon.

Kate McCafferty convincingly argues that Pauline grows
Wa'bano "in opposition to Fleur." McCafferty defines *Wa-bano* as
evil shamanism. Leopolda/Pauline is also *windigo*: a person with a
psychic disorder who projects her own maladies onto others and

then proceeds to vindicate herself through various forms of violence (743). In *The Last Report on the Miracles at Little No Horse*, Father Jude Miller comes to Little No Horse to collect stories that can either confirm or deny the possibility of Sister Leopolda's sainthood. Fragments of his attempts to write a book about Leopolda appear in a section called "Leopolda's Passion" (336). "Father Jude understood that to tell the story as a story was to pull a single thread, only, from the pattern of this woman's life, leaving the rest —the beautiful and brutal tapestry of contradictions—to persist in the form of a lie" (337).

However, it is the dead Leopolda who appears to Eleanor—the night she is telling her tale of burning love—and provides the most stunning insight into Christ and love's medicine (*Tales of Burning Love*). (Eleanor is a college professor interested in the lives of saints; she interviews Leopolda to gain insights into her Christian odyssey). Leopolda listens to the tales of burning love, and she tells Eleanor:

> You and your sisters are blind women touching the vast body of the elephant, each describing the oddness beneath the surface of her hands. Love is brutalizing, a raw force, frail as blossoms, tough as catgut wire. Lost, found, sprinkled with the wild sweet oils, love changes and is immutable. You have all been students of habitual, everyday contentment. You have all known the deep and twisting nights, the scarves of the magician threaded through the body, changing colors, knotted and then separate. And too, you know and understand the love a child bears its mother, its father, a parent bears its child. It is a love that is no other thing but pure salvation, and by it, Christ's balancing trick was inspired and foretold (371).

This "balancing trick" is further explained as the ability to not be crucified by one's own desires. Such desire often comes in the guise of wanting "abiding rightness, an assurance of your course. You will *not* find all that in a man. No, that imaginary conviction is a cross that will break his back," Leopolda explains (372–373). Nor must a man find his "abiding rightness" in a woman. Such expectations project/deflect "rightness" onto the body of another.

And yet, as Father Damien comes to understand in *The Last Report on the Miracles at Little No Horse*, Christ is revealed in the acts of kindness of those surrounding him. However, such actions propel Father Damien toward a kind of religious life that contests traditional Christianity as well as traditional gendered constructions of "abiding rightness." In actuality, Father Damien has gone through several "transfigurations" or shifts in identity. She/he "takes upon her" many names: Sister Cecilia, Agnes DeWitt, Agnes Brendt, and finally, Father Modeste Damien. Each name reveals one aspect of identity—nun, daughter, wife, and priest. The four sections of this novel—"The Transfiguration of Agnes," "The Deadly Conversions," "Memory and Suspicion," "The Passions"—each reconfigure traditional religious life. Especially critical in this work seems to be the essential religious conflict between right action and religious sanctions: the "priest was in the service of the spirit of goodness, wherever that might evidence itself." And yet, "were he known to have fooled, deceived, and hidden his most fundamental nature [as a passionate woman] all would be lost" (276). Baptisms, marriages, funerals, and forgiven sins would be annulled. In Catholicism, too often goodness is assigned/designed to be disseminated and authenticated through and by male religious authority. This novel challenges all that in favor of the "Ojibwe mind. . . . unprejudiced by gender distinctions" or distinctions such as "alive or dead." "For the Anishinaabeg, the quality of animation from within, or harboring spirit, is not limited to animals and plants" (257).

Prior to Father Damien's death, he concedes:

> The old man [Nanapush] was my teacher, my confidant, my priest's priest, my confessor, my friend. Plus, he was funny and you don't get funny much in this life. God, how we used to laugh. Even his funeral was hilarious—I miss him. There is no one I want to visit except in the Ojibwe heaven, and so at this late age I'm going to convert . . . and become at long last the pagan that I always was at heart before I was Cecilia, when I was just Agnes, until I was seduced and diverted by the music of Chopin (310).

Still, there is something about the quality of Father Damien's forgiveness and his ability to truly commune that is constantly informed by Christian symbolism—he is at once the bride and the bridegroom.

Erdrich's novels are complex networks of characters, themes, and theological concerns caught up in a kind of demythologized Postmodern mythology: the possibility of healing through narratives, telling stories. Perhaps one final example might serve to underscore this project. In *The Antelope Wife*, Scranton Roy conceives:

> *Who knows whose blood sins we are paying for? What murder committed in another country, another time? The black-robe priests believe that Christ allowed himself to be nailed high on the cross in order to pay. Shawanos think different. Why should an innocent god, a manitou spirit, have to settle for our bad drunks, our rage, our heart-sown angers and mistakes?* (238)

Personal atonement is another hard-worked theme—another ethical obligation—inferred throughout Erdrich's prose. And yet again, Erdrich is not doctrinaire in her accounts. Consider, for example, her sections in *The Antelope Wife* dealing with "Father's milk." At the end of the novel, Scranton Roy falls ill. Over a period of a hundred nights, Roy is visited in his feverish dreams:

> She was there, the old woman, stumbling toward him with a grandmotherly anxiety, her face not ferocious but pleading, hopeless, satisfied to divert his attention, shot, pistol, from the running children. She threw herself toward him, a sacrifice. With shame, he saw again her sight rush inward to meet her death. . . . On the hundredth night that she visited him, exhausted and fearful, Scranton Roy made a promise to the now familiar old woman. He would find the village and the people he had wronged. He would bring along the son of the boy nursed on Father's milk. His grandson, Augustus (238).

The novel begins and ends with Father's milk. And the lives in between are tangled and conflicted—perhaps as a consequence of the violence that generates the generations of lives tangled together in urban settings. Against his parents' counsel, Roy enlists in "the U.S. Cavalry at Fort Sibley on the banks of the Mississippi in St. Paul, Minnesota" (4). Shortly after enlisting, Roy finds himself and his company engaged in warfare against a Chippewa village of mostly women and children. He has a "sudden contempt" for the people—an "unexpected," "frigid hate" (4). And so he shoots two and bayonets a third—the old woman in his fevered dreams. Shortly after killing the old woman, Roy sees a child strapped to a dog's back running off into open space. He chases after the two. He finally gains possession of the child, and therefore deserts his company. In the days that follow, Roy attempts to feed the child; but the baby is too young to eat. And so he puts the baby to his breast in what he thinks to be a vain attempt to comfort a dying infant. "The baby kept nursing and refused to stop. His nipples toughened. Pity scorched him, she sucked so blindly, so forcefully, and with such immense faith. It occurred to him one slow dusk as he looked down at her, upon his breast, that she was teaching him something." Readers are told that the idea that this baby could teach him something "seemed absurd when he first considered it, and then, as insights do when we have the solitude to absorb them, he eventually grew used to the idea and paid attention to the lesson." This baby had a "pure supply" of faith:

> She nursed with utter simplicity and trust, as though the act itself would produce her wish. Half asleep one early morning, her beside him, he felt a slight warmth, then a rush in one side of his chest, a pleasurable burning. He thought it was an odd dream and fell asleep again only to wake to a huge burp from the baby, whose lips curled back from her dark gums in bliss, whose tiny fists were unclenched in sleep for the first time, who looked, impossibly, well fed (7).

Throughout this novel, human relationships are likened to beadwork. In seemingly "random patterns," beads are woven together into new strands. This novel involves complexes of marriages and offspring drawn together by incredible circumstances. "Who are you and who am I, the beader or the bit of colored glass sewn onto the fabric of this earth?" Erdrich asks. "All these questions, they tug at the brain. We stand on tiptoe, trying to see over the edge, and only catch a glimpse of the next bead on the string, and the woman's hand moving, one day, the next, and the needle flashing over the horizon" (240). Much in Erdrich's works is generated by the child's need for mother's milk—for inseparable kinship ties. Erdrich's unfathomable, yet biologically possible, response to the suffering of any innocent child can be recognized in her complex symbol: "Father's milk."

In her most recent novel *Four Souls* (2004), Erdrich writes about the effects of exploitation and retribution on human souls. Fleur, the central character in the novel, seeks vengeance on the lumber baron, John James Mauser, who stole her lands. In an ironic turn of events, Fleur marries Mauser and they produce an autistic son. Like a worried father, Nanapush anguishes over Fleur's exploits. During one of his elaborate and wise moments of reflection, Nanapush asserts what might be the central ethical position in Erdrich's novels: Fleur "should have known that it is wrong to bear a child for any reason but to surrender your body to life" (72).

Linda Hogan (b. 1947)

This study now moves from Chippewa authors Vizenor and Erdrich to two authors whose Native homelands, histories, and literary contributions are located in their filial associations with the Five Civilized Tribes: Linda Hogan (Chickasaw) and Louis Owens (Choctaw-Cherokee) (see next section). A number of award-winning writers come from this heritage, including Ralph Salisbury (Cherokee), Joy Harjo (Creek), Diane Glancy (Cherokee), Craig Womak (Creek), and Gary Hobson (Cherokee-Quapaw/Chickasaw). Entire books could be written about all of these authors. Notwithstanding, the novels of Hogan and Owens are more frequently studied.

To date, Linda Hogan has eleven books, one play, and numerous anthologized short stories and essays to her credit. Her novel *Mean Spirit* and a collection of her poetry *Book of Medicines* were both finalists for Pulitzer Prize awards. Hogan also won an American Book Award from the Before Columbus Foundation (1985) and was a finalist for a National Book Critics Circle award (1993). To support her various writing projects, Hogan applied for and received prestigious research grants, among them a D'Arcy McNickle Memorial Fellowship (1980), a National Endowment for the Arts grant (1986), a Guggenheim (1990), and a Lannan Award (1994). Hogan has been a writer-in-residence for several associations and councils as well as a college professor. She currently (2003) teaches in the American Indian Studies Program and English department at the University of Colorado at Boulder.

Hogan recounts, "I come from two different people, from white pioneers who crossed into Nebraska plains and from Chickasaw Indian people from south central Oklahoma" ("The Two Lives" 233). Hogan's father, Charles Henderson, is Chickasaw, and her mother, Cleona Bower Henderson, is Anglo. On the Chickasaw side of her ancestry, Hogan traces her lineage to her great-grandmother Addie who was "the granddaughter to Winchester Colbert, head of the Chickasaw Nation." Addie "married Granville Walker Young, a rancher and politician of French-Indian (Métis) ancestry, and as such, in Indian Territory, was considered to be White. As a White intermarried citizen of the Chickasaw nation, he was given land, and later a place on the Chickasaw legislature, and they built a large home" (236). Hogan describes her ancestors, however, as a "people who have not had privilege" (237). Indian Removal, explains Hogan, "was followed by the Dawes Act, by other wars, by one tragedy laid down upon another, by land loss and swindles during the oil boom and the Depression, by continuing struggle, poverty, and loss" (236). Were it not for her desire to learn and be able to analyze what happens to Indian people on a "daily basis in the form of classism and racism," declares Hogan, "I would have destroyed myself out of frustration, pain, and rage" (240).

In her biographical essay on Hogan, Kathryn W. Shanley claims:

> As a writer of Chickasaw heritage, Linda Hogan centers her-self and, consequently, her readers on what nature has to teach human beings and on the regenerative female forces that shape the world. The Chickasaw were matrilineal and matrilocal in precontact times; other tribes, though patriar-chal, revered their women as the creative life force of the universe. Domination by Christian Europeans has altered the traditional tribal balance between male and female power in American Indian life. In her works, Hogan seeks to restore that balance and to offer ancient wisdom about nature in mythological yet contemporary terms (123–124).

Shanley's assessment of Hogan's motives for writing thrusts Hogan's work into an important critical arena. Today, critical theory and literature are interactive to an unprecedented extent. Certainly, Hogan's works are more profoundly understood in light of various contemporary theories. For example, in "The Terrestrial and Aquatic Intelligence of Linda Hogan," Donelle N. Dreese aligns Hogan's works with ecofeminism and ecocriticism. Ecofeminists equate the degradation of the earth, the abuse of women, and the ill-treatment of indigenous people with the Western/patriarchal/Christian need to subordinate and control. Dreese explains that subordination arises from "The alienating and destructive dichotomies nurtured by Western metaphysical ideologies." Dreese states: "Culture/nature, mind/body, black/white, man/woman, intellect/emotion are all structures which lie at the root of subordination and are perpetuated by those who benefit from them." Moreover, "the ecofeminist agenda involves healing these artificial separations" through various means—including "challenging existing power structures" (12). However, in her novels, Hogan does not perpetuate the us/them duality—us (the Indian good guys and victims) versus them (the power-mongering White bad guys and perpetrators).

In *Dwellings*, for example, Hogan explains,

> It has been my lifelong work to seek an understanding of the two views of the world, one as seen by native people and the other as seen by those who are new and young on this continent. It is clear that we have strayed from the treaties we once had with the land and with the animals. It is also clear, and heartening, that in our time there are many —Indian and non-Indian alike—who want to restore and honor these broken agreements (11).

This move by Indian and non-Indian people to understand and restore broken treaties with the Earth could clearly be defined as both ecofeminist and environmentalist in nature. However, Hogan explains that her "lifelong love for the living world and all its inhabitants" has "grown" out of her "native understanding that there is a *terrestrial intelligence* that lies beyond our human knowing and grasping" (italics added; 11).

Postmodern physics clearly supports Hogan's notion of *terrestrial intelligence*. Fritjov Capra's the *Tao of Physics* and *The Turning Point* plus David Peat's *Synchronicity: The Bridge Between Matter and*

Mind and *Turbulent Mirror: An Illustrated Guide to Chaos Theory and the Science of Wholeness* offer physicists' explorations into the idea of terrestrial intelligence. And yet, simply amassing evidence for understanding that the natural world behaves similarly to other thinking organisms might not get at the power of Hogan's novels. Perhaps ecopsychology is the field that most nearly corresponds to Hogan's assertions that humans continually risk their own sanity by alienating themselves (or others) from appropriately interacting with the earth and her creatures. Ecopsychology is a combination of Western and Indigenous psychologies. While the tenets of ecopsychology are complex, perhaps a rehearsal of some of the major contentions in this field might shed light on Hogan's novels as literary expressions of ecopsychology. "Biomedical reductionism" (Theodore Roszak), "original trauma" (Chellis Glendinning), "species arrogance" (John E. Mack), "ontogenetic crippling" (Paul Shepard), and "ecological groundedness" (William Cahlahan) are terms used by professionals in the field to help practitioners and scholars understand the causes and effects of a neurosis causing untold damage to humans and the natural world.

Biomedical reductionism is a term Theodore Roszak applies to theories, since Sigmund Freud, that promote the idea that "The normally functioning ego [is] an isolated atom of self-regarding consciousness that [has] no relational continuity with the physical world around it" (10). Such theories continue the false self/environment, culture/nature, interior/exterior dichotomies that are generally accepted as the ground of reality throughout Western civilization. Roszak claims: "Whatever else has changed in mainstream psychological thought, the role Freud assigned to psychotherapy, that of patrolling the 'boundary lines between the ego and the external world,' remained unquestioned in the psychiatric mainstream until the last generation" (11). Roszak notes that participants at a conference held at Harvard in 1990 ("Psychology as if the Whole Earth Mattered" sponsored by the Harvard-based Center for Psychology and Social Change) concluded that "if the self is expanded to include the natural world, behavior leading to the destruction of this world will be experienced as self-destruction" (12). Roszak, among many others, draws on the Gaia hypothesis for his assertions concerning sanity.

Gaia [the ancient Greek word for Earth as mother], taken simply as a dramatic image of ecological interdependence, might be seen as the evolutionary heritage that bonds all things genetically and behaviorally to the biosphere. *Just that much is enough to reverse the scientific worldview and all psychology based upon it.* In place of the inevitable heat death, we have the deeply ordered complexity of natural systems holding out indefinitely against entropic exhaustion. In place of cosmic alienation, we have life and mind as fully at home in the universe as any of the countless systems from which they evolve. More hypothetically, we have the possibility that the *self-regulating biosphere 'speaks' through the human unconscious*, making its voice heard even within the framework of modern urban human culture (italics added; 14).

Roszak further suggests that "Whether one accepts or rejects the concept of an ecological unconscious, ecopsychology as a field of inquiry commits itself to understanding people as actors on a planetary stage who shape and are shaped by the biospheric system" (14). Who could argue, nonetheless, against *every*one's dependence on air, water, plants, animals, the seasons, gravity, planetary motion, and the labors of other peoples for their daily survival?

In other words, ecopsychology is engaged in paradigm shifts—shifts in the scientific, philosophic, and psychological ways people in the Western world have been taught to perceive, and therefore, interact with the world. And this shift is informed by indigenous ways of viewing the world.

Original trauma is a term employed by Chellis Glendinning to explore the "disconnection from the Earth" as the origin of subsequent traumas—such as the abuse of children and indigenous peoples. Glendinning avows that the dissociation from the earth likewise leads to various kinds of addictions. Glendinning asserts that the characteristics of addictive behaviors are denial, dishonesty, control, grandiosity, disconnection from feelings, and a multiplicity of thinking disorders. Furthermore, Glendinning contends that these behaviors are systemic or collective (stemming from basic systems of thought):

> The trauma endured by technological people like ourselves is the systemic and systematic removal of our lives from the

natural world: from the tendrils of earthly textures, from the rhythms of sun and moon, from the spirits of the bears and trees, from the life force itself. This is also the systemic and systematic removal of our lives from the kinds of social and cultural experiences our ancestors assumed when they lived in rhythm with the natural world (52).

This split from the earth causes *madness* because it cuts humans off from the "primary sources of satisfaction once found routinely in life in the wilds, such as physical nourishment, vital community, fresh food, continuity between work and meaning, unhindered participation in life experiences, personal choices, community decisions, and spiritual connection with the natural world." When such needs are not satisfied, claims Glendinning, "the psyche finds some temporary satisfaction in pursuing secondary sources like drugs, violence, sex, material possessions, and machines" (53).

Glendinning notes that "the world is awash in a sea of both personal and collective addictions: alcoholism, drug abuse, sex addiction, consumerism, eating disorders, codependence, and war making." Glendinning explains: "As the world has become less organic and more dependent on techno-fixes for problems created by earlier techno-fixes, humans have substituted a new worldview for one once filled with clean rushing waters, coyotes, constellations of stars, tales of the ancestors, and people working together in sacred purpose." As Western peoples attempted defining their relation to the world "in a state of psychic dislocation," says Glendinning, "they ended up projecting a worldview that reflects the rage, terror, and dissociation of the traumatized state" (54). The film *Koyaanisqatsi* (the Hopi term for the world out of balance) is an excellent visualization of these ideas. *Mindwalk*, a film based on *The Turning Point* by Fritjof Capra, is another motion picture dedicated to exposing this malady. However, *Mindwalk* offers scientific, psychological, political, and artistic solutions to *Koyaanisqatsi*.

Species arrogance is defined by John E. Mack as "a prevailing attitude, conscious and unconscious, toward the Earth":

> We regard it as a thing, a big thing, an object to be owned, mined, fenced, guarded, stripped, built upon, dammed, plowed, burned, blasted, bulldozed, and melted to serve the

material needs and desires of the human species at the expense, if necessary, of all other species, which we feel at liberty to kill, paralyze, or domesticate for our own use (282).

Postmodernism is engaged with exposing the *narcissism* at the heart of thought from the Enlightenment through the Modernist periods. However, "this form of species arrogance has received little scrutiny," claims Mack (282). Mack says, "One must wonder how or why we have done it ['cut off consciousness from a connection with nature'], how we have so overdeveloped the use of reason at the expense of feeling, in the service of a fear-driven need to conquer other peoples and the material world on a planet with a growing population that is perceived as yielding finite, diminishing resources" (283). Holy wars of earlier periods have justifiably engendered mistrust for traditional spiritual approaches to the natural world. However, such mistrust has likewise robbed contemporary industrialized nations of access to the roots of sanity.

Ontogenetic crippling is a term that Paul Shepard uses to describe the arrested development experienced by most adults in the modern era. "The whole of growth through the first twenty years (including physical growth) is our ontogenesis or ontogeny, our 'coming into being,'" claims Shepard. Shepard conjectures that the ontogeny of tribal peoples "is healthier than ours . . . and that it may be considered a standard from which we have deviated" (26). Shepard claims that the traditional celebration of life-stages among tribal societies promotes participation in creation. Furthermore, growth stages require viewing the world as a secondary womb if maturity is to be attained. Shepard explains:

> Maturity emerges in midlife as the result of the demands of an innate calendar of growth phases, to which the human nurturers—parents, friends, and teachers—have responded in season. It celebrates a central analogy of self and world in ever-widening spheres of meaning and participation, not an ever-growing domination over nature, escape into abstractions, or existential funk (30).

Shepard demonstrates that when the stages of development aren't marked by increased understanding of one's place within the context of the larger environment, that the "normally healthful features of adolescent narcissism" will be "pathologically extended into adulthood" (31).

Such "arrested development" promotes an "ontogenetic crisis"—a crippling brand of dependence that eventuates in "childish adults." Modern society continues to function, despite this condition. "But the private cost," says Shepard, "is massive therapy, escapism, intoxicants, narcotics, fits of destruction and rage, enormous grief, subordination to hierarchies that exhibit this callow ineptitude at every level, and perhaps worst of all, a readiness to strike back at a natural world that we dimly perceive as having failed us." Shepard shows that the "erosion of human nurturing" stems from "the failure of the passages of the life cycle and the exhaustion of our ecological accords" (35).

Ecological groundedness is a term used by Gestalt therapists. William Cahlahan says:

> Groundedness is a dynamic state of the person that includes the sense of confidence, pleasure, and wonder resulting from progressively deepening contact with the wild and domesticated natural community of the person's neighborhood and larger land region: with unpaved ground, soil, or landscape; with weather and the diversity of native plants and animals; and with human family, neighbors, and local cultural activities (217).

When humans have "empathic engagement with the world," claims Cahlahan, "the Earth tends to be sensed as the all-embracing, enduring Self of which the individual is one unique but temporary expression." Cahlahan further posits that humans have a "genetically based need . . . for such rootedness or sense of place, in which our very nervous system requires this face to face, balanced giving and taking, a self-corrective interchange within the human and nonhuman life community." As individuals experience life with an "intimate sense of belonging," they can "discover, in the seasonal turning" of life "within this larger life, the deep urge to grow and mature, to ripen and 'leave seed' to a wider community—and to anticipate death as the final resigning or giving back of self to the elements and beings of the land community that have birthed and sustained the self" (217).

These few precepts of ecopsychology could well be drawn directly from Native American traditions. And yet, the words of the above experts in the field underscore the seriousness with which many modern psychologists approach traditional Native American wisdom with regard to the ecological foundations of mental health. It is no coincidence, in other words, that Linda Hogan's novels *Mean Spirit* (1990), *Solar Storms* (1995), and *Power* (1998) have gained widespread acceptance and acclaim during the period surrounding the rise of ecopsychology.

Mean Spirit is a historical/mystery novel grounded on the consequences of species arrogance. Such arrogance is the "mean spirit" that pervaded Oklahoma following the discovery of oil on Indian allotments in the early 1920s. Floods of lawyers, policy makers, and White citizens congregated in Oklahoma in order to legitimize placing Indian women and children in the hands of money-hungry men. During this period, Anglos became legal guardians or custodians of Indian people and lands under the ruse that Indian people were incompetent to handle their own affairs. Hogan based much of the historical portions of her novel on the research of John Joseph Mathews (Osage) and Angie Debo. Debo's work *And Still the Waters Run* has long been a classic historical work unveiling the corrupt practices of Anglos during Oklahoma's formative years as a state. An *American Experience* documentary, *Indians, Outlaws, and Angie Debo* is available for those interested in the legal shenanigans of corrupt legislators during the oil boom in Oklahoma.

Many characters in Hogan's novel are also drawn from actual tribal family histories. Hogan combines history, politics, and mythology in *Mean Spirit*. References to Jack Wilson (founder of the Ghost Dance Religion), Black Elk (the Sioux holy man), and Peacemaker (the Iroquois prophet) as well as the Trail of Tears and Wounded Knee place the spirit of this work in that era of Indian history when all was being either taken away from or denied Native peoples. Indian Removal Policies and the Dawes Allotment Act are juxtaposed in this work—the first act made to remove the Five Civilized Tribes from the eastern homelands to Indian Territory (Oklahoma) and the next act made to remove tribal lands from community ownership to private property. When oil was "discovered" on Indian allotments, further policies were made to remove private Indian lands into the control of greedy men. Money garnered from oil boom profits was portioned out to Native individuals on a percentage basis. Naturally, those "handling" the economic affairs of Natives took the largest percentages of the wealth.

Mean Spirit is also a complex mystery novel—murders are committed, Natives are falsely accused of crimes and then put in jail, and local Anglos take out insurance policies on Natives who then show up dead. And this "mean spirit" extends to crimes against the earth. The crime that brings awareness that all these events are linked, is the murder of Grace Blanket. Grace is the daughter of Lila, a Hill Indian and river prophet—"a listener to the voice of water, a woman who interpreted the river's story for her people" (5). Lila sent her daughter to Watona (meaning "the gathering place") to learn about White man's laws and ways in order to "ward off" the "downfall" of Indian people. Upon her death, Grace's "half-crazed" daughter Nola becomes subject to government policies, including forced attendance at boarding school. Nola also becomes subject to illegal plots to achieve guardianship over her and her inherited allotments. Michael Horse, the spiritual leader in the novel, writes endless letters to government officials and the news media informing them of "a conspiracy against Indian people"(126). Numerous newspapers and radio stations, from Boston to Dallas, begin to comment on problems in Oklahoma's Indian Territory.

Inevitably, the Federal government must do something. And so federal investigators are brought onto the scene. Stace Red Hawk, a Sioux and also a federal investigator, is sent from Washington to find out who is responsible for all these crimes. Stace soon comes to realize "The people he was up against . . . in Indian Territory were the ones who did not love the earth and her creatures. Much of what these people believed to be good, was not good. What they believed was evil, was not" (205). Lionel Tall, a Sioux activist, is also drawn to Oklahoma and the suffering Natives there. Lionel wants to "set up an altar and perform a sing, a ceremony for healing everyone, even the injured earth that had been wounded and bruised by the oil boom." However, Lionel can't stay in Oklahoma for long because "he, too, would lose his inner core of harmony. This was the problem with places in the world that had been broken" (213). Lionel knows first hand the consequences of radical evil—his family did not survive Wounded Knee. In such desperate circumstances, Lionel recognizes that "survival was their religion" (221). Much of the novel unravels the countless murderous plots to gain Indian wealth. Leading perpetrators (like Hale "the oil man") are brought to trial and convicted. And yet the aggression against Indian people persists.

Survival *is* the religion of the people at this time. And yet, it is through the vision of central characters that many Native people are saved or restored to their former beliefs. Belle and Moses Graycloud are the matriarch and patriarch of the novel. Their home provides shelter and solace for numerous characters—including Nola and Stace. Belle continually intuits the needs of her loved ones and of the earth—she has ecological consciousness. Belle also has the unending support of her husband. Their intelligence, wit, and perseverance make them emblems of what can be achieved when there is "balance between male and female power" (Shanley 123–124). For example, when Belle comes upon a truck full of 317 eagle carcasses, she assaults the men responsible—she screams, curses, spits, hisses, and keeps hitting the men until they subdue her and take her to jail. She dares Jess Gold, the police chief, to arrest her. When the episode is resolved and Belle is released from jail, Michael Horse asks her, "What were you doing in jail, anyway?" Moses answers for her. "'She attacked some hunters.' It wasn't unusual for Belle. She'd put up quite a fight for bears not long ago, though she hadn't been arrested for it. 'Again,' Moses added. 'I'm proud of her'" (113). When Belle tries to save the lives of the bats in Sorrow Cave from being slaughtered because locals fear the bats, Moses joins his wife in a standoff against all comers (280).

Place matters in this novel. There are three major communities as well as sacred places, like Sorrow Cave, that come to symbolize the relationship between land, tradition, and sanity. The village of Hill People, Watona, and Tar Town are the principle dwelling places for people in this novel. The Hill people live secretly and away from the congress of "civilization." "A different kind of peace prevailed at the old settlement of the Hill People. A silence lived there, one that went deep down into the fiery bones of earth" (253). Despite their seclusion, the Hill People continually respond to what occurs in the places where Indian people suffer. For example, the Hill People send "watchers" to protect Nola and the Graycloud's home following the death of Grace. However, the watchers "didn't want to be around the broken earth's black blood and its pain" (229). Watona is the "gathering place" of Indians and Whites. This is the place where Indian people gathered "to sign for their royalty payments and lease checks." Up the road from Grace's house, "was an enormous crater a gas well blowout had made in the earth. It was fifty feet deep and five hundred feet across" (53). Tar Town is a "settlement of the dispossessed" —those addicted to alcohol, barroom society, and the illusive American Dream (252). Tar Town is surrounded by trees "killed by bagworms. Many of the fields had been burned black, and those that were not burned had been overgrazed by hungry cattle the world-eaters raised" (274). When Belle goes there in search of her grandson, Ben, she looks at the people. She thinks, "Pain had a way of changing the body. Human skin became something else, a wall, a membrane between the worlds of creation and destruction" (275). The earth, in this novel, has a will of her own, however. Oil wells often burn because the earth resists the loss of her life's blood (186).

Sorrow Cave is sacred space in this work. In *Dwellings*, Hogan writes that there are "events and things that work as a doorway into the mythical world, the world of first people, all the way back to the creation of the universe and the small quickenings of the earth, the first stirrings of human beings at the beginning of time." Furthermore, Hogan contends her tribal elders "believe this to be so, that it is possible to wind a way backward to the start of things, and in so doing find a form of sacred reason, different from ordinary reason, that is linked to the forces of nature" (19). The events in Oklahoma during this time lead many of the characters in the novel to Sorrow Cave as a place where "sacred reason" can be discovered. Belle and Moses Graycloud, Stace Red Hawk, Martha and Joe Billy, and Michael Horse all find themselves retreating to Sorrow Cave for solace and reflection. Hogan explains that caves are often "places of healing for Indian people, places where conflict between tribes and people [are] left behind, neutral ground, a sanctuary outside the reign of human differences, law, and trouble." Hogan suggests that caves are also "a feminine world, a womb of earth, a germinal place of brooding. In many creation stories, caves are the places that bring forth life" (*Dwellings* 29–31). Sorrow Cave gains these distinctions in *Mean Spirit*.

In *Mean Spirit*, bats are the arbiters between two worlds—day and night; sound and silence; the womb and body of the earth; the spiritual past and the troubled present. Joe Billy says, "One of the best things about bats is that they are a race of people that stand in two worlds like we do. . . . And they live in earth's ancient places" (257). They are the keepers of the cave.

In *Dwellings*, Hogan explains: "Bats hear their way through the world. They hear the sounds that exist at the edges of our lives. Leaping through blue twilight they cry out a thin language, then listen for its echo to return." For bats, says Hogan, "the world throws back a language, the empty space rising between hills speaks an open secret then lets the bats pass through, here or there, in the dark air. Everything answers, the corner of a house, the shaking leaves on a wind-blown tree, the solid voice of bricks" (*Dwellings* 25–26). In *Mean Spirit*, then, bats become a symbol for earth consciousness— a tangible symbol of the possibility that the world speaks if we know how to listen. As the world-weary Natives in *Mean Spirit* explore Sorrow Cave, they discover numerous chambers, like a heart. Joe Billy finds "a ceremonial room." He finds the fur of bears who "once populated the region." He finds a mummified body and realizes this space is also a burial site. He finds rock art on the walls—"paintings of red bats," "blue fish," "black buffalo." "It was a sacred world they entered and everyone became silent and heard a distant dripping of water in the caveways, the echoing sounds of the breathing earth" (284). However, it is Martha Billy, Joe Billy's Anglo wife, who realizes that the bat medicine is still alive—filling her dreams with wisdom and warnings.

Michael Horse, the comic prophet, is, like the bats, able to live in two worlds. He is brilliant, a writer, a dreamer, and the keeper of the sacred fire of his people. Michael Horse keeps histories of everything happening in Oklahoma; he writes letters to powerful government officials and media resources. Horse, however, has another writing project. At the end of the novel, when several of the characters have taken Nola and her infant to live among the Hill People, Horse is asked what he has been writing. "First," says Horse, "I have to tell you about the book they call the Bible. It is a holy book for the European people, like those who live in the towns. It carries visions, commandments, and songs. I have added what I think is missing from its pages" (361). The women ask Horse why he doesn't just speak his revisions. "They don't believe anything is true unless they see it in writing," he answers. Then Horse reads his additions:

> Honor father sky and mother earth. Look after everything. Life resides in all things, even the motionless stones. Take care of the insects for they have their place, and the plants and trees for they feed the people. Everything on earth, every creature and plant wants to live without pain, so do them no harm. Treat all people in creation with respect; all is sacred, especially the bats (361).

Perhaps Horse's next words might be taken as the theme in *Mean Spirit*. "Live gently with the land. We are one with the land. We are part of everything in our world, part of the roundness and cycles of life. The world does not belong to us. We belong to the world. And all life is sacred" (361–362).

Father Dunne, the Hog Priest, tells Horse, "You can't add a new chapter to the Bible."

"Hmmm," muses Horse, "do you think I need more thou shalts?" And yet, Hogan has not written a bipolar novel. Peacemaker, Christ, and the Creator are acknowledged, along with Horse, as those who preach: "Keep peace with all your sisters and brothers. Humans whose minds are healthy desire such peace and justice" (362). And because many characters restore themselves, remake their spirits, or continually respond to the world with the desire to live "in harmony with the rest of nature and the universe," they survive desperate times.

Solar Storms is loosely based on history—on recent events (the mid-1970s), when companies attempted to reroute rivers and create dams in the name of progress and without the permission of the people who dwelt on the land. In *Solar Storms*, Hogan moves from concerns with the earth, oil, and fire to concerns with the power of water. Historical events provide the context, notwithstanding, for a more elegant tale about the journey of four women:

> Four women, each of us with a mission. I [Angela Wing] was going to meet my mother, who lived near the Fat-Eaters. Bush was going to see what was happening to the water, to see if what the two men had said was true, to help

the people. Dora-Rouge was going, first, after plants that were helpful to the people, and then to die in her ancestral homeland. It was Agnes whose task was going to be the hardest. She was going to deliver her mother to that place and grieve (138).

Home base for these women is "Adam's Rib." And as they journey to the north, they travel the ancient waterways. Angela says that her life, "before Adam's Rib, had been limited in ways I hadn't even known. I'd never have thought there might be people who found their ways by dreaming." Angela wonders how "people who came from their own Earth, who lived there for tens of thousands of years, could talk with spirits, could hear land speak, and animals?" (189).

The first third of the novel, through various episodes, acquaints the readers with the character of each of these women. And these women are related. Dora-Rouge is the mother of Agnes Iron and Harold. Harold married Bush, but then Harold ran off with Loretta Wing (a woman with a bad spirit) and they produced Hannah Wing. And Hannah Wing produced Angela, the novel's protagonist and narrative voice. The genealogy, however, is almost tangential. Kinship is freely given and gracefully earned between these women. Bush, for example, is the woman who held a mourning ceremony for Angela—when civil service workers took her away from Hannah and placed her into foster care.

Although this novel is primarily about these women, it is not a radically feminist text. Each of these women yearns for and receives the love of worthy men. The novel is poetically dense. And although the stories told therein span much of the twentieth century, Angela's place in the story begins in 1972 when she writes a letter. Angela writes to Agnes, saying, "Dear Mrs. Iron, I am Angela Jensen, the daughter of Hannah Wing, and I believe you are my great-grandmother." Agnes writes back, "Come at once." "Along with her note," explains Angela, Agnes sent "fifty-five dollars in old one-dollar bills. They were soft as cloth and looked for all the world as if they'd been rolled, folded, counted, and counted again. When I opened the envelope, the smell of an old woman's cologne floated up from the bills" (23). Over the expanse of the novel, Angela moves from being an emotionally and physically scarred teenager to being renamed— or given the name—Maniki, meaning "a true human being" (347).

Then she marries Tommy. "I believed Tommy and I were our ancestors reunited in their search for each other and we loved deeply, in the way they had loved. I thought how gods breathe on people and they come to life. Something had breathed on us." Both Agnes and Dora-Rouge die before the end of the novel. Although their deaths are mourned, both women return to the earth as part of the cycle of life. And yet, Angela continually hears their stories and teachings. "The voice of Agnes floats toward me," and tells her stories of creation. And she feels Dora-Rouge touch her. "I hear her say that a human is alive water," says Angela, and "that creation is not yet over" (350).

Hannah Wing is the symbol of the people's woundedness. "Whenever she walked by a person," the story goes, "they felt what lived in her. They felt the world that was ruined and would never be whole again." She is "the sum total of ledger books and laws. Some of her ancestors walked out of death, out of a massacre. Some of them came from the long trail of dying, people sent from their world, and she was also the child of those starving and poisoned people on Elk Island." Hannah wounded and scarred her own and other people's children. She received strange men to her bed—men compelled by her empty, yet strangely attractive, soul. "There was a word for what was wrong with her," an old healer explains, but "no one would say it. They were afraid it would hear its name and come to them." The old healer also explains that Hannah's body is the place where "time and history and genocide gather and move like a cloud above the spilled oceans of blood" (101). *Solar Storms* is also the story of Hannah, her life, and death. Her story is the story about "the frozen heart of evil that was hunger, envy, and greed, how it had tricked people into death or illness or made them go insane." Angela's grandmothers knew Hannah "stood at the bottomless passage to an underworld. She was wounded. She was dangerous. And there was no thawing for her heart" (12–13). And yet, in the end, Angela attends her mother's death and receives her mother's last child as a sister to be loved and given a chance for life.

Throughout the novel, Dora-Rouge, Agnes, and Bush try to figure out where Angela's story begins. They search for stories, explanations, and understanding; they search for the "original trauma." They feel that the story might have started in 1938 when hunters started "killing the wolves," "when the people were starving," when the beaver were all trapped out, when loggers had "just logged the last of the pine forests," and when Harold "vanished off the face of earth" (37). In the words of ecopsychologists, Hannah's insanity was created when the Earth's resources were depleted through the actions of ignorant and arrogant men. Hannah, however, is not the only casualty of these circumstances. Such conditions create whole communities of estranged people. When Dora-Rouge returns home, her return

> was not what she'd hoped or imagined. It was nothing like the place she remembered. . . . Dora-Rouge had gone home to die in a place that existed in her mind as one thing; in reality it was something altogether different. The animals were no longer there, nor were the people or clans, the landmarks, not even the enormous sturgeon they'd called giants; and not the water they once swam in. Most of the trees had become nothing more than large mounds of sawdus (225).

Such loss causes "ontogenetic crippling"—not only in Hannah and her offspring, but in the lives of the majority of Fat-Eaters who survived the catastrophes.

Dora-Rouge is shocked and grieved by the madness she sees:

> The young children drank alcohol and sniffed glue and paint. They staggered about and lay down on streets. Some of them had children of their own, infants who were left untouched, untended by their child-parents. Sometimes they were given beer when they cried. It was the only medicine left for all that pain. Even the healing plants had been destroyed. Those without alcohol were even worse off, and the people wept without end, and tried to cut and burn their own bodies (226).

Dora-Rouge asks the generative question of this novel: "How do conquered people get back their lives?" The text tells that "she and others knew the protest against the dams and river diversions was their only hope. Those who protested were the ones who could still believe they might survive as a people" (226). This is only partially

true. What the novel suggests, more fully, is that the grandmothers
—Dora-Rouge, Agnes, Bush—know how to heal. And they do so
through storytelling, through teaching Angela how to read the maps
of the earth, and more particularly, they heal through loving well.
In her poem, "The Grandmother Songs," Hogan writes: "The grandmothers were my tribal gods. / They were there / when I was born.
Their songs / rose out of wet labor / and the woman smell of birth."
Hogan says that at death, "grandmothers pass, / wearing sunlight /
and thin rain, / walking out of fire / as flame / and smoke / leaving
the ashes." Hogan concludes that "the grandmothers / keep following the creation / that opens before them / as they sing" (*The Book
of Medicines* 57–58).

Hogan's latest novel *Power* (1998) moves to Florida and another
dying tribe whose continuity is assured through the actions of a
young Tiaga woman named Omishto. Although Hogan generally
focuses on the lives of women in her novels, she does so with the
intent of demonstrating the roles women have had and can have in
world renewal and the promotion of sanity. This work has yet to
become required reading on university syllabi. Perhaps as further
study becomes available, *Power* will gain popularity equal to that of
Mean Spirit and *Solar Storms*.

Louis Owens (b. 1948, d. 2002)

Gerald Vizenor has called Louis Owens the "most original scholar
in [Native American] critical theory," "an inspired, original literary
artist," "a masterful storier," and an "exceptional teacher" ("In Memoriam" 1). In truth, no other Native author has dealt more critically
with multicultural identity than Owens. Although he teases about
not being an "enrolled" Indian, Owens explains that by the time he
reached midlife, he had "learned to inhabit a hybrid, unpapered,
Choctaw-Cherokee-Welsh-Irish-Cajun mixed space in between. I
conceive of myself today not as an 'Indian,' but as a mixedblood, a
person of complex roots and histories." The ontology of Owens's
identity is further defined as "liminal." "Along with my parents and
grandparents, [eight] brothers and sisters, I am the product of liminal space, the result of union between desperate individuals on the
edges of dispossessed cultures and the marginalized spawn of

invaders. A liminal existence and a tension in the blood and heart must be the inevitable result of such crossing. How could it be otherwise?" (*Mixedblood Messages* 176). "Liminal space," "desperate individuals on the edges of dispossessed cultures," and "marginalized spawn of invaders" are phrases Owens uses to indicate not his attitude toward his ancestry but rather his attitude toward the social, political, and economic space people of mixed-blood have been constrained to occupy in American history. Owens was born in California to Hoey and Ida, who were migrant workers. He spent his childhood moving from California to Mississippi and back—always living and working in poverty.

Owens's inquiry into mixedblood identity permeates his fiction and critical works. Such inquiry is caught up in genealogical research that is also an archeology of place and displacement. Owens's projects are informed equally by family histories and Postcolonial/Postmodern literature and theory—a blend of personal and professional concerns. Owens has five "mystery" novels to his credit: *Wolfsong* (1991), *The Sharpest Sight* (1992), *Bone Game* (1994), *Nightland* (1996), and *Dark River* (1999). Although Owens's novels are often classified as mysteries, the traditional definition of mystery/detective novel does not adequately delineate Owens's texts.

It is true that Owens's works are caught up in solving crimes, but the surface investigations into the whodunits are actually literary probes into the nature of crimes against the Earth and humanity within a Postcolonial context. Other conceptions of *mystery* apply to Owens's works. Mystery, in the way that Owens implements the genre, is analogous to the French *mystère* plays, early medieval dramas based on sacred narratives and rituals. However, in Owens's texts, the sacred narratives and rituals are a complex of Native American traditions along with some allusions to Christian patterns. Owens also plays with the connections between *mystery* and *mysticism* in his works. Mysticism is the belief that reason and logic are not the only means of gaining knowledge (solving crimes). Knowledge of events—of relationships between people and the earth—is also attainable through myths, dreams, and ecological consciousness. Such consciousness is collective rather than individual. This means that others have access to similar dreams—are even called to share similar dreams, particularly dreams that help resolve psychological, sociological, and ecological ruptures that damage whole peoples and the earth. The ultimate mystery, in a modernist sense, is death. And mystery novels, while they engage in death as the ultimate trauma/drama, also attempt to explain death and, in so doing, the meaning of life. Owens's sophisticated type of "detective" work has drawn international acclaim. His novels have been translated into French, German, and Japanese. In fact, Owens was given the prestigious Roman Noir Prize for *The Sharpest Sight*—deeming it the most outstanding mystery novel published in France in 1995. Other awards for his fiction include the 1993 PEN-Josephine Miles Award for *The Sharpest Sight* and the 1997 American Book Award for *Nightland*.

Owens's critical/autoethnographic texts include *Other Destinies: Understanding the American Indian Novel* (1992), *Mixedblood Messages: Literature, Film, Family, Place* (1998), and *I Hear the Train: Reflections, Inventions, Refractions* (2001). Owens's critical works combine his knowledge of Western philosophic/literary traditions with Native traditions in what Postmodern critics call dialogic thought—conversations across cultural boundaries. Owens's title *Mixedblood Messages*, for example, is a metaphor for the recognition that multiple narratives from mixed genealogies converge in a person who is the product of mixed bloodlines. For instance, Owens uses the thoughts of Roland Barthes to come to terms with family photographs of Native ancestors whose stories are primarily like negatives—images of absence rather than presence. He says, "I enter the labyrinth in search of what I already know to be at the center: the monster of my own hybridization"(*I Hear the Train* 98). Hybridization is a term used widely in Postcolonial discourse. When bloodlines mix, pluralism (multiple views of the world) conflicts in one person, or multiple epistemologies compete for ascendance in one mind. In addition, the conflicts between self and other converge in the face that looks back from the mirror.

Owens is also a well-renowned John Steinbeck scholar; his books on Steinbeck include *John Steinbeck's Re-Vision of America* (1985) and *The Grapes of Wrath: Trouble in the Promised Land* (1989). Owens was drawn to Steinbeck's works because of his familiarity with the life-ways and history of the Salinas Valley. As the titles of

Owens's works on Steinbeck indicate, Owens is likewise concerned with reimagining the American experience from the position of the disenfranchised and dispossessed. Owens's ability to help students understand the complexities of writing creatively and reading contemporary theory and literature also achieved recognition. Owens was awarded several teaching awards including the "University of New Mexico's Alumni Award for Teaching Excellence, the University of California Santa Cruz Alumni Association Distinguished Teaching Award, the UCSC Student Alumni Council Favorite Professor Award, and the Outstanding Teacher of the Year Award from the International Steinbeck Society" ("In Memoriam" 3).

Although it is tempting to discuss the complex of Owens's novels, perhaps an introduction to the relationship between *The Sharpest Sight* and *Bone Game* might serve to demonstrate the excellence of Owens's writings. In an interview with John Purdy, Owens calls *Bone Game* the "favorite of my novels" (10). And Gerald Vizenor includes *Bone Game* on his list of "visionary novels" written by Native Americans (*Postindian Conversations* 166). *Bone Game* continues the narrative, albeit twenty years later, told in *The Sharpest Sight*. Each novel, however, needs to be contextualized. In fact, Postmodernism establishes the necessity of realizing that all tellings (truth claims) can only be understood *in context* and that every context reveals the contingent nature of any narrative construct. In other words, Postmodern narratives reveal the "messy" nature of interpreting characters and events. Many factors must be taken into account—especially the realization that every character involved in any given event will have a unique, yet limited, point of view. As a result, truths must be concerned with *difference*. In Owens's works, polyvocal approaches to events are also multicultural. Margaret Dwyer says of *The Sharpest Sight*, for example, "The intertextual nature of the novel allows members of disparate cultures, joined in the story, to observe and remark on the attitudes and values of 'the other'" (46). Moreover, for each character, "knowledge and truth are determined by beliefs," Dwyer contends (48).

Furthermore, Margaret Dwyer argues that *The Sharpest Sight* moves "beyond the frequently used issues of poverty, alcoholism, and the victimization of Native people. Instead, myths, cultures, and autobiography mix on a dynamic frontier in which no one voice dominates. Unwilling to simply offer up a work in which Choctaw spice flavors a complex, frequently humourous murder mystery, Owens appropriates and subverts the colonists' canonized literature" (45–46). Owens himself maintains, he "began to write novels as a way of figuring things out for myself. I think my works are about the natural world and our relations with that world, with one another, and, most crucially, with ourselves. Though each of my novels begins and ends with place itself, the mysteries of mixed identity and conflicted stories, both the stories we tell ourselves and the stories others tell about us and to us, are what haunt my fiction" (*Mixedblood Messages* 181).

Owens often reflects on the stories he writes, "using the raw material" of his family's lives "for fantastic fictions" (*I Hear the Train* 14). Owens recounts that *The Sharpest Sight* draws heavily on elements from his own family history:

> I wrote of a young Choctaw-Cherokee-Irish mixedblood [Cole McCurtain] who must learn who he is and how to balance a world that has led his brother [Attis] to madness and destroyed him, a world of stories in deadly conflict. I used my father's name, Hoey, and my grandfather's name, Luther, in that novel, and I created a powerful old Choctaw lady named Onatima whom I modeled upon what I remembered and imagined of my grandma. Onatima, too, ran away with a gambler on the great river. I also based a major character [Attis] in that novel on my brother Gene, who had come back from three tours in Vietnam with such pain that he became one of the psychological casualties who disappeared into the Ozark Mountains of Arkansas (*Mixedblood Messages* 182).

Owens reports that "after a quarter of a century of silence," Gene called him. "He had found a copy of *The Sharpest Sight*, had seen my name and read the book. . . . He had read it and had known at once that it was about him, had read past layers of metaphor and myth, through a complex 'mystery' plot, to see that I'd written a novel about the loss of my own brother" (*I Hear the Train* 13).

Although Gene did not kill his girlfriend nor get sent to a mental institution (like Attis in *The Sharpest Sight*), Gene's experiences in Vietnam became a symbol for Owens of the effects of killing, even in war, on the human psyche. Gene told his brother, "he'd shot a child, a little girl running toward them with a satchel charge while his CO shouted at him to fire. That was when all the pieces began to separate for him" (9). Owens remembers, "Gene had left for the same war I had planned to go to before his warnings, and then he'd come back only to vanish. It was as though he'd never come back at all, as though they'd killed him and sent something else home" (11). When Owens asked his brother why he had stayed for three tours of duty in "what his letters had described as worse than any hell a person could imagine," Gene answered, "I stayed so that someone wouldn't have to take my place." Owens further explains the ravages of war on two uncles who were "murdered years after coming home. Neither case [was] solved, or perhaps even investigated" (*I Hear the Train* 11). On one hand, *The Sharpest Sight* explores the indeterminacy of such lives. On the other, this novel establishes the worth of such lives through telling stories about the complex reactions of those kin whose lives are impacted by such tragic loss.

Chris LaLonde clearly explains the complexity of this novel in his essay, "Discerning Connections, Revising the Master Narrative, and Interrogating Identity in Louis Owens's *The Sharpest Sight.*"

> The work is an intricately crafted murder mystery that tells the stories of Vietnam veteran Attis McCurtain, the victim; Cole and Hoey McCurtain, Attis's brother and father; Luther and Onatima, Mississippi Choctaws to whom Cole goes for help; the Nemi family, whose oldest daughter was killed by Attis after his return from Vietnam; Mundo Morales, a mestizo deputy sheriff and friend of the McCurtains; and various other inhabitants of Amarga, California (306).

An FBI agent, Lee Scott; Diane Nemi, the sister of the murdered girl; and Jessard Deal, a redneck opportunist, ought to also be listed in the cast of characters.

Each character interprets and responds to Attis's crime and mental illness differently. Lee Scott's attitudes toward Attis stem from the noble/savage paradox that has, historically, prompted U.S. public policies. In Scott's mind, Attis is a strange type of deranged warrior shaman—a ghost-dance type of Indian who could cause trouble, even in death. As Mundo's name indicates—Mundo (world) Morales (values)—ethical concerns are often tangled in the face of such a crime. Mundo is a mix of Mexican-American, Chinese, and Native American heritages—with a healthy dose of Catholicism mixed in. While Mundo has been taught (by his dead grandfather) to be suspect of Native mysticism, he, nevertheless, has sympathy for Attis because they shared their youth, loves, and experiences in Vietnam. Dwyer notes that Diane Nemi is named after Diane of Nemi, a Roman fertility goddess (50). This possibility would indicate that Diane is the heir of several complex traditions. Her behavior is consistent with those of characters within Senecan tragedies. These dramas focus on unnatural crimes, and characters are often motivated by revenge as a means of getting even. Furthermore, rapacious behaviors abound in these dramas—incest, rape, and infanticide being typical behaviors. In *The Sharpest Sight*, Diane is incested by her father, raped by Jessard Deal, desired by Mundo and Cole, and viewed as a sorceress. These men, to some degree, want to control Diane's sexuality. Luther tries, however, to break the vengeance/sexual violence cycle exemplified in Diane's life. When he finds out that Diane is both the killer of Attis and an incest/rape survivor, he offers her a healing ritual. Those characters who know Attis attempt to heal the ruptures made by his delusional behaviors. Those who don't know Attis want his crime avenged (the Nemi family) or buried (the FBI).

Owens takes his title, *The Sharpest Sight*, from a 1741 sermon delivered by Jonathan Edwards entitled "Sinners in the Hands of an Angry God." Chris LaLonde speculates that Owens's novel is a commentary on the assertions Edwards makes in his discourse. LaLonde says, "With his sermon Edwards attempted to coerce his listeners into religious commitment and conversion by describing the control God has over their life and death." The God Edwards believes in is "a vengeful God," who watches sinners "lose their footing and fall to hell." In Edwards's theology, such sinners become invisible; "the arrows of death fly unseen at noonday" and even "the sharpest sight cannot discern them." Owens's novel challenges the ideas of sin, discernment, and the Creator's motives proffered by Edwards. "Such discerning sight, Owens makes clear, is associated with a different worldview than that held by subjects of the dominant culture," claims LaLonde ("Discerning Connections" 310).

Luther tells Cole, "the great spirit don't want churches and hullabaloo, he just wants us to stay awake and look with more than our eye" (*The Sharpest Sight* 112). Luther contends: "Most people's asleep all the time, just walking around in their sleep, fighting in their sleep, making children and dying without ever waking up. Wars like that one Hoey's other son went to is fought by men in their sleep. They shoot and stab and die without ever waking up." Furthermore, "Most people think dreams is only for the time we're asleep, they don't know that dreams is how we see in the dark" (112). With the aid of Luther, Onatima, Hoey, and his own dreams and intellect, Cole is able to gain "sharper sight." Cole is able to discern Attis's *shilombish* and *shilup*—"inside and outside shadows"(113). Cole is able to understand why he must collect the bones of his brother and bury them in Mississippi. Such a burial returns Attis to the Choctaw people, the tribal lands, and the tribal ways of releasing the dead from their torturous lives. Without such release, Attis's *shilup* would remain on earth, lonely, and seeking for a loved one to join him.

The Sharpest Sight is a complex novel. Only a part of that complexity can be discussed in such a short essay. However, such complexity is rendered more familiar in *Bone Game*. Both novels address the response of the earth to those evils committed on her. Colonial violence still penetrates the soil, invades the forests, and hangs heavy in the atmosphere. As violated cultures are buried in the earth, their stories persist. In his interview with Purdy, Owens conveys that he wanted *Bone Game* "to be a story in which all times and all actions coexisted simultaneously. I felt that I couldn't convey the fabric of violence in that place any other way." Purdy responded to this statement by clarifying, "So, it's a geospecific place that is deep with the history of violence." Owens responds in the affirmative: "I wanted to explore that sense, the enormous sense of loss that the indigenous people of the Santa Cruz area, the Ohlone, experienced. Within a single generation—the matter of a few years, even months—so much was lost, changed forever, as the result of the coming of Europeans. That is why the novel begins with the lines, 'Children. Neófitos. Bestes. And still it is the same sky, the same night arched like a reed house, the stars of their birth.' I wanted to convey in those lines the extraordinary shock of recognizing that the world has not changed at the deepest, most important levels, though one's people or culture may have vanished" (Purdy "Clear Waters: A Conversation with Louis Owens" 11).

Two independent paragraphs serve as prologue to this novel. These paragraphs contain excerpts from two seemingly unrelated historical events. On October 15, 1812, "six armed men" are reported to have been "dispatched" to "exhume the body" of "Padre Andrés Quintana at the mission of Santa Cruz." He is found to have been "tortured" and "hanged." And on November 1, 1993, the "dismembered body of a young woman begins washing ashore on the beaches of Santa Cruz, California" (*Bone Game* 3). The novel shows how these two events are related. Following these paragraphs (on the next page) come what Purdy and Owens call "the first lines of the novel"; they are words uttered by Padre Quintana. He molested children, violated his sacred trust, and ended up murdered by an Ohlone man (Venancio Asisara) who wanted the destruction of his people and culture to stop. "Then the killing of the priest is the apt, the perfect act to precipitate the events in the novel, the evil that came with the change," Purdy comprehends. "Yeah," answers Owens. "That's how I felt. And in a way, Santa Cruz is a microcosm for the U.S. There's been so much violence perpetrated in its history" ("Clear Waters" 11).

The major plot of the novel traces Cole McCurtain's growing consciousness of the violence present in Santa Cruz and the role he must play in addressing that violence. Cole is a professor of literature at UC Santa Cruz. He teaches courses on Modernism and Native American Literature. But his teaching is affected by his loneliness, drinking, and troubled dreams. Cole is divorced, separated from his daughter Addy, and living half a continent away from Hoey, Luther, and Onatima. At the beginning of the novel, dreams come to Cole for six nights. Asisara Venancio sends the dreams. These dreams are infused with a sense of urgency and malice, exemplified by these dream images: "At the crest of the ride," Venancio "feels himself rising to full height, the bear in him reaching to embrace this new life and shatter its bones." Venancio wonders why he has been awakened to "such hate." He asks where his father's world is.

And, "He holds forth his hands, wondering who will gamble for a world, the blood of the old priest still fresh and sweet in his nostrils" (*Bone Game* 7). Cole's dreams become so menacing that he sends for his father, great uncle, and grandmother. (Their journey to Cole constitutes another plot line.) However, they have already been informed, by their dreams, of Cole's impending danger.

Cole befriends Alex Yazzie, a new Navajo faculty member, a Harvard graduate in anthropology, and a cross-dresser. It is Alex who begins to share the history of the Ohlone people with Cole. And slowly, Cole recognizes the frightening figures in his dreams as being historically accurate characters—the Ohlone, the Padre, and Asisara. In Cole's dreams, Asisara has taken upon himself the role of the painted gambler—the one who plays the bone game. The plot thickens when a number of female bodies begin to show up—decapitated and ravaged. LaLonde suggests that "Cole fears his dreams because they deal with violence, death, and loss—that is, because they are all too easily connected to Attis" (*Grave Concerns, Trickster Turns* 118). In other dreams, Cole is given clues to his own survival. However, his anguish persists for most of the novel.

Much of the novel hinges on an understanding of the inexhaustible nature of violence/evil; the centrality of death to any comprehension of life; and the psychological, and often radical, effects of conflicting ideologies on students of those ideologies. The historicity of these intellectual concerns are housed in the fiber of courses taught at universities. These issues, therefore, are exemplified by the classes Cole teaches on Modernism and Native American Literature. The painted, evil gambler is the living, yet ghostly, presence of origins of such issues. Half of him is dark, the other half light. "He holds his hands in front of him, showing the bones, one pale and one dark"—"The painted bone lies in the palm of the right hand, the white bone in the left" (106–107). Two refrains in Spanish run throughout the novel: "*Gente de razón*"(5)—People of reason, and "*eran muy crueles*"(7, 243)—they were very cruel. The second phrase comes from the sentence: "*Los padres españoles eran muy crueles con los indios*"—the Spanish priests were very cruel to the Indians (107). Onatima recognizes the nature of the gamble in her waking dream of the gambler: "'Desire and death. The bone game. . . . He wants his world,' she whispers" (107). The gambler is a variation of the Choctaw *nalusachito*—souleater (132). The larger purposes of those surrounding Cole—Luther, Hoey, Onatima, Alex, and Abby—is to help Cole prepare to meet the gambler.

Three other plot lines (stories) run parallel to, and often impose on or intersect, those of Cole; Hoey and Luther (who take a side trip to the Navajo reservation and discover that souleater is there too); Onatima and Abby (grandmother/matriarch and daughter—the sources of wisdom and love); and Abby and Alex (the possibility of gendered love). These other plot lines offer character sketches of two students: Paul Kantner (an unattractive, burly, red-headed, embattled Vietnam veteran who is in Cole's Modernism class) and Robert Malin (Cole's broody teaching assistant in the Native American Literature class). Part of the intellectual appeal of this novel is the commentary it makes on the distressing responsibilities of university professors given the diverse and often unstable needs of students. Cole vents:

> A modernism class, with all the requisite talk of hanged gods and Christ and human responsibility, tended to fertilize their imaginations. It could be even worse in a Native American literature course, where they imagined themselves reincarnations of Crazy Horse and descendants of Indian princesses. Everyone had a Cherokee great-grandmother, never Paiute or Lummi. On weekends they found a feathered huckster to take their hundred bucks for a sweat ceremony or three hundred for a vision quest, and they returned hungry and dazed with an Indian name like Willow or Redbird (21).

Perhaps *Kantner* is a name invented by Owens to represent Kant and those philosophies that led to the crisis of modernism and the development of the deracinated protagonist in much of modern fiction. In Kantian philosophy, the human mind can not substantiate the nature of reality, but even so, must affirm the existence of absolute moral law ("human responsibility"): the categorical imperative—a paradox that seems to lead to schizophrenia. The deracinated individual is alienated, torn from his/her roots, estranged from family ties, forced to live in an absurdist world bereft of meaning ("hanged gods"), and filled, therefore, with enormous anxiety. Ironically, the modernist also expects mastery of mind, nature, and society. The consummate modernist is the structuralist who looks for universal patterns. Moreover, as authors such as D. H. Lawrence and T. S. Eliot so rightly predicted: the modern, technological, post-industrial person would become most harmed in his/her sexuality. Paul Kantner is obsessed with T. S. Eliot's Prufrock who desires the recognition of women but can't obtain it.

In a violent exchange with Robert, Kantner declares: "I hate violence. It's pointless. I mean here we are at the University of California at Santa Cruz, where language is god, so wouldn't it be ridiculous if we substituted physical conflict for intellectual discussion?" Further on, Kantner reveals his displeasure with the Postmodern condition.

> I'm sick of these professors playing their language games. We pay money to sit there and listen to a bunch of faggots tell us everything is just language. That's because they don't know a fucking thing about reality, do they? They've never been hungry or had to kill so they could stay alive. They go to some goddamned prep school and then Yale or Harvard, and then they come here to teach us how to live. What a joke. Sometimes I want to stick a knife in their guts and ask them what that signifies (172).

While Owens fictionalizes the Postmodern condition in *Bone Game*, he defines it in *Other Destinies*. For example, Owens quotes David Harvey on Postmodern schizophrenia—the "inability to unify [the] past, present, and future . . . of our own biographical experience or psychic life." Furthermore, "Postmodernism typically strips away that possibility by concentrating upon the schizophrenic circumstances induced by fragmentation and all the instabilities (including those of language) that prevent us even picturing coherently, let alone devising strategies to produce, some radically different future" (*Other Destinies* 98–99). Similar ideas lead Kantner to perpetrate crimes against women; he becomes a psycho-sexual slayer projecting his rage onto women who shun him. Abby, Alex, and Robert discover Kantner is the serial killer when Kantner tries to take Abby and Alex hostage. Robert shoots Kantner ostensibly to save Alex and Abby and then is given a hero's write-up in the press. This "brave act" is a cover-up; no one knows the role that Robert Malin is playing in the local murders.

Perhaps the name Robert Malin is also indicative of the character's attributes. Maybe the name *Malin* is related to male; malign; malignant; Malinowski (the father of "participant observation" in anthropology); or more noticeably the name of a point off the coast of Ireland and Scotland (an allusion to European ancestry). Robert is obsessed with Cole—and Abby. Robert is also a strange kind of romantic who is caught up in extrasensory readings. Cole says of Robert, "He's one of those white people who suspect all the evil their ancestors have done to the earth and feel the need to atone somehow. What he really wants is to be a white Indian, the Natty Bumppo of Santa Cruz. I guess that would make me his Chingachgook and Alex his Unca. Only thing missing is Magua." And to Abby he adds, "And you must be Cora, the beautiful maiden with the cross in her blood" (206). Early in the novel, Cole asks the overachieving Robert if he remembers his dreams. "Always," he answers. "Edgar Cayce [a famous psychic reader] said that in every man there exists a vast expanse, unfamiliar and unexplored, which sometimes appears in the guise of an angel, other times a monster. This is man's unconscious mind, and the language we call dreams. But I wonder sometimes how we know which is speaking to us, which voice we obey" (18).

Robert has this conversation with Cole just prior to Cole's lecture on Black Elk. Cole tells Robert he is going to "deconstruct *Black Elk*" (19). Cole's lecture on Black Elk is "a failure. In trying to free Black Elk from the romantic visions of John Neihardt and the students, he'd confused everything. He could tell the students felt cheated, missing the truth of the beautiful, troubled old man, Nicholas Black Elk, the angry Catholic who had been born on the boundary of one world and survived far into another" (35). Robert advises Cole that the students feel "like you cheated them. That you took away the Black Elk they believed in and gave back nothing in return." Cole, angry, replies, "They like to think Nicholas Black Elk was a one-dimensional holy man, Neihardt's romantic, tragic creation. That's what the whole fucking world wants, isn't it Robert? To see Indians as noble and mystical and, most important of all, impotent and doomed?" (42) Robert wants Cole to feel the students' needs because "their parents haven't given them anything at all. Neihardt's Black Elk lets them think that the world is holy, filled with dreams, not just an empty place we fill with things we possess." Cole wants to rescue the students from "ethnostalgia" (43). But in Robert's case, this is an impossible task. What Cole doesn't realize is that Robert Malin's dreams are also haunted by the painted gambler. Robert is seduced by the monster in his dreams; he carries out the evil gambler's wishes through the sacrifice of innocence.

Just before Malin lays his own body—painted after the fashion of the gambler—onto Abby's in a violent attempt to control her future, Robert explains: "The most effective sacrifices are those things we value most. Maybe one [meaning Alex] will be enough this time" (232). Robert has sacrificed thirteen people to appease crimes against the earth. And he has just shot Alex as well. In addition, he forces Abby to strip and paints her body after the image of the gambler. When Robert unintentionally places his gun beside the prostrate body of Abby (the symbol of his *pure* [?] sexual desires), Abby reaches for the gun and shoots Robert.

What role does Cole act in playing the bone game? He is the desired victim of the evil gambler as well as the impetus for expiating the extensive violence. However, this task is not a solitary task; Cole is not a typical hero. His kindred and other empathic healers are drawn to help Cole survive his ordeal; together they form an active community that recognizes how to rid the entire environment from historical/contemporary violence. Much of the novel is concerned with healing rituals. In *Grave Concerns, Trickster Turns*, LaLonde suggests "that liminality can be both an accurate term to describe the position in which Cole finds himself and a necessary position for one seeking healing and the recovery and/or reaffirmation of identity" (111). However, Cole must come to terms with death and radical evil in order to be made whole. "Although Cole is caught in a liminal, betwixt-and-between state, it is liminality as it functions in traditional ceremonies and passage rituals that can enable him to emerge from that state healed," LaLonde conjectures (111–112).

LaLonde explains that anthropologists have repeatedly shown how ceremonies help whole "communities and individuals confront and deal with crises." Lalonde quotes Victor Turner who declares that traditional rituals and ceremonies grant actors the freedom: "to contemplate for a while the mysteries that confront all men, the difficulties that peculiarly beset their own society, [and probable causes for] their personal problems" (Turner in LaLonde 112). Cole is called to a ritual site in Cueloze Pueblo to gain knowledge of his solitude, of the Pueblo striped ones, and of the crimes committed against Pueblo peoples at that site (74); and Alex brings powerful Native friends to Cole's home in Santa Cruz to perform a sweat ceremony to purify Cole (163) and to hold a peyote service to help give Cole visions (196). Each of these three ceremonial experiences fulfills the three purposes of traditional rituals outlined by Turner.

Luther tells Cole, "You have prepared yourself well, Grandson. For many months now you have put away the appetites of men. You have fasted and gone into the sweat lodge, and you have prayed and been given a vision" (208). Cole's response to Luther is typical of Cole's wry personality:

> 'I think we may be dealing with semantics here, Uncle Luther. The truth is that I haven't been with a woman for all these months not because I was being pure, but because I was afraid.' He glanced at Onatima. 'I've done what you call fasting only because until Abby came I was too sick to eat. Alex dragged me into the sweat lodge and into another ceremony in which I ate a hallucinogenic drug that nearly killed me. To call all of that purification is wish fulfillment, I'm afraid' (208).

Luther retorts, "What you call it don't matter. Onatima always says the Good Lord works in mysterious ways." Onatima reminds Cole the gambler is "part of something too big. It's everywhere now. We all have to live with this thing." Onatima counsels Cole, "People got to live with what they made here, just like everywhere." Onatima also clarifies why the gambler is obsessed with Cole: "The gambler wants power, Grandson. And he thinks you brung it to him. He thinks you are a warrior like him" (209).

Onatima's role in the novel communicates an important character established in many Native works: the wise old woman who, through her wisdom and nurturing capacity, is given the honorary status of grandmother. Onatima and Luther work as a team, revealing the necessity of harmony between the sexes if there is to be harmony in the world. Luther's reputation is impressive. While Luther and Hoey are en route to Cole, they stop among the Navajo to rescue a Navajo woman, Kate Begay, from an attempted kidnapping. Robert Jim (a Navajo elder) tells Kate: "Granddaughter, do you know who saved you? Luther Cole is a famous medicine man, known all over the world, and this here's his nephew, Hoey, a great hunter" (169).

Onatima's grandmotherly love, wisdom, and intuition run through this novel with a comic seriousness worthy of mention. For example, Onatima arrives at Cole's home just in time to rescue Abby from a frightful confrontation with the gambler lurking outside the window of her father's house. Onatima tells Abby, "Perhaps the man who frightened you today wants to make you see yourself only through his eyes, so that you can only imagine yourself from outside the window looking in. That way, every time you look in a mirror you will see only what the man sees. You will always be outside yourself, and your own reflection will be a trap. When that happens we become like ghosts who can't see our own bodies." Onatima's speech voices insight into colonial psychology: the imposition of the colonizer on the colonized. Such incursions require that Native peoples must either exclaim their own identity or accept the identity forced upon them. Onatima says: "Then we have to make others see us so we can know we exist, or we have to use others' lives as our own. That's what they want. It's a matter of power. They would imprison us in their vision and their stories, and we can't let them do that. We have to have our own stories" (140). Onatima, however, contextualizes her wisdom within the story of her own journey and that journey's relationship to her own grandmother.

In an exchange between Cole and Onatima, Onatima asks Cole if she can watch him lecture. "I haven't been in a classroom in thirty years. I think I would enjoy hearing you lecture. Elders teach, and I want to see you function as an elder," Onatima says. This conversation thrusts Cole into a new position with regard to his understanding of his expected role as an elder. Onatima, however, is the actual instructor in this circumstance. Onatima reveals that she has telephoned Cole's former wife, Mara (the root word for marriage), shortly before coming to see Cole. Cole is puzzled. "My former wife. Why?" he asks. Then the lessons come:

> 'Mara's my friend, and women have to help each other when you men screw everything up. She sounded relatively happy. Life's just like that, Grandson, and the sooner you adjust the better. It's time you got some perspective on this midlife crisis and stopped feeling sorry for yourself. You're very fortunate. You have a wonderful daughter and a wonderful former wife who will remain your friend if you let her. You have an education. If I had a Ph.D., I'd be in Washington, D.C., giving everybody hell. Indian male menopause is a terrible thing.'
>
> 'And I have a ghost. You left that part out.'
>
> 'We all have ghosts, Grandson.'

Onatima smooths "her dress with fragile hands." And then she lets Cole have it:

> 'Isn't it wonderful that life is interesting? Incidentally, you'll stop drinking alcohol, too. That's the worst Indian cliché of all. It's time to quit feeling sorry for yourself and start thinking about this situation here. It's your story, after all, and people are dying' (144–145).

Cole, in the end, does face the gambler, who is an actual presence. The gambler has influenced Robert to do his bidding. And yet, Cole and his community resist. In the finish, Venancio Asisara smiles at Cole and says, "*Eran muy crueles*," as he retreats, in the form of a bear, into the forest. Cole and Abby move back to New Mexico where Cole will resume his former teaching position and also where Alex will join them when he is finished with a Navajo healing ceremony. Onatima and the Choctaw contingent will return to their home in Mississippi, far away, but as close as dreams. While the sun beautifies the sky in New Mexico, however, such natural beauty is not possible in Santa Cruz. The novel ends with these two sentences: "It is a world so like his [Asisara's] own, of black streams and changeless skies. His shadow falls across the town and bay, undulating with the slow waves. *Eran muy crueles*" (243). In other words, such evil will persist in "geospecific" places until the larger population becomes aware that historical evils are coeval—part of particular geographies.

Sherman Alexie (b. 1966)

A discussion of Sherman Alexie (Coeur d'Alene/Spokane) moves us back to the Northwest yet forward to the career of a prolific, yet controversial, *Indian* (Alexie's preference) writer. Between 1992 and 2004, Alexie published sixteen books and wrote screenplays for two motion pictures: *Smoke Signals* (1998), based on a collection of his short stories *The Lone Ranger and Tonto Fistfight in Heaven*; and *The Business of Fancydancing* (2002), based on his poetry collection of the same name. During this period, Alexie also contributed lyrics to five CDs and appeared at numerous venues as an author and standup comedian. Alexie has worked on screenplays for his two novels, *Reservation Blues* (1995) and *Indian Killer* (1996), as well. Alexie's adaptation of texts to film indicates his awareness of film as one of the most viable mediums for reaching large audiences. Alexie, while grateful for his success in elitist circles, would also like his books/films to be accessible to reservation "kids" whose heroes have typically been created by the "white" media (Spencer 2–3).

Alexie was born in October of 1966 to a Coeur d'Alene father (Sherman Joseph Alexie) and a Spokane mother (Lillian Agnes Cox). He grew up in Wellpinit, Washington on the Spokane Indian Reservation—fifty miles northwest of Spokane. Alexie's poetry, short stories, and novels most often take place either on or near the Spokane Indian Reservation. Characters with familiar family names reappear in Alexie's works formulating a fascinating social field of reservation and urban Indian life within the state of Washington. Alexie was born hydrocephalic, survived brain surgery at the age of six months, and lived to prove doctors' prognoses incorrect — doctors assumed Alexie would either die or be severely retarded. Even though he did suffer seizures and unmanageable bed-wetting throughout his childhood, Alexie went on to excel academically and to become a star basketball player during his high school years. Alexie was a lover of books in his youth. By the age of five, he was reading works by major American authors. Alexie attended Gonzaga University (in Spokane) and Washington State University (in Pullman); he graduated in American Studies. Alexie wrote two books of poetry, under the tutelage of Alex Kuo (his poetry professor at WSU), during his college years. Both collections—*The Business of Fancydancing* (1992) and *I Would Steal Horses* (1992)—were published shortly after Alexie graduated (*cum laude*) from college in 1991. Alexie intended to be a doctor, but his success as a writer altered his career plans. Early success also caused Alexie to give up drinking at the age of twenty-three. His "official biography" claims that Alexie has been "sober ever since" (2).

In a biographical article on Alexie, Ron McFarland rehearses the wide range of Alexie's kudos. McFarland notes that in 1992, *The New York Times Book Review* by James R. Kincaid "singled out" Alexie as "'one of the major lyric voices of our time'" (3). Alexie's first collection of short stories *The Lone Ranger and Tonto Fistfight in Heaven* (1993) won a PEN-Hemingway Award "for the best first book of fiction," states McFarland (6). Alexie transformed one of the short stories, "The Lone Ranger and Tonto Fistfight in Heaven," from this short story collection into the film *Smoke Signals*. *Smoke Signals* is the first film in the United States to be written (Alexie), directed (Chris Eyre), and acted in (Adam Beach, Evan Adams, Gary Farmer, and Tantoo Cardinal) wholly by Native Americans. *Smoke Signals* received three awards at the 1998 Sundance Film Festival where it premiered: the Audience Award for Dramatic Films, the Filmmakers Trophy, and a nomination for the Grand Jury Prize.

Three of Alexie's works are taught on a regular basis at universities throughout the United States: *The Lone Ranger and Tonto Fist Fight in Heaven*, *Reservation Blues*, and *Indian Killer*. Alexie, however, continues to produce quality texts; his latest collections of short stories *The Toughest Indian in the World* (2000) and *Ten Little Indians* (2003), for example, are now appearing on course syllabi. Notwithstanding, a brief introduction to the three major texts will demonstrate the complexity of Alexie's prose as well as the controversy generated by his works.

Stephen F. Evans claims that Alexie "came under fire from certain quarters for his purportedly negative use of irony and satire—namely, literary connections to (white) popular culture and representations of Indian stereotypes that some consider 'inappropriate' and dangerously misleading for mainstream consumption" (47). Evans quotes Louis Owens who finds that Alexie's fiction reinforces

> stereotypes desired by white readers: his bleakly absurd and aimless Indians are imploding in a passion of self-destructiveness and self-loathing; there is no family or community center toward which his characters . . . might turn for coherence; and in the process of self-destruction the Indians provide Euramerican readers with pleasurable moments of dark humor of the titillation of bloodthirsty savagery (Owens 79–80).

However, film reviewers Siskel & Ebert disagree—at least about Alexie's enormously popular film *Smoke Signals*. Gene Siskel says:

> Obviously, *Smoke Signals* is not, in any way, a standard film involving Native Americans. These are very specific characters, but not every utterance and every event in the film revolves around their Indian heritage. The result is to expand our notion of just who Native Americans are and can be. This thoroughly entertaining film . . . could turn out to be a milestone in Native American cinema (2).

Roger Ebert agrees: "I felt I was seeing real Native Americans everyday, talking to each other, living life, without all kinds of filters of history and tradition and archetypes and stereotypes between me and the screen. These are just two people" (2). John Warren Gilroy claims that this film "represents a radical departure for indigenous actors, screenwriters, and filmmakers through its appropriation and manipulation of the very medium that has done so much to create our false impressions of American Indian cultures. We can begin to imagine the further import of Alexie's desire to subvert stereotypes by approaching the film with sensitivity to the pervasive nature of these false impressions" (30–31).

The two people that Ebert refers to are two young men, Victor Joseph (a Coeur d'Alene Reservation basketball hotshot raised by his mom) and Thomas Builds-the-Fire (a reservation geek and storyteller raised by his grandmother). When Victor's mother tells him his father has died in Arizona, Victor decides to go claim his ashes.

Because Victor has no money to support such a trip, Thomas offers
to pay the way—if Victor will take him along. Both boys are, in
some respects, "sons" of Victor's father. Victor, the natural son, is tor-
mented by his father's abandonment while Thomas idolizes Victor's
father as a father substitute. Thomas, at one point in the film/story,
tells Victor of a dream he had about Victor's father:

> I remember when I had this dream that told me to go to
> Spokane, to stand by the Falls in the middle of the city and
> wait for a sign. I knew I had to go there but I didn't have a
> car. Didn't have a license. I was only thirteen. So I walked
> all the way, took me all day, and I finally made it to the Falls.
> I stood there for an hour waiting. Then your dad came
> walking up. *What the hell are you doing here?* He asked me.
> I said, *Waiting for a vision.* Then your father said, *All you're
> going to get here is mugged.* So he drove me over to Denny's,
> bought me dinner, and then drove me home to the reser-
> vation. For a long time I was mad because I thought my
> dreams had lied to me. But they didn't, your dad was my
> vision. *Take care of each other* is what my dreams were say-
> ing. *Take care of each other* (*The Lone Ranger and Tonto
> Fistfight in Heaven* 69).

Thomas looking for a vision in a place where he might get mugged
is a trope—a Trickster image. In an interview with John Purdy,
Alexie decries the romantic sentimentalism attending much Native
fiction. "It's not corn pollen, eagle feathers, Mother Earth, Father
Sky," Alexie scoffs. "It's everyday life" (12). Going to Denny's for
dinner is an example of that everydayness.

   Smoke Signals is comically subversive throughout. Gilroy, in fact,
calls the film a subversion of the formula buddy/road movie (31).
First of all, the lead duo aren't White males; they are Indians. In fact,
Victor's and Thomas's comic exchanges are intended to challenge
White conceptions of Indianness. What is more, both members of
the team are of equal import. This is not a Lone Ranger (hero) and
Tonto (sidekick) team. As the dialogue suggests, this is a "Tonto and
Tonto" team. Furthermore, no male lead has a love interest. Women
do play significant roles—mother, grandmother, and friend. But the
film is actually about father/son relationships.

The film begins and ends with voiceover narrations. The opening voiceover reveals the crucial event in the story: the death of Thomas's parents. Between this revelation and the closing scene, Thomas and Victor learn what actually happened during the fire that killed Thomas's parents on the Fourth of July, 1976 (American Independence, ironically, means dependence for Natives). After a day of boozing, many reservation families converge on Thomas's home. Victor's father stumbles through the yard, trying to arouse the sleeping drunks by setting off fireworks. The fireworks, however, go astray and set fire to the house—killing Thomas's parents. Before the home is completely destroyed, Victor's father manages to save both Thomas and Victor from becoming victims of the fire. Guilt plagues Victor's father who eventually leaves his family in search of some peace of mind. Victor learns, from Suzy Song (his father's neighbor in Arizona), that his father continually spoke of him, bragged about his prowess on the basketball court, and longed to return home. In light of these revelations, the final voiceover narration recites Dick Lourie's poem, "Forgiving Our Fathers."

Before recounting Lourie's poem, perhaps reference to another of Alexie's short stories, "Because My Father Always Said He Was the Only Indian who Saw Jimi Hendrix Play 'The Star-Spangled Banner' at Woodstock," will demonstrate Alexie's concern with fatherloss. At one point, the narrator explains: "On a reservation, Indian men who abandon their children are treated worse than white fathers who do the same thing. It's because white men have been doing that forever and Indian men have just learned how. That's how assimilation can work" (*The Lone Ranger and Tonto Fistfight in Heaven* 34). When readers review the entire body of Alexie's works, the significance of good fathers becomes more apparent. And yet, the last poetic voiceover in *Smoke Signals* establishes why this film transcends reservation sociality. Alexie might be suggesting here that fatherloss is one of the central forces generating human angst. The poem "Forgiving Our Fathers" asks: should we forgive our fathers

> maybe for leaving us too often or
> forever when we were little maybe
> for scaring us with unexpected rage

or making us nervous because there seemed
never to be any rage there at all
for marrying or not marrying our mothers
for divorcing or not divorcing our mothers
and shall we forgive them for their excesses
of warmth of coldness shall we forgive them
for pushing or leaning for shutting doors
for speaking only through layers of cloth
or never speaking or never being silent
in our age or in theirs or in their deaths
saying it to them or not saying it—
if we forgive our fathers what is left? (1)

Smoke Signals constantly challenges distorted images of reservation life. In this film, the reservation is not a dismal, socially impoverished space, but the actual Coeur d'Alene Reservation—"depicted as dynamic and life affirming: an impression that is further supported by the cinematography's sweeping depiction of the beautiful landscape that the characters inhabit," says Gilroy. Gilroy also suggests that this film "simultaneously insists on not only the differences inherent in the cultures [Coeur d'Alene/Anglo], but also the radical differences between the actuality of contemporary American Indian life and the stereotypical pictures a non-Native viewer might hold in their minds" (33). However, both Anglos and Natives have inherited skewed images of Native people from popular culture. The following scene underscores the absurdity of these images:

Thomas: Hey, what do you remember about your dad?

Victor ignores Thomas.

Thomas: I remember one time we had a fry bread eating contest and he ate fifteen pieces of fry bread. It was cool.

Victor sits up in his seat and looks at Thomas.

Victor: You know, Thomas? I don't know what you're talking about half the time. Why is that?

Thomas: I don't know.

Victor: I mean, you just go on and on talking about nothing. Why can't you have a normal conversation? You're always trying to sound like some damn medicine man or something. I mean, how many times have you seen *Dances With Wolves*? A hundred, two hundred times?

Embarrassed, Thomas ducks his head.

Victor: Oh, jeez, you have seen it that many times, haven't you? Man. Do you think that shit is real? God. Don't you even know how to be a real Indian?

Thomas: (*Whispering*) I guess not (Gilroy 23–25).

Victor then moves from the film stereotypes in *Dances with Wolves* to other falsely held images.

Victor offers Thomas the "stoic Indian" alternative to the romantic notions in *Dances*. "First of all, quit grinning like an idiot. Indians ain't supposed to smile like that. Get stoic," Victor advises Thomas. Gilroy says of this scene, "By creating a film steeped in classical Hollywood norms, yet rooted in an American Indian epistemology, the filmmakers have created a space that invites Euroamerican viewers in and then uses humor as a tool for incisive political commentary. The palliative effect of humor works to dissolve racist stereotypes even as it softens the blow of social commentary" (25–26).

Versions of Victor and Thomas are characters in Alexie's *Reservation Blues* as well. Joseph L. Coulombe's commentary on the relationship between these two characters applies to both texts, however. Victor and Thomas aren't simply opposing versions of Indian stereotypes. Their relationship is actually mutually edifying —their exchanges expose the limitations of both their ways of viewing the world. Coulombe, for example, claims: "Recognizing his separation from his ancestors, [Victor] ultimately accepts (albeit uneasily) the importance of their traditions, particularly that of story-telling. He acknowledges the value of Thomas's vision of sobriety and traditionalism . . ." (97).

Reservation Blues is a problematic text for many Native critics. The novel is a polyglot—drawing images, narratives, and musical styles from a wide range of resources. Briefly, the novel is the story of the rise and disintegration of an unusual rock-and-roll reservation band called Coyote Springs. Spokane Indians Thomas Builds-the-fire, Victor Joseph, and Junior Polatkin are the original members of the band. Two White backup singers, Betty and Veronica (comic book names) join the band followed by two Flathead Indian women, Chess and Checkers (names of games). Both backup duos are rejected by local reservation gossips—the first for being White, the second for being Indians from another tribe.

The novel clearly reflects Alexie's training in American Studies. The novel begins, "In the one hundred and eleven years since the creation of the Spokane Indian Reservation in 1881, not one person, Indian or otherwise, had ever arrived there by accident. Wellpinit, the only town on the reservation, did not exist on most maps, so the black stranger surprised the whole tribe when he appeared with nothing more than the suit he wore and the guitar slung over his back" (3). The black stranger is the legendary (albeit dead) blues guitarist and singer Robert Johnson who has come to the reservation to be healed/freed from his afflictions by "Big Mom," a tribal healer living on a remote part of the reservation. Johnson sold his soul to the devil, as the story goes, who endowed Johnson with superior musicianship in exchange for his soul. Victor inherits Johnson's guitar—a guitar that can't be destroyed. Victor has no real talent, but possessed by this guitar, Victor becomes another Jimi Hendrix. The epigram to the novel comes from another Jazz musician, Charles Mingus: "God's old lady, she sure is a big chick."

American popular culture seeps through every level of this novel demonstrating the degree to which pop culture informs every corner of this continent. Alexie's treatment of popular culture, however, has a unique density of purpose. His novel is at the *crossroads* of numerous American racial/cultural narratives. Each of the ten chapters in the novel is prefaced with lyrics to a song—a red version of the blues. Titles of lyrics include: "Reservation Blues," "Treaties," "Indian Boy Love Song," "Father and Farther," "My God Has Dark Skin," "Falling Down and Falling Apart," "Big Mom," "Urban Indian Blues," "Small World," and "Wake." (Alexie and singer Jim Boyd produced a soundtrack for *Reservation Blues* in 1995.) Each lyric focuses on particular reasons for lamentation among the Spokane. And each lyric also announces the theme content of the following chapter. For example, the chorus of "Reservation Blues" (the chapter where Thomas and Johnson meet), reads: "I ain't got nothing, I heard no good news / I fill my pockets with those reservation blues

/ Those old, those old rez blues, those old reservation blues / And if you ain't got choices / What else do you choose?"(1).

When Johnson tells Thomas he "Made a bad deal years ago. Caught a sickness I can't get rid of," the narrator explains: "Thomas knew about sickness. He'd caught some disease in the womb that forced him to tell stories. The weight of those stories bowed his legs and bent his spine a bit. Robert Johnson looked bowed, bent, and more fragile with each word" (6). Thomas wants to "take Johnson to the Indian Health Service Clinic, for a checkup and the exact diagnosis of his illness" but he knows that health care on the reservation is deficient. "Indian Health only gave out dental floss and condoms, and Thomas spent his whole life trying to figure out the connection between the two" (6). Johnson tells Thomas the reservation is "a beautiful place," to which Thomas responds, "But you haven't seen everything." Thomas remembers "all the dreams that were murdered here, and the bones buried quickly just inches below the surface, all waiting to break through the foundations of those government houses built by the Department of Housing and Urban Development" (7).

This kind of archeology of place is furthered in this chapter with reference to actual historical events. As Douglas Ford reminds us, Big Mom's memories "go back to the horrific slaughter of Indian horses by US Calvary soldiers, an event that continues to overshadow, the contemporary events of the novel. The horses' screams follow [Coyote Springs] through traumatic events, usually perpetrated by the same soldiers who re-enter the text as record produces" (198). In 1858, Ford explains, Colonel George Wright's soldiers rounded up and slaughtered close to 900 horses belonging to the Spokane in order to render the Indians powerless (198). The novel explains that this event was recorded in Big Mom's DNA. She "saw the Indian horses shot and fallen like tattered sheets." But, readers are told, "After she counted the dead, she sang a mourning song for forty days and nights, then wiped the tears away, and buried the bodies. But she saved the bones of the most beautiful horse she found and built a flute from its ribs." The novel informs readers that with "each successive generation, the horses arrived in different forms and with different songs, called themselves Janis Joplin, Jimi Hendrix, Marvin Gaye . . . and turned to Big Mom for rescue" (10).

This juncture, between horrific memory, mourning, and song, is what the blues are about. And yet, contained in the singing of the blues is the possibility of beauty and, therefore, renewal: "Big Mom played a new flute song every morning to remind everybody that music created and recreated the world daily" (10). Alexie reworks cultural expectations of the blues as Johnson and Thomas Builds-the-Fire—bluesman and storyteller—are recognized as individuals who carry the pain of a people in their voices. As lead singer for Coyote Springs, Thomas also writes the lyrics for most of their songs and, therefore, the lyrics that precede each chapter. In a jam session on Big Mom's mountain, when all his wounds are healed, Johnson sings: "Ah, blues walkin' like a man / I's up this mornin' /Ah, blues walkin' like a man." The reservation can hear the music sung on Mom's mountain; but when the music stops, the narrator explains: "Those blues created memories for the Spokanes, but they refused to claim them. Those blues lit up a new road, but the Spokanes pulled out their old maps. Those blues churned up generations of anger and pain: car wrecks, suicides, murders. Those blues were ancient, aboriginal, indigenous" (174).

Associate editor of *Wicazo Sa Review*, Gloria Bird (Spokane) voices concern with Alexie's treatment of alcoholism and pop culture in this novel. The agents in the novel who want to spiral Coyote Springs to stardom are also named after two historic figures, Calvary officers Phil Sheridan and George Wright who campaigned against Indians following the Civil War. In *Reservation Blues*, these men are the rock agents from Calvary Records who launch a monetary-gain campaign with Coyote Springs as their asset. However, their presence sponsors horrific nightmares for Checkers. They corrupt Coyote Springs by exposing it to the damaging side of the rock world. They simply want to use Coyote Springs to advance their own materialistic aims. Bird worries that mainstream readers will get a false impression of reservation life from *Reservation Blues*. Stephen F. Evans claims Bird challenges Alexie as an artist with regard to three ethical positions: the "'right' of authors to write new Indian fiction, the moral obligations of those authors to Indian cultures, and how that art may be perceived and received by 'reservation tourist' and Indian readers" (Evans 50).

General editor and founder of *Wicazo Sa Review,* Elizabeth Cook-Lynn (Crow/Creek/Sioux) also finds fault with Alexie's work. She says that *Reservation Blues* is one of "several new works in fiction that catalogue the deficit model of Indian reservation life." Cook-Lynn is offended by such works because "they reflect little or no defense of treaty-protected reservation land bases as homelands to the indigenes, nor do they suggest a responsibility of art as an ethical endeavor or the artist as a responsible social critic, a marked departure from the early renaissance works of such luminaries as N. Scott Momaday and Leslie Marmon Silko" (126). *Reservation Blues* addresses these expectations and criticisms. When Native individuals show promise, much is expected from them. Thomas, for example, says, "When any Indian shows the slightest hint of talent in any direction, the rest of the tribe starts expecting Jesus. Sometimes they'll stop a reservation hero in the middle of the street, look into his eyes, and ask him to change a can of sardines into a river salmon" (*Reservation Blues* 97).

In several of his interviews, Alexie responds to the criticism of traditionals like Bird and Cook-Lynn. In one interview, for instance, Alexie asserts, "They ask me to represent them, until the point where I'm not an artist. I'm a politician, or not even that, a propagandist. I'm supposed to be making public-service announcements, rather than creating art" (Spencer 6). Indeed, throughout *Reservation Blues,* Alexie exposes the insistence on the part of reservation leaders that artists represent the reservation favorably. Frequent editorials are sprinkled throughout the novel from such venues as *The Wellpinit Rawhide Press.* In an open letter to the tribe, Tribal Chairman David WalksAlong repudiates the band: "I'm beginning to seriously wonder about Coyote Springs's ability to represent the Spokane Tribe. . . . First of all, they are drunks. Victor and Junior are such drunks that even Lester FallsApart thinks they drink too much. . . . Do we really want people to think that the Spokanes are a crazy storyteller, a couple of irresponsible drunks, a pair of Flathead Indians, and two white women? I don't think so" (175–176). Imbedded in WalksAlong's editorial is a particular kind of reverse Native racism—against whites, against Indian drunks, and against people from other tribes. Such racism is yet another cause for lamentation.

Furthermore, the very particular life-stories of characters from dysfunctional families show just cause why many Indians sing the reservation blues. Thomas's father Samuel, a former tribal basketball hero, eventually gains the nickname "Drunk and Disorderly." Samuel is a good man, *when* he is sober. Chess and Checkers hate to see Samuel "so helpless and hopeless; they hated to see the father's features in his son's face. It's hard not to see a father's life as prediction for his son's" (96). Victor and Junior inherit their parents' faces. The chapter "Wake," for example, is about the suicide of Junior—who doesn't want to be drunk anymore. Junior's heritage is dysfunction. And his only love interest was a White student who aborted their mixedblood child. When Victor sobers up, following Junior's suicide, he applies to WalksAlong for Junior's job and is turned down. As Victor leaves WalksAlong's office, he steals money from the secretary's purse to buy "a six-pack of cheap beer at the Trading Post" (292). When Victor opens "the first can. That little explosion of the beer can opening sounded exactly like a smaller, slower version of the explosion that Junior's rifle made on the water tower" (293). *Reservation Blues*, in typical blues fashion, sorts through many of the causes for suffering among *rez* Indians—and alcoholism is only one cause.

Ford claims that *Reservation Blues* is a novel that "inscribes a crossroads similar to those in the blues, a juncture where we can see indigenous Native American oral tradition still at work, but now in a hybrid form, informed by the other discursive forms that have crossed its path" (197). In his extensive study of the blues in African American literatures, Houston Baker defined the "matrix" of practices and forms that are absorbed in the blues: "Combining work songs, group seculars, field hollars, sacred harmonies, proverbial wisdom, folk philosophy, political commentary, ribald humor, elegiac lament, and much more," the blues "constitute an amalgam that seems always to have been in motion in America—always becoming, shaping, transforming, displacing the peculiar experiences of Africans in the New World" (Ford 199). Alexie accomplishes such an amalgamation in his novel. However, while Alexie sorts through rhetorical forms and tribal socio/political contradictions, many critics take various characters' enunciations of these complex concerns for Alexie's beliefs.

Hybridity is a difficult Postcolonial concept. It deals with the complexity of inheriting a bipolar world—us/them; black/white; savage/civilized; mixedblood/pureblood, colonized/colonizer—and posits the possibility of another dimension, a new combination or recombination of elements, a third thing. P. Jane Hafen (Taos Pueblo), for example, says the "composition of the [Coyote Springs] figuratively represents an ideal tribal community where the parts are greater than the whole, where the harmonizing of singular voices with instruments, melodies, and rhythms assemble together. In addition to the specific instrumentations, the individuals in the band represent a wholeness by balancing points of view and gender" (75). This, traditionally, has been the role Trickster (Coyote) plays in tribal life—exposing false dichotomies (with humor and pathos) and pointing the way to less crazy, or debilitating, behaviors.

And yet, Hafen takes Alexie on for the words of one character, Checkers Warm Water, who is definitely against biological hybrids:

> *Those quarter-blood and eighth-blood grandchildren will find out they're Indian and torment the rest of us real Indians. They'll come out to the reservation, come to our powwows, in their nice clothes and nice cars, and remind the real Indians how much we don't have. Those quarter-bloods and eighth-bloods will get all the Indian jobs, all the Indian chances, because they look white. Because they're safer* (Alexie's emphasis; 283).

Hafen explains her concerns with this kind of sentiment. "The reservation where I grew up was, like most, tribally ethnocentric. I and a handful of other Indians and mixedbloods were outsiders to both the tribe and the white community. We had to forge our own identities" (76). Hafen chose to find her identity through education. She is a professor of Native Literatures at the University of Nevada, Las Vegas. Hafen continues, "Every time I return to the 'rez' I am aware of my economic and educational privileges" (78). Hafen and her children meet a kind of reverse discrimination when they return to the reservation. Hafen, who enjoys Alexie's works, also accuses him of being "uncomfortably essentialist" (78). With Hafen's argument, a dichotomy arises between the criticism of Bird and Cook-Lynn on one side and Hafen on the other.

Bird and Cook-Lynn would like Alexie to be more essentialist (supporting a purer vision of Native peoples—a pure blood version) while Hafen would like him to be less essentialist. And yet hybridity studies underscore these very tensions. Historical treatment of Natives might argue for a retreat from interaction with colonizers; and yet particular human responses to life argue both for and against such retrenching. From Thomas Builds-the-Fire's journal comes a particularly hybrid version of the Reservation's Ten Commandments (154–155). Certainly Catholicism has been both a curse and blessing to tribal peoples. "The church does have a lot to atone for," says Chess, a devout Catholic (166). Thomas rehearses the massacre at Wounded Knee to Chess at this point in the novel. To which Chess rejoins: "Don't you understand that God didn't kill any of us? . . . Jesus didn't kill any of us." Thomas retorts, "But they allowed it to happen, enit?" Chess's next logical retort concerns human will and responsibility. "They [God and Christ] didn't allow it to happen. It just happened. Those soldiers made the choice. The government made the choice. That's free will, Thomas" (168).

Religion exists in *Reservation Blues* at a particularly interesting crossroads. Ford claims that *Reservation Blues* "simulates Baker's idea of 'a point of ceaseless input and output, a web of intersecting, crisscrossing impulses always in productive transit'"(200). Father Arnold, for example, is an interesting character in this regard. He is a celibate priest who is in love with Checkers. He also challenges essentialist patriarchal notions. In the chapter "My God has Dark Skin," Father Arnold tells Checkers that Jesus was Jewish and "probably had dark skin and hair" (141). An old Spokane Indian Catholic gives Father Arnold a dreamcatcher "decorated with rosary beads" (250). Father Arnold cherishes this dreamcatcher even though, or especially because, it combines Indian mysticism with Catholic iconography. When Junior commits suicide, both Father Arnold and Big Mom want to attend to the funeral services. Big Mom asks Father Arnold if he intends to help. He doesn't know what to do. "You're not even Catholic, are you?" he asks. Big Mom tells Father Arnold he should "cover all the Christian stuff; I'll do the traditional Indian stuff. We'll make a great team." Father Arnold resists Big Mom's invitation because he doesn't have his collar or cassock along. Big Mom enlightens Arnold with this retort: "You don't need that stuff. That's a very powerful t-shirt you have on" (289). The site of this humorous exchange is human suffering. Neither Father Arnold nor Big Mom turn sufferers away. Both Big Mom and Father Arnold engage in activities that promote the welfare of those in their circle of care. For example, Big Mom insists that the tribe contribute money to Thomas, Chess, and Checkers so that they can leave the reservation to better establish themselves in the world. Alexie also subverts patriarchal norms through his characterization of God's wife: Big Mom. Hybridity theory is, at heart, a call to reconfigure gender identity at the mythic level.

In her apt assessment of Alexie's seminal works, Hafen claims:

> Alexie's sharp edge of essentialism and tribal awareness unmasks institutional and historical racism. As American Indians we have the collective historical and genetic memory of Phillip Sheridan, Mr. Armstrong, and George Wright from *Reservation Blues*. We play with popular cultural images like those found in *Lone Ranger*. Like the characters in *Indian Killer*, we live with the exploitative novelist wanabees like Jack Wilson, professors like Dr. Clarence Mather who fill our children and students with misdirected Noble Savage romanticisms, and those well meaning individuals who like Olivia and Daniel Smith want to possess us in the name of rescuing us (78).

Hafen's comments move us nicely into a discussion of *Indian Killer*, a novel that might be Alexie's most essentialist work.

According to Arnold Krupat, *Indian Killer* "insists that continued violence directed by whites against Indians will be productive of anger, rage, and a desire for murderous revenge that must be expressed, not repressed or channeled into other possible action, and this, I think, is indeed something new, and also something frightening" (103). The first and last chapters of this novel are titled "Mythology" and "A Creation Story"—both stories are allusions to a new world era that is apocalyptic in nature. The first chapter describes the theft of an infant from his fourteen-year-old Indian mother for adoption by White parents, Olivia and Daniel Smith. They name their son John Smith. Certainly Alexie's choice of names for this "adopted" son is more than generic. Captain John Smith, of early Jamestown fame, wrote a much disputed narrative of his capture by the Powhatans in 1607 and his subsequent rescue by Pocahontas. The capture/rescue theme is inverted by Alexie's use of the name John Smith.

On the level of a murder mystery, *Indian Killer* is about a serial killer in Seattle whose mode of operation is to randomly kill White males, scalp them, and leave owl feathers behind as a reminder of "who done it." (Although the killer does kidnap a male child and returns him unharmed.) Chapter 3, "Owl Dancing at the Beginning of the End of the World," certainly takes the murderous intentions of the serial killer into a mythic realm. In that chapter, the narrator writes that the now-adult Indian John Smith, "Knew many Indian tribes believed the owl was a messenger of death. For those Indians, the owl was death itself. Yet, those same Indians who feared the owl still owl danced" (37). A local radio talk show host, Truck Schultz, incites the Seattle public to action. He has an informant in the Seattle Police Department who keeps him informed about the killings. Schultz, however, puts his own spin on events. "My sources say that the man [who died in Fremont early this morning] was scalped and ritually mutilated. . . . My sources say certain evidence makes it clear that an American Indian might be responsible for this crime. . . . or a person intimately familiar with Indian culture" (56). Retaliation for these crimes come from whites and Indians alike—random beatings and rage.

In the course of the novel, three suspects are revealed—Marie Polatkin (an urban Spokane Indian attending the University of Washington), Reggie Polatkin (Marie's cousin and former university student), and John Smith (an Indian who doesn't know his tribe or parentage and is now mentally unstable). Each of these Native characters expresses a desire to kill White people. John, for example, feels that the most important decision in his life will be to find out which "white man had done the most harm to Indians" and kill him (29). John thinks "about the beauty of myths and the power of lies, how myths told too often become lies. . . . John knew there was one white man who should die for all the lies that had been told to Indians" (132). As Krupat points out, Alexie's novel "is about the anger and rage Indian people feel toward whites who have hurt and in the present continue to hurt them" (113). Krupat's discussion of

Indian Killer, however, is convincing along two further lines. None of the Indian suspects are guilty of the murders; as a result, the novel is more likely about the rage and violence that attends decolonization.

Although numerous whites in the novel continue to colonize Natives, four characters in particular represent contemporary colonizing tendencies: University professor and anthropologist Dr. Clarence Mather; Jack Wilson, former police officer turned "native" novelist; and Daniel and Olivia Smith, the adoptive parents of John. One of these characters is chosen by John as "the one white man who should die for all the lies . . . told to Indians" (132). So often colonizers assume they know what is best for tribal peoples. White arrogance coupled with naïveté humiliates Natives. Continued humiliation often turns into irrational violence. Reductive thought occurs on both sides of the equation—whites assuming superior knowledge (or totalizing Natives) and Natives responding to whites as a collective. The novel tells us that "Dr. Clarence Mather, the white professor, supposedly loved Indians, or perhaps his ideas of Indians, and gave them good grades. But he was also a Wannabe Indian, a white man who wanted to be Indian, and Marie wanted to challenge Mather's role as the official dispenser of 'Indian education' at the University" (58). Dr. Mather is the nemesis of both Marie and Reggie. For example, Marie is "completely shocked by the course reading list" in Mather's Introduction to Native American Literature class.

> One of the books, *The Education of Little Tree,* was supposedly written by a Cherokee Indian named Forrest Carter. But Forrest Carter was actually the pseudonym for a former Grand Wizard of the Ku Klux Klan. Three of the other books, *Black Elk Speaks, Lame Deer: Seeker of Visions,* and *Lakota Woman,* were taught in almost every Native American Literature class in the country, and purported to be autobiographical, though all three were co-written by white men. . . . The other seven books included three anthologies of traditional Indian stories edited by white men, two nonfiction studies of Indian spirituality written by white women, a book of traditional Indian poetry translations edited by a Polish-American Jewish man, and an

Indian murder mystery written by some local white writer
named Jack Wilson, who claimed [falsely] he was a
Shilshomish Indian (58–59).

Throughout the semester in which Marie is enrolled in Mather's
class, she continually challenges his assertions. The two finally have
an altercation, and Marie is dismissed from Mather's class.

Reggie is also a victim of Mather's need to control the flow of
information about Natives. Reggie, a former student of Mather's, is
courted/consumed by Mather. Mather exoticizes Reggie, takes
Reggie into his circle of care, uses him to get into Native gatherings,
uses Reggie to get girls, and so on. When Mather discovers some old
recordings of an elder Native woman, he wants to use them to further his career. Reggie takes a hostile stand (he punches Mather)
against such appropriation, and is, therefore, expelled from the
University of Washington. The name Clarence Mather is also
cribbed from early American history. The Calvinist Cotton Mather
believed he had an errand from the Lord to purify the wilderness,
to gather the elect into a covenant community, and to redeem or
destroy the Natives. Indeed, Alexie often draws on the names of
actual historical figures to demonstrate how their attitudes are perpetuated down to the present. They are perpetrators/predators—
and yet, often unconsciously so.

P. Jane Hafen summarizes best how Daniel and Olivia Smith
perpetuate aggression against Native peoples. Their role in the novel
is very difficult to unravel. They are loving, kind, and dutiful parents. When John becomes mentally unstable, they seek medical care
for him. They train him in Native art, literature, and history. The
support and love him; they want him to be successful and happy.
When he disappears among the homeless in Seattle, they go looking for him. What White arrogance, therefore, do they perpetuate?
Hafen calls Olivia and Daniel Smith "well meaning individuals who
. . . want to possess us [Natives] in the name of rescuing us" (78).

Stuart Christie says that John Smith's "mental illness represents
. . . the despair and hopelessness engendered by cross-cultural
American Indian identities" (2). For Christie, John Smith is the "tribal
schizophrenic" who becomes a "caricature of narrative futility." John
Smith "comes dangerously close to signifying the fate of not only

mixed-bloods, but also schizophrenics, whose postmodernity invites not discourse but destruction. Accordingly, John Smith's eventual suicide signifies the ultimate postmodern signifier of mixed-blood madness: the nothing of nothing" (3). In other words, the cause of John Smith's malady is twofold: he has no knowledge of his origins —his birth parents or their tribal affiliation; and he has a brain chemistry disorder that heightens and distorts his longing for identity. Furthermore, he is silenced by his anxieties and, therefore, cannot communicate any of his internal narratives.

The "narrative futility" Christie speaks of is especially potent in *Indian Killer*. John Smith, like Junior Polatkin in *Reservation Blues*, has no stories. Both commit suicide. Some of the most painful chapters in *Indian Killer* are those in which John Smith imagines an Indian identity. Chapter four, "How He Imagines His Life on the Reservation," is full of longing. In this chapter, John imagines he is a grassdancer. His entire family gathers to watch him at a powwow. "John's mother watches from the bleachers. She loves her son and cannot believe she almost gave him away. But that was so long ago, a million years ago, and she would never give him away now. Not for anything. . . . She is a dancer, too, but wants this moment to be her son's. If she were dancing, she would not be able to see him make his first circle." John imagines that he spots his mother in the crowd. "She waves her arms wildly. He sees her. He tries not to smile. Grassdancing is serious business. But he cannot help himself and grins with all of his teeth" (45). John's dreams are futile dreams —unrealizable, futile narrative constructs. This "narrative futility" is projected onto Jack Wilson, the Wannabe Indian novelist.

The title *Indian Killer* can be read two ways: the Indian who kills (the mystery level of the novel) or those who kill Indians (the colonists who continue to exert their control over Indians). Franz Fanon, the black Algerian psychiatrist who wrote *The Wretched of the Earth*, identified types of madness in both colonizers and the colonized. He furthermore noted several stages in the decolonization process: (1) Native intellectuals, in anger and rage, "renew contact . . . with the oldest and most pre-colonial springs of life of their people"; (2) next, their anger is "kept up or at least directed by the secret hope of discovering beyond the misery of today, beyond self-contempt, resignation, and abjuration, some very beautiful and splendid era whose existence rehabilitates" them; (3) then they move toward a nationalism that "believes it can discover the people's true nature" (essentialism); (4) next they attempt to write to "the oppressor" and then to their own people; (5) then they make a conscious effort to write a literature that expresses a will to "combat"—a will to reciprocal violence; and (6) finally they attempt to create new epic forms, and so forth (Fanon 154–156). This movement, from romanticism or essentialism, through violence, and then toward renewed identity is preempted in *Indian Killers*. In this novel, Marie Polatkin, Reggie Polatkin, and John Smith are arrested at the stage where Native people respond to colonization with rage. Ironically, both John Smith and Jack Wilson represent a kind of romanticism—John in his dreams and Jack in his novels. Both characters are arrested at that stage; their romanticism exoticizes violence. Rather than kill Jack Wilson, however, John commits suicide as a way out of his narrative prison. Clarence Mather and Jack Wilson live in negative space with regard to their narratives—their stories lie, and therefore, do untold damage. They perpetuate or project their own brand of madness onto the world.

Jack Wilson desires to appropriate John's life for his Indian hero Aristotle Little Hawk, that is until he discovers John will make a better villain. Wilson's agent tells him, "Publishers are looking for that shaman thing, you know? The New Age stuff, after-death experiences, the healing arts, talking animals, sacred vortexes, that kind of thing. And you've got all that, plus a murder mystery. That's perfect" (162–163). Marie Polatkin condemns him: "Wilson is a fraud. . . . He claims to be Indian, yet has no documentation to prove it. His novels are dangerous and violent." When asked if she thinks Wilson's novels "have an influence on the Indian Killer," she says: "I don't know. . . . But I do think books like Wilson's actually commit violence against Indians" (264).

Again, the name Jack Wilson is a reference to an actual historical figure. Jack Wilson is the Anglo name of the Paiute prophet, Wovoka. Wovoka was "unofficially" adopted by the Wilsons who trained him in Christian millennialism. Out of that training, Wovoka resurrected the Ghost Dance "to raise the Paiutes out of their spiritual cellar" (Peterson 97). Wovoka prophesied that if tribal peoples would follow the Ghost Dance religion, their dead ancestors would be restored to them and White people would be purged from America. Wovoka claimed to be a savior. Ghost Dance activity, as a result, caused the U.S. government to ban Native religions in 1890. Such allusions to Jack Wilson in *Indian Killers* makes the character Jack Wilson especially problematic. At the end of the novel, when Wilson says "that Indian children shouldn't be adopted by white parents" or that "those kids commit suicide way to often" or that "John's suicide was a good thing," references to Wovoka's history take on a sardonic irony (415). This is especially pertinent when the last chapter of *Indian Killer* is taken into account. The actual Indian killer hasn't been caught; he/she/it dances in the darkness. "The killer dances and will not tire. The killer knows this dance is over five hundred years old." Hundreds of Indians join the killer in this dance. The last line of the novel reads, "The tree grows heavy with owls" (420).

Christie suggests "Alexie's novel might have achieved a more than postmodern success, particularly by problematizing how social constructions of tribal identities in wider Anglo-European culture can provoke despair to the point of seeming pathology" (4). Alexie's novels are complex; and they have engendered significant critical debate. A thorough study of Alexie's novels, therefore, will bring readers to a clear apprehension of contemporary Native issues, including causes for Native lamentation, rage, and despair. As Krupat so ably suggests, Alexie's *Indian Killer* is "about the unsettling and frightening fact," to quote Fanon, that "'decolonization is always a violent phenomenon'"(113)—both for the colonized and colonizers.

Thomas King (b. 1943)

Ending a chapter on the best and best known Native authors with Thomas King (Cherokee/Greek/German) is indicative of an important move in Native Studies. King's fiction, like that of Louis Owens, Gerald Vizenor, Leslie Silko, and Louise Erdrich, takes on the implications of multiculturalism in the Postcolonial movement. What are the implications, for example, of being conscious of inhabiting multiple cultures at any given moment? If an individual has inherited several bloodlines, which gains ascendance? Furthermore, what occurs

when several of those bloodlines are Native? Which mythological system does an individual adhere to? Are Native individuals attracted to
or repelled by Christianity? Are Native individuals inclined toward
individualism and away from tribalism? Contemporary Native individuals inhabit multiple other systems of value—professional, political, aesthetic, and social (including gender). With such a barrage of
information systems, what emerges as being of lasting value? Or are
individuals constrained by such diversity to survive as social schizophrenics? And, finally, does the interaction between biological and
cultural strains lead to hybridity and syncretism?

King was born in Northern California to a Cherokee father and
Greek and German mother. He was raised and educated in
California, received his doctorate in English literature from the
University of Utah, and then became a university professor, first in
the United States and then in Canada. King taught for numerous
years at the University of Minnesota where he was Chair of the
American Indian Studies program. He then took teaching positions
in Canada, first at the University of Lethbridge and subsequently at
the University of Guelph where he now teaches Native Literature
and Creative Writing. King is currently a Canadian citizen. Much of
King's fiction, as a result, is about boundary crossing. His most widely
known novels—*Medicine River* (1990), *Green Grass, Running Water*
(1993), and *Truth and Bright Water* (1999)—are about tribal peoples
living on and moving between boundaries, constantly in the process
of renegotiating their identities. Although King is not Blackfoot, his
novels are about Blackfeet characters whose tribal lands are divided
between the U.S. and Canada. Such borders are imposed rather than
actual; yet such imposition is indicative of the many kinds of psy-
chological/social/cultural/geographic/political splittings that occur
among Native individuals/peoples.

Thomas King has come under attack for not writing about tra-
ditionally sanctioned Native themes. Elizabeth Cook-Lynn includes
King on her list of Native intellectuals—Gerald Vizenor, Louis
Owens, Wendy Rose, Maurice Kenny, Michael Dorris, Diane Glancy,
Thomas King, Joseph Bruchac, and Paula Gunn Allen—who "pay lip
service" to the "condemnation of America's treatment of the First
Nations," but do not create "useful expressions of resistance and
opposition to the colonial history at the core of Indian/White rela-

tions." Cook-Lynn accuses these authors of creating "an aesthetic that is pathetic or cynical, a tacit notion of the failure of tribal governments as Native institutions and of sovereignty as a concept, and an Indian identity which focuses on individualism rather than First Nation ideology" (124–125). Cook-Lynn hopes that "responsible" critics "will challenge the generic development of what is called Native American fiction by using the idea that there are such concepts as (1) moral fiction and (2) indigenous/tribally specific literary traditions from which the imagination emerges" (131).

Cook-Lynn would like King to write morally responsible fiction from his own "indigenous/tribally specific literary traditions," which are Cherokee. Certainly Cherokee history is full of colonial violence and indigenous resistance. For example, the Indian Removal policy of Andrew Jackson (1834–1835) forcibly removed Cherokee, Creek, Choctaw, Chicasaw, and Seminole Indians—the Five Civilized Tribes—from their traditional lands in Alabama, Florida, Georgia, Tennessee, Mississippi, Kentucky, and North Carolina to Indian Territory in Oklahoma. King could explore the fate of the Cherokee during these horrific times. There is much to lament— four thousand Cherokee people died during this forced removal, known as the Trail of Tears.

Several noted Native novelists have written about the complex historical and generational consequences of Indian Removal on the Five Civilized Tribes. Of Robert Conley's (Cherokee) thirty-four novels, ten are devoted to Cherokee history; these novels are collectively known as The Real People Series (the meaning of *Cherokee* is "Real People"). Poet and novelist Geary Hobson (Cherokee-Quapa/Chikasaw) published *The Last of the Ofos* (2002), a tale told from the point of view of the last member of the Mosopelea Tribe (known as the Ofos) who once resided on the Mississippi Delta. Devon Abbot Mihesuah's (Choctaw) first novel *Roads of My Relations* (2000) is based on eleven generations of her own family history. And Craig S. Womack's (Creek) novel *Drowning in Fire* narrates the life of a character who relies on his memories of tribal elders to shape his identity. If readers want novels based on tribal histories, many abound.

Louis Owens counteracts Cook-Lynn's criticism of King. Owens claims that: "The fiction of a Gerald Vizenor or a Thomas King" is "replete with the humor that has kept Indians alive for generations" and that these authors frequently draw on "the enduring power of story" which "directly counter [the] entropic tales" of Indian "defeatism" so abhorrent to Cook-Lynn. Owens contends that by "including Thomas King" as a villain who writes "awful . . . new fiction," Cook-Lynn "demonstrates a refusal or inability to acknowledge the crucial role of humor in the long survival of Native American peoples" (159–160).

Certainly *Medicine River* and *Truth and Bright Water* attain "to the hopeful, life-affirming aesthetic of traditional stories, songs, and rituals" that Cook-Lynn craves (125). Both novels are about various families in crises; and yet many members survive because of their capacity to love and create community. *Medicine River* is the story of two Blackfoot friends—Will Horse Capture (the narrator) and Harlen Bigbear. Will returns to Medicine River to attend a funeral. While Will is home, Harlen tricks him into staying and becoming involved in the lives of various members of the community. "Harlen Bigbear was one of the most charitable people I had ever known," thinks Will. "No matter who it was, Harlen would always go looking for the good in a person" (151). Furthermore, whenever anyone has a special need, Harlen finds a way/someone to fulfill it. Of special note is Louise Heavyman; she is an unwed, expectant mother who wants to remain single. But she needs to be cared for; so Harlen tries to orchestrate connections between Louise and various unwed men in the community. Even though Will would like to berate Harlen for his constant meddling, Will accepts the invitation to be part of Louise's life—with humor and good will.

When Louise's daughter is born, the nurses in the hospital keep mistaking Will for the father. One nurse asks him for the baby's new name. Will looks at the signs above his head and says, "South Wing" (as a joke). The nickname sticks. Before South Wing's first birthday, Harlen tricks Will into going to see Martha Oldcrow to get South Wing a suitable birthday gift. "Martha was a doctor. People with problems went to see her. She was known as the 'marriage doctor' because that was what she fixed best" (137). Martha lives on a remote part of the reserve, so the journey is difficult. Martha offers Will a "leather rattle made out of willow and deer hide." Martha offers the rattle at no charge—along with a song. Martha tells Will, "give this to your daughter. Everything will be fine. You'll see. No cost. Next time you come maybe bring a book or maybe some oranges. Better learn that song" (140–141). Harlen also hoodwinks Louise into making the same trip for the same gift (with marital advice included).

In the "middle of the night," following her birthday party, South Wing starts to cry. When Will goes in to comfort her, South Wing is "standing in her crib. One of the rattles was on the floor. I picked it up and shook it, and South Wing smiled and reached out. I took her out of her crib. Her diaper was wet, so I changed it. She didn't make a sound. She lay there playing with the rattle, watching, and it reminded me of the morning she was born." Will is hardly the failed male that Cook-Lynn imagines people King's fiction. The care for a child, the next generation, is fundamentally a moral posture. When Will puts South Wing back in her crib, he stays in her room until it gets light trying "to remember the song" (143).

Harlen also tempts Will into becoming a father-figure for several of the local youth on the basketball team. And so the story goes. *Medicine River* moves back and forth in time and also contains brief vignettes about numerous characters within the community. Herb Wylie identifies *Medicine River* as "associational literature." Wylie suggests that Will's "gradual immersion in the community . . . avoids the bourgeois individualism associated with the novel in the Western tradition." King accomplishes this by "consistently breaking up the focus on Will as protagonist" (111–112). Even as Will reclaims memories of his dead mother or tries to reconnect with his estranged brother, the focus is on associations. (*Medicine River* was made into a film starring Graham Greene in 1993.)

Truth and Bright Water has a more tragic element; yet the novel is also life-affirming. The towns of "Truth and Bright Water sit on opposite sides of the river, the railroad town on the American side, the reserve in Canada." A ramshackle bridge joins the two Blackfoot towns. "At a distance, the bridge between Truth and Bright Water looks whole and complete, a pale thin line, delicate and precise, bending over the Shield and slipping back into the land like a knife. But if you walk down into the coulees and stand in the shadows of the deserted columns and the concrete arches, you can look up through the open planking and the rusting webs of iron mesh, and see the sky" (1). This bridge serves as a metaphor—describing the condition of boundary crossings between the past and present; the restraint caused by family secrets and the possibility of a future; art and reality; religion and life. . . .

Truth and Bright Water is a novel about two young Blackfoot friends—Techumseh (being raised by a single mom) and Lum (being raised by an unscrupulous and abusive father who is also, through corrupt means, the tribal chief). Techumseh and Lum's adventures uncover several communal and family secrets. But Techumseh has a loving home to curtail his exploits and Lum does not. Techumseh survives and Lum, abandoned to his own devices, does not. Lum, a talented runner, destroys himself running on/ through the bridge. The story is told by Techumseh, whose knowledge of the truth is piecemeal and naïve. Much of the intrigue in the novel stems from the readers' need to put the pieces together from Techumseh's limited point of view. His desire for truth and his inability to tell lies drives the plot. And Techumseh's plucky and hard-working mother helps him come to terms with all that he encounters by the sheer force of her constant concern. Satire abounds in this novel, including a Buffalo hunt on motorcycles. Again, many of the characters are likeable; they try to repair past mistakes and create a future for themselves, often through humor.

King's *Green Grass, Running Water* is probably the novel that has given King his mixed reputation among Native critics. The novel is irreverent—few sacred paradigms are free from Coyote's dissembling gaze. As Herb Wyile proposes, "Myth, reality, the sacred, and the absurd are generally recognized in Western thought as different and distinct orders of being, but in this book, as in much native orature and literature, they are constantly merged in playful, creative, and purposeful ways" (115). The novel has multiple narrative threads, including mythic narratives seen through the filter of Coyote (Trickster). The prologue in the novel begins: "So. In the beginning, there was nothing. Just the water" (1). And yet, Coyote is there, dreaming. And his dream is noisy; it wakes him up. Coyote challenges his dream: "It thinks it is in charge of the world," says Coyote. "I *am* in charge of the world, says the silly Dream" (2). An argument ensues. Coyote claims superior intelligence over his own dream. However the dream claims he is very smart and so he must be Coyote. "No," says Coyote, "You can't be Coyote. But you can be a dog." Coyote's dream doesn't want to be a dog, especially a little dog. But then the dog becomes contrary and begins getting everything backwards. He is, therefore, not a dog, but GOD.

This "beginning" is only one of five that are told throughout the novel. Each time a genesis story is retold, the story teller is rebuked for getting her story muddled or wrong. "How many times do we have to do this?" Coyote asks Thought Woman. She answers, "Until we get it right" (256). Each of the four major chapters begin with a creation story told by a mythological character—First Woman (the Lone Ranger), Changing Woman (Ishmael), Thought Woman (Robinson Crusoe), and Old Woman (Hawkeye), who gain other names throughout their autobiographies.

Each of these mythological characters is given multiple pseudonyms dependent on the social situation she inhabits at any given moment in her narrative. These pseudonyms conflate the meaning of the story being told. These sacred women also inhabit the stories of tribal peoples other than their own. Readers unfamiliar with creation narratives will not notice the degree of play King engages in throughout the novel. Some creation stories describe human creation as emergent (coming forth from the earth) while others picture human creation as ascendant (coming from the skies). Often readers will not recognize the mistakes the tellers make. Moreover, King draws tribal creation narratives into dialogue with biblical narratives, often with hilarious consequences.

Anglo names given these mythic women are taken from American and British literary works. Such names allude to secular mythologies. The Lone Ranger, for example, refers to the masked White hero whose identity is only known by his Indian sidekick. Ishmael is a reference to Abraham's disavowed son as well as to the narrator of Herman Melville's *Moby Dick*. In *Moby Dick*, Ishmael is thrust onto the Pequod (named after a Native American culture) adrift on the ocean under the leadership of Ahab (a biblical king) who is confronting cosmic evil (in the form of a white whale) in a racially and culturally complex environment (crew members of the ship). Hawkeye is the nickname given to Natty Bumpoo from James

Fenimore Cooper's *The Last of the Mohicans*. Hawkeye is a pre-revolutionary scout who represents both the spirit of the wilderness as well as a person who is more caught up in doing what is just than in aligning himself with tribal or colonial powers. And Robinson Crusoe is the central character in Daniel Defoe's *Robinson Crusoe*. Crusoe is a shipwrecked voyager who is the consummate colonial: he adapts to his new environment (or conquers that environment) and domesticates a native man (on whom he imposes the name, Friday) who becomes his servant/sidekick. Over the course of the novel, Crusoe's friendship with Friday causes him to revoke his master/slave, Christian/heathen narrative.

Marlene Goldman draws attention to the titles of each of the four chapters indicating that they create a map for the journey implied in the novel. She notes,

> *Green Grass, Running Water* serves as a map—a tool with which one can reckon one's place in the world. To come to grips with the nature of this map, readers must pay attention to Native codes. For example, at the beginning of each section is a word in Cherokee. Rather than signify a linear progression, such as chapter one, two, and so on, each word announces one of the four directions and the sacred colour associated with it. The narrative begins with the east and red, then proceeds to south and white, west and black, and north and blue, in that order (37).

In actuality, the entire novel moves from St. Augustine, Florida (southeast) to Blossom, Alberta, Canada (northwest). Indeed, the goal of the journey is Blossom.

The pseudonyms given to the sacred women who retell creation narratives reveal the hybrid nature of King's novel. First Woman's story references the Adam and Eve tale (the Lone Ranger); Changing Woman is the noted savior figure among the Apache and Navajo (Ishmael); Thought Woman is the female originator of creation among Pueblo Indians (Robinson Crusoe), and Old Woman is a figure noted in Blackfoot cosmology (Hawkeye). Wyile suggests that King is playing with the "formations of multiculturalism" which have "been radically revised in recent decades under the influence of a number of factors." These factors include:

greater consciousness of the diversity of those communities, growing resistance to the notion of cultural purity, and
the increasing influence of postcolonial notions of hybridity and cross-fertilization. As a result, cultural production
in Canada, as elsewhere, is increasingly being recognized as
syncretic, as a heterogeneous complex in which different
cultural elements are neither absolutely discrete nor
absolutely blended (105).

Each chapter in this novel is interspersed with several narrative
threads, only one of which is an ongoing, revisionist, story of
creation. These creation stories, however, are full of images from
various tribal creation stories of how this earth began; most often
these stories contain the waters of creation or chaos. And each story
of creation also tells how each narrator received Anglo names and
came to be imprisoned/placed in the mental institution at Fort
Marion in Florida. The mental hospital is run by Dr. Joseph (Joe)
Hovaugh (Jehovah, if you combine the names). Collectively, these
four "inmates" escape, time and again, in an attempt to fix things in
the world. Each chapter, therefore, also narrates the stories of contemporary characters whose lives need fixing.

James Mooney, in *Myths of the Cherokee*, includes the Cherokee
story of how the world was made. "The earth is a great island floating in a sea of water, and suspended at each of the four cardinal points
by a cord hanging down from the sky vault, which is of solid rock.
When the world grows old and worn out, the people will die and the
cords will break and let the earth sink down into the ocean, and all
will be water again. The Indians are afraid of this" (239). One refrain
that runs throughout *Green Grass, Running Water* is "Where did all
this water come from?" (104). Indeed, in this novel, characters find
themselves standing ankle deep in water, cars inexplicably float away,
bathrooms flood, and a damn is being built on the Blackfoot reserve
in Blossom—the goal of the journey for Coyote and the four sacred
women. Perhaps these four women are the four cords that keep the
earth from sinking, once again, into the ocean. Whoever they are,
these women often recount falling through the sky onto a turtle's
back (Iroquois creation story) or into a canoe, or. . . .

One of the funniest revision narratives in the novel is Changing
Woman's (a.k.a. Ishmael from *Moby Dick*). Changing Woman falls

from the sky and lands in a canoe full of animals; she also falls on Old Coyote:

> It must be a party, says Changing Woman as she falls through the sky. But as she gets closer, what she sees is poop. There is poop everywhere. There is poop on the side of the canoe. There is poop on the bottom of the canoe. There is poop all around the canoe. That canoe isn't all white, either, I can tell you that (158–159).

Before Changing Woman can apologize to Old Coyote for falling on him, "give him some tobacco or some sweet grass, a little man with a filthy beard jumps out of the poop at the front of the canoe" and asks Changing Woman who she is. "Any relation to Eve? says the little man. She sinned, you know. That's why I'm in a canoe full of animals. That's why I'm in a canoe full of poop" (160). When Changing Woman continues her conversation with Old Coyote, the bearded man asks her, "Why are you talking to animals? . . . This is a Christian ship. Animals don't talk. We got rules" (160). When the canoe is finally beached, Noah spends his time chasing Changing Woman along the beach telling her it is time for procreation. She won't, so Noah loads the boat and leaves Changing Woman on the island alone. There are so many versions of creation; so many ideas about woman's place in creation. And when the logical implications of these versions are teased out, readers can see why critics have been uncomfortable with *Green Grass, Running Water*. Who wouldn't wonder how much feed Noah would have to amass to feed two of every kind of animal on an ark for forty days and nights? And, biologically speaking, who wouldn't wonder what happened to the waste produced by so many animals? Christianity certainly takes a hit in this novel—especially for the insistence that the Christian narrative is the one true story. The linear nature of the Old/New Testaments—from genesis to the apocalypse—is also challenged as it coexists with more cyclical sacred stories.

The title of this novel is a reference to treaty language that promised Native peoples, time and again, that treaties made between the United States and Native Nations would be kept as long as the waters flow and the grasses grow. The notion that governments, members of cultures, or partners in a love relationship are engaged in making promises that repeatedly fail is an extension of the concept of treaties. The gap between theory (covenant promise) and practice (the vagaries of actual life) is continually underscored by King. Patricia Linton suggests that the title "resonates throughout the narrative as a code for betrayal, but betrayal compounded so many times that it has become predictable" (218).

One of the primary tales in the novel is about the love triangle between three Blackfoot friends: Lionel Red Dog, Alberta Frank, and Charlie Looking Bear. Lionel has remained on the reserve, works for a local TV salesman, and is nearing forty. He continually wants to revise the story he is living. He claims that his life has been misdirected by three fundamental mistakes. As a youth, Lionel was supposed to get his tonsils removed; while at the hospital for this procedure, a nurse mistakes him for another child who needs to be life-flighted to another hospital for heart surgery. The mistake is discovered, just in time, but the false record of Lionel having heart problems goes with him throughout his life. He is turned down for jobs because of his medical history. Tribal leaders know Lionel's mishaps and eventually give Lionel a job. In a freaky series of events, Lionel goes to Salt Lake City to present a paper for his boss, gets caught up with AIM activists who get Lionel arrested (on false charges); he consequently gets felony charges assigned to his record and finally loses his tribal job over a legal error. The only option for Lionel at this point is to go to college and get some training. But he decides to work for a while (to get out of debt) at the local appliance mart; he never manages to leave the job for a college career. Alberta Frank dates both Lionel and Charlie, but does not want to marry either one of them. She already had one failed marriage to a control freak and is leery of men. Alberta is a college history professor who likes her job, but also wants to be a mother—even if she has to rely on artificial insemination to accomplish her goals. Charlie is a lawyer for the firm (Duplessis [duplicitous] International Associates) that is trying to overturn the injunctions against the completion of the Grand Baleen Dam near Blossom. Each character in this triad is related to a complex of other characters who find their home of origin in Blossom.

For example, Lionel has a sister, Laticha, who is a single mother raising three children. In order to provide for them, Laticha opens a café called the Dead Dog. To attract tourists, Laticha names her cuisine Old Agent Puppy Stew, "Dog du Jour, Houndburgers, Puppy Potpourri, Hot Dogs, Saint Bernard Swiss Melts, with Doggie Doos and Deep-Fried Puppy Whatnots for appetizers" (117). Laticha married George Morningstar. He goes from job to job, can't provide or be a good father, abuses Laticha, and ends up leaving his family in search of some dream of success.

Lionel's aunt Norma and Uncle Eli (brother and sister) play significant roles in the development of the novel. Norma is a human Trickster who teases her loved ones into doing what is in their best interest. Eli, a college professor of English, retires and returns to the reservation following the deaths of his wife and mother. He lives in his mother's old log cabin on lands required by the government to complete the dam near Blossom. Eli spends his days getting injunctions against the completion of the dam. Eli's life, before returning to Blossom, was devoted to White notions of success. The narrator explains:

> It was a common enough theme in novels and movies. Indian leaves the traditional world of the reserve, goes to the city, and is destroyed. Indian leaves the traditional world of the reserve, is exposed to white culture, and becomes trapped between two worlds. Indian leaves the traditional world of the reserve, gets an education, and is shunned by his tribe (317).

At first, Eli had a hard time leaving the reserve, but after he did, each year away "laid more space between who he had become and who he had been. Until he could no longer measure the distance in miles" (317). He became, the "Indian who couldn't go home," until his mother and wife died (316). Eli missed his mother's death because Norma didn't want to inform him; she wanted Eli to come to his senses about the losses his choices had created. Karen, Eli's beloved wife, got him to take her to one Sun Dance where she met and fell in love with Eli's family and former lifestyle. Karen wanted to return yearly to the Sun Dance; but Eli always found an excuse not to return. After twenty years of coaxing, Eli finally agrees to take Karen back. But Karen is killed in a car accident before she can return.

Every character reveals a complex of historical/cultural/gender information. For example, Alberta Frank teaches Native American history at the University of Toronto. One of her lectures identifies the historical origins of Fort Marion:

> In 1874, the U.S. Army began a campaign of destruction aimed at forcing the southern Plains tribes onto reservations. The army systematically went from village to village burning houses, killing horses, and destroying food supplies. They pursued the Cheyenne, Kiowa, Comanche, and the Arapaho relentlessly into one of the worst winters of the decade. Starvation and freezing conditions finally forced the tribes to surrender (15).

During this period of American history, seventy-two Natives were identified by the government as being rebellious and, therefore, dangerous. As a result, these people were taken from Fort Sill in Oklahoma and imprisoned in Fort Marion. In King's novel, First Woman, Changing Woman, Thought Woman, and Old Woman are among those incarcerated. These seventy-two were given ledger books to draw on; they created, from their imprisonment experiences and yearnings for freedom, what is known as Ledger Art. Henry Dawes, John Collier, Richard Pratt, Mary Rowlandson, Elaine Goodale, and several other famous or infamous names in Native history are referenced as indifferent or incredulous students in Alberta's class.

Alberta's memories of her upbringing also help create a complex social field with regard to various characters' motives for either staying or leaving Blossom. Amos, Alberta's alcoholic father, is not simply his disease. At one point, Alberta recalls when her father's sacred ceremonial regalia was illegally confiscated by boarder guards because they had eagle feathers on them. When the clothing is finally returned, it has been soiled, crumpled into garbage bags, and many of the feathers attached to the robes have been irreparably damaged. Alberta's father has just cause for grief; but his repugnant alcoholic behavior causes Alberta's mother to wish him gone. Alberta's relationships with men are complicated by her father and former husband. As a result, she has intimacy issues. In order to avoid further intimacy with Charlie, for instance, Alberta decides to go to Lionel's fortieth birthday party in Blossom. Charlie finds out, and so he also heads for Blossom. For all intents and purposes, Charlie should be the man of Alberta's choice. He went to college, became a lawyer, and has a good car and nice apartment. And he is better-looking than Lionel.

Charlie's father is Portland Looking Bear, a former Hollywood actor who played Indians (and then Indian Chiefs) in notable movies staring John Wayne and Richard Widmark, among others. When Charlie's mother dies, Portland leaves Hollywood only to return when he can no longer get parts. Hollywood images of Indians abound in this novel as well. Bill Bursam, Lionel's boss, creates an entire wall of televisions in the shape of a map of the United States and Canada. And he continually shows Westerns on these televisions. Westerns, according to Bursam, are the "best romances" (210). The trouble is, the Indians are generally defeated in all the old Westerns. This is another problem that needs "fixin." In one hilarious scene (the four inmates are in the store too), Bursam demonstrates the power of his TV map to those assembled. He chooses his favorite Western, one staring Charlie's father. In the scene, with John Wayne, that generally shows how cowboys defeat Indians, the ending is reversed and Portland Looking Bear leads a successful charge against the whites. Somehow, the four inmates can be seen riding with Looking Bear's band of Indians. This movie has also been inexplicably changed from black-and-white into color.

Green Grass, Running Water is a complex novel full of themes and characters too intricate to fully unpack in a short essay. However, one major point must be made. As Marlene Goldman so aptly claims, King's novel can be "set apart from other fictions":

> *Green Grass, Running Water* succeeds in articulating a Native cosmography, and . . . serves as a map in the traditional, Native sense of the word. More specifically, through its allusions to, and depictions of, the Sun Dance, the novel inscribes an aboriginal conception of the world in which the individuals can locate themselves at the centre of a land-based, communal, and non-hierarchial spiritual practice that involves both body and soul (20).

As has been noted, Blossom, Alberta, Canada is the destination of many characters. The four inmates go there to fix things. Dr. Hovaugh goes there to track down the inmates. Alberta goes there to celebrate Lionel's birthday. Charlie goes there to meet up with

Alberta. It just so happens, however, that Lionel's birthday corresponds with the Sun Dance. And through a series of coincidences,
all of the major characters end up at the Sun Dance at the same
time. Eli, on the insistence of Norma, fulfills his duty as an uncle by
taking Lionel to lunch on his birthday where he can, as is his
obligation, impart a vision of futurity to his nephew. Eli takes Lionel
to the Sun Dance for lunch. On the way, Eli recounts his own life-
story and, by implication, tells Lionel his future can be found among
his people. Alberta, with all the symptoms of pregnancy, goes to the
Sun Dance with Latisha.

Latisha's mucked-up husband also shows up at the Sun Dance;
however, he shows up to take unlawful pictures of the ceremony.
He has become a photojournalist. He sees the Sun Dance as being
"not exactly sacred" but rather more "like a campout or a picnic"
(42). At any rate, Lionel is the person who sends George packing.
When the incident is resolved, the Lone Ranger says, "Well, grandson, . . . that's about as much as we can do for you. How do you
feel?" Lionel responds with incredulity. "That's it?" he says. "This is
how you help me fix up my life?" Ishmael responds this time, "Pretty
exciting isn't it?" Lionel then asks, "Have I missed something?"
Robinson Crusoe suggests, "you'll be able to tell your children and
grandchildren about this" (424). Dramatic irony plays a large role at
this juncture. Only the readers can see all that has conspired to get
the principle players at the same place and time for a simple altercation that will change their lives. Alberta's immaculate conception,
like Mary's, is the one miracle few but the readers can fathom. And
the four inmates, they say, have done it before.

Three cars are stolen at various times throughout the novel:
Alberta's Nissan, Charlie's rental car, a Pinto, and Dr. Hovaugh's
Karmann-Ghia (an allusion to the ships of Columbus). All three
ships can be seen floating on the dam waters. The dam breaks, flooding the lands around it; and Eli and his cabin go with the flood
waters. The four sacred women/clowns return to Fort Marion to
await their next adventure. Dr. Hovaugh attempts to chart what has
just happened "on graph paper, turning the chart as" he goes, inscrib-
ing the words "literal, allegorical, tropological, anagogic" at the top
of four columns (430). Charlie goes to visit his father in Hollywood.
Life goes on. Although Eli dies, he came home in every way

imaginable; and Lionel is going to stay home and rebuild Eli's cabin. And Alberta? She stays close to Lionel.

On a literal level, the stories are clear. Allegorically, the novel is replete with multiple meanings for a single symbol. Certainly the tropological level, the level of values, is more difficult to deduce. The anagogic level, the level of sacred transformation, is left to the reader to negotiate. Nonetheless, *Green Grass, Running Water* is clearly a novel worth the multiple critical responses is has received. Certainly the idea that the sacred wears many masks is still a thought that engages contemporary readers who want to know how to live in a multicultural, Postmodern, world.

Works Cited

What Can Be Understood by "the Best"?

Allen, Paula Gunn, "The Great Vision," in *Voice of the Turtle: American Literature 1900–1970*, Paula Gunn Allen, ed. (New York: Ballantine Books, 1994).

Beebee, Thomas O., *The Ideology of Genre* (University Park: Pennsylvania State University Press, 1994).

Black Elk, *Black Elk Speaks*, as told through John G. Neihardt (1932; repr., Lincoln: University of Nebraska Press, 1979).

Dorson, Richard M., *Handbook of American Folklore* (Bloomington: Indiana University Press, 1986).

Eastman, Charles, *The Soul of an Indian: An Interpretation* (1911; repr., University of Nebraska Press, 1980).

Harmon, William and C. Hugh Holman, *A Handbook to Literature*, eighth ed. (Upper Saddle River, NJ: Prentice Hall, 2000).

Hirsch, E. D., *Validity in Interpretation* (New Haven, CT: Yale University Press, 1965).

Kleymeyer, Charles David, "Introduction," in *Cultural Expression & Grassroots Development* (Boulder, CO: Lynne Rienner, 1994).

Krupat, Arnold, *For Those Who Come After* (Berkeley: University of California Press, 1985).

———, *The Voice in the Margin: Native American Literature and the Canon* (Berkeley: University of California Press, 1989).

Lincoln, Kenneth, *Native American Renaissance* (Berkeley: University of California Press, 1983).

Nussbaum, Martha C., *Poetic Justice: The Literary Imagination and Public Life* (Boston: Beacon Press, 1995).

Purdy, John Lloyd, *The Legacy of D'Arcy McNickle: Writer, Historian, Activist* (Norman: University of Oklahoma Press, 1996).

Rice, Julian, *Black Elk's Story: Distinguishing Its Lakota Purpose* (Albuquerque: University of New Mexico Press, 1991).

Turner, Victor W., "Dewey, Dilthey, and Drama: An Essay in the Anthropology of Experience," in *The Anthropology of Experence*, Victor W. Turner and Edward M. Bruner, eds. (Urbana: University of Illinois Press, 1986).

Vickers, Scott B., *Native American Identities: From Stereotype to Archetype in Art and Literature* (Albuquerque: University of New Mexico Press, 1998).

Vizenor, Gerald and A. Robert Lee, *Postindian Conversations* (Lincoln: University of Nebraska Press, 1999).

The Best and Best Known Native Writers Before 1969

Allen, Paula Gunn, "Mourning Dove (Humishuma)," in *Voice of the Turtle: American Literature 1900–1970*, Paula Gunn Allen, ed. (New York: Ballantine Books, 1994).

Bataille, Gretchen M., "Black Elk—New World Prophet," in *A Sender of Words: In Memory of John G. Neihardt*, Vine Deloria, Jr., ed. (Salt Lake City, UT: Howe Brothers, 1984).

Black Elk, Benjamin, "The Legacy," in *Black Elk Lives: Conversations with the Black Elk Family*, Hilda Neihardt and Lori Utecht, eds. (Lincoln: University of Nebraska Press, 2000).

Bruner, Edward M., "Experience and Its Expressions," in *The Anthropology of Experience*, Victor W. Turner and Edward M. Bruner, eds. (Urbana: University of Illinois Press, 1986).

Deloria, Vine, Jr., "Introduction," in *Black Elk Speaks* (1932; repr., Lincoln: University of Nebraska Press, 1979).

DeMallie, Raymond J., "Introduction," in *The Sixth Grandfather: Black Elk's Teaching Given to John G. Neihardt*, Raymond J. DeMallie, ed. (Lincoln: University of Nebraska Press, 1984).

Eastman, Charles A., *From Deep Woods to Civilization* (1916; repr., Lincoln: University of Nebraska Press, 1977).

Levinas, Emmanuel, *Collected Philosophical Papers*, Alphonso Lingis, trans. (The Hague: Martinus Nijhoff, 1987).

———, *Totality and Infinity*, Alphonso Lingis, trans. (Pittsburgh: Duquesne University Press, n.d.).

Marybury-Lewis, David, "Foreword: Culture and Development," in *Cultural Expression & Grassroots Development*, Charles David Kleymeyer, ed. (Boulder, CO: Lynne Rienner, 1994).

McNickle, D'Arcy, *Wind from an Enemy Sky* (San Francisco: Harper & Row, 1978).

Miller, David Reed, "Charles Alexander Eastman, Santee Sioux, 1858–1938," in *American Indian Intellectuals of the Nineteenth and Early Twentieth Centuries*, Margot Liberty, ed. (Norman: University of Oklahoma Press, 2002).

Momaday, N. Scott, "To Save a Great Vision," in *A Sender of Words: Essays in Memory of John G. Neihardt*, Vine Deloria, Jr., ed. (Salt Lake City, UT: Howe Brothers, 1984).

Owens, Louis, *Other Destinies: Understanding the American Indian Novel* (Norman: University of Oklahoma Press, 1992).

Peyer, Bernd C., "Introduction," in *Singing Spirit: Early Short Stories by North American Indians*, Bernd C. Peyer, ed. (Tucson: University of Arizona Press, 1989).

Ruoff, A. LaVonne Brown, "Native American Writing: Beginnings to 1967," in *Handbook of Native American Literature*, Andrew Wiget, ed. (New York: Garland, 1996).

Steltenkamp, Michael F., *Black Elk: Holy Man of the Oglala* (Norman: University of Oklahoma Press, 1993).

Treat, James, "Native Christian Narrative Discourse," in *Native and Christian*, James Treat, ed. (New York: Routledge, 1996).

Warrior, Robert Allen, *Tribal Secrets* (Minneapolis: University of Minnesota Press, 1995).

Wilson, Terry P., "John Joseph Mathews," in *Handbook of Native American Literature*, Andrew Wiget, ed. (New York: Garland, 1996).

Wiget, Andrew, "The Historical Emergence of Native American Writing," in *Handbook of Native American Literature*, Andrew Wiget, ed. (New York: Garland, 1996).

The Best and Best Known Native Writers from 1969 to the Present

Lyotard, Jean-François, *The Postmodern Explained*, Julian Pefanis and Morgan Thomas, trans. (Minneapolis: University of Minnesota Press, 1992).

Roemer, Kenneth M., "Introduction," in *Dictionary of Literary Biography*, vol. 175, *Native American Writers of the United States*, Kenneth M. Roemer, ed. (Detroit: Bruccoli Clark Layman, 1997).

Works Cited for N. Scott Momaday

Allen, Paula Gunn, "Bringing Home the Fact: Tradition and Continuity in the Imagination," in *Recovering the Word: Essays on Native American Literature*, Brian Swann and Arnold Krupat, eds. (Berkeley: University of California Press, 1987).

Bonetti, Kay, "N. Scott Momaday: Interview," in *Conversations with N. Scott Momaday*, Matthias Schubnell, ed. (Jackson: University Press of Mississippi, 1997).

Bruner, Edward M., "Introduction," in *The Anthropology of Experience*, Victor W. Turner and Edward M. Bruner, eds. (Urbana: University of Illinois Press, 1986).

Coltelli, Laura, "N. Scott Momaday," in *Conversations with N. Scott Momaday*, Matthias Schubnell, ed. (Jackson: University Press of Mississippi, 1997).

Hirsch, Berenard A., "Self-Hatred and Spiritual Corruption in *House Made of Dawn*," *Western American Literature* 17 (Winter 1983) 307–320.

Kerr, Baine, "The Novel as Sacred Text: N. Scott Momaday's Myth-Making Ethic," *Southwest Review* 63 (1978) 172–179.

Momaday, N. Scott, *House Made of Dawn* (New York: Signet, 1969).

————, "Man Made of Words," in *Religion and the Humanizing of Man*, James M. Robinson, ed. (Waterloo, Ontario, Canada: Waterloo Lutheran University, 1973) 191–204.

————, *The Names: A Memoir* (New York: Harper and Row, 1976).

————, *The Way to Rainy Mountain* (1969; repr., Albuquerque: University of New Mexico Press, 1976).

————, "The Native Voice in American Literature," in *The Man Made of Words* (New York: St. Martin's Griffin, 1997).

Roemer, Kenneth M., ed., *Approaches to Teaching Momaday's "The Way to Rainy Mountain"* (New York: The Modern Language Association of America, 1988).

Sandner, Donald, *Navajo Symbols of Healing* (Rochester, VT: Healing Arts Press, 1991).

Scarberry-Garcia, Susan, *Landmarks of Healing: A Study of "House Made of Dawn"* (Albuquerque: University of New Mexico Press, 1990).

Schubnell, Matthias, "Tribal Identity and the Imagination," in *Approaches to Teaching Momaday's "The Way to Rainy Mountain"* (New York: The Modern Language Association of America, 1988).

Turner, Victor, "Dewey, Dilthey, and Drama: An Essay in the Anthropology of Experience," in *The Anthropology of Experience*, Victor W. Turner and Edward M. Bruner, eds. (Urbana: University of Illinois Press, 1986).

Zolbrod, Paul, "When Artifacts Speak, What Can They Tell Us?" in *Recovering the Word: Essays on Native American Literature*, Brian Swann and Arnold Krupat, eds. (Berkeley: University of California Press, 1987).

Works Cited for Leslie Marmon Silko

Cutchins, Dennis, "Leslie Marmon Silko," in *Dictionary of Literary Biography*, vol. 256, *Twentieth-Century Western Writers: Third Series*, Richard H. Cracroft, ed. (Detroit: Bruccoli Clark Layman, 2002).

Dinome, William, "Laguna Woman: An Annotated Leslie Silko Bibliography," *American Indian Culture and Research Journal* 21:1 (1997) 207–280.

Lincoln, Kenneth, *Native American Renaissance* (Berkeley: University of California Press, 1983).

Owens, Louis, *Other Destinies: Understanding the American Indian Novel* (Norman: University of Oklahoma Press, 1992).

Silko, Leslie Marmon, *Ceremony* (New York: Penguin Books, 1977).

Zolbrod, Paul G., "When Artifacts Speak, What Can They Tell Us?" in *Recovering the Word: Essays on Native American Literature*, Brian Swann and Arnold Krupat, eds. (Berkeley: University of California Press, 1987).

Works Cited for James Welch

Bevis, William, "Native American Novels: Homing In," in *Recovering the Word*, Brian Swann and Arnold Krupat, eds. (Berkeley: University of California Press, 1987).

Deloria, Vine, Jr., *Spirit & Reason: The Vine Deloria, Jr., Reader*, Barbara Deloria, Kristen Foehner, and Sam Scinta, eds. (Golden, CO: Fulcrum, 1999).

Irwin, Lee, "Native American Spirituality: An Introduction," in *Native American Spirituality*, Lee Irwin, ed. (Lincoln: University of Nebraska Press, 2000).

Owens, Louis, *Other Destinies: Understanding the American Indian Novel* (Norman: University of Oklahoma Press, 1992).

Pritzker, Barry M., *A Native American Encyclopedia: History, Culture, and Peoples* (Oxford: Oxford University Press, 2000).

Velie, Alan R., *Four American Indian Literary Masters: N. Scott Momaday, James Welch, Leslie Marmon Silko, and Gerald Vizenor* (Norman: University of Oklahoma Press, 1982).

Welch, James, *Fools Crow* (New York: Penguin Books, 1987).

———, with Paul Stekler, *Killing Custer* (New York: Norton, 1994).

Works Cited for Gerald Vizenor

Blaeser, Kimberly M., "Gerald Vizenor," in *Dictionary of Literary Biography*, vol. 175, *Native American Writers of the United States*, Kenneth M. Roemer, ed. (Detroit: Bruccoli Clark Layman, 1997).

Hauss, John, "Real Stories: Memory, Violence, and Enjoyment in Gerald Vizenor's *Bearheart*," *Literature and Psychology* 41:4 (1995) 1–16.

Owens, Louis, "Afterword," in Gerald Vizenor, *Bearheart: The Heirship Chronicles* (1978; repr., Minneapolis: University of Minnesota Press, 1990).

Velie, Alan R., "Gerald Vizenor," in *Four American Indian Literary Masters: N. Scott Momaday, James Welch, Leslie Marmon Silko, and Gerald Vizenor* (Norman: University of Oklahoma Press, 1982).

Vizenor, Gerald, *Bearheart: The Heirship Chronicles* (1978; repr., Minneapolis: University of Minnesota Press, 1990).

———, *Interior Landscapes: Autobiographical Myths and Metaphors* (Minneapolis: University of Minnesota Press, 1990).

Vizenor, Gerald, and A. Robert Lee, *Postindian Conversations* (Lincoln: University of Nebraska Press, 1999).

Works Cited for (Karen) Louise Erdrich

Bruchac, Joseph, "Interviews with Louise Erdrich and Michael Dorris," in *Louise Erdrich's "Love Medicine": A Case Book*, Hertha D. Sweet Wong, ed. (New York: Oxford University Press, 2000).

Caputo, John D., *Against Ethics* (Bloomington: Indiana University Press, 1993).

Dooling, D. M., "Foreword," *The Sons of the Wind*, D. M. Dooling, ed. (New York: Parabola Books, 1984).

Erdrich, Louise, *Love Medicine* (New York: Holt, Rinehart, and Winston, 1984).

———, *Tracks* (New York: Harper & Row, 1988).

———, *The Bingo Palace* (New York: HarperCollins, 1994).

———, *The Blue Jay's Dance: A Birth Year* (New York: Harper Perennial, 1995).

———, *Tales of Burning Love* (New York: HarperCollins, 1996).

———, *The Antelope Wife* (New York: HarperFlamingo, 1998).

———, "Where I Ought to Be: A Writer's Sense of Place," in *Louise Erdrich's "Love Medicine": A Case Book*, Hertha D. Sweet Wong, ed. (New York: Oxford University Press, 2000).

———, *The Last Report on the Miracles at Little No Horse* (New York: HarperCollins, 2001).

———, *Four Souls* (New York: Harper Collins, 2004).

Hafen, Jane, "We Anishinaabeg are the Keepers of the Names of the Earth: Louise Erdrich's Great Plains," *Great Plains Quarterly* 21 (Fall 2001) 321–332.

Jaskoski, Helen, "From the Time Immemorial: Native American Traditions in Contemporary Short Fiction," in *Louise Erdrich's "Love Medicine": A Case Book*, Hertha D. Sweet Wong, ed. (New York: Oxford University Press, 2000).

McCafferty, Kate, "Generative Adversity: Shapeshifting Pauline/Leopolda in *Tracks* and *Love Medicine*," *American Indian Quarterly* 21 (Fall 1997) 729–352.

Rosenburg, Roberta, "Ceremonial Healing and the Multiple Narrative Tradition in Louise Erdrich's *Tales of Burning Love*," *Melus* (Fall 2002) 113–331.

Sands, Kathleen M., "*Love Medicine*: Voices and Margins," in *Louise Erdrich's "Love Medicine": A Case Book*, Hertha D. Sweet Wong, ed. (New York: Oxford University Press, 2000).

Sarvé-Gorham, Kristan, "Games of Chance: Gambling and Land Tenure in *Tracks, Love Medicine*, and *The Bingo Palace*," *Western American Literature* 34:3 (Fall 1999) 276–300.

Storhoff, Gary, "Family Systems in Louise Erdrich's *The Beet Queen*," *Critique* 39:4 (Summer 1998) 341–362.

Works Cited for Linda Hogan

Cahlahan, William, "Ecological Groundedness in Gestalt Therapy," in *Ecopsychology*, Theodore Roszak, Mary E. Gomes, and Allen D. Kanner, eds. (San Francisco: Sierra Club Books, 1995).

Dreese, Donelle N., "The Terrestrial and Aquatic Intelligence of Linda Hogan," *SAIL* 11:4 (Winter 1999) 11–23.

Glendinning, Chellis, "Technology, Trauma, and the Wild," in *Ecopsychology*, Theodore Roszak, Mary E. Gomes, and Allen D. Kanner, eds. (San Francisco: Sierra Club Books, 1995).

Hogan, Linda, "The Two Lives," in *I Tell You Now*, Brian Swann and Arnold Krupat, eds. (Lincoln: University of Nebraska Press, 1987).

———, *Mean Spirit* (New York: Ballantine Books, 1990).

———, *The Book of Medicines* (Minneapolis: Coffee House Press, 1993).

———, *Dwellings* (New York: Touchstone, 1995).

———, *Solar Storms* (New York: Scribner Paperback Fiction, 1995).

Mack, John E., "The Politics of Species Arrogance," in *Ecopsychology*, Theodore Roszak, Mary E. Gomes, and Allen D. Kanner, eds. (San Francisco: Sierra Club Books, 1995).

Roszak, Theodore, "Where Psyche Meets Gaia," in *Ecopsychology*, Theodore Roszak, Mary E. Gomes, and Allen D. Kanner, eds. (San Francisco: Sierra Club Books, 1995).

Shanley, Kathryn W., "Linda Hogan," in *Dictionary of Literary Biography*, vol. 175, *Native American Writers of the United States*, Kenneth M. Roemer, eds. (Detroit: Bruccoli Clark Layman, 1997) 123–130.

Shepard, Paul, "Nature and Madness," in *Ecopsychology*, Theodore Roszak, Mary E. Gomes, and Allen D. Kanner, eds. (San Francisco: Sierra Club Books, 1995).

Works Cited for Louis Owens

Dwyer, Margaret, "The Syncretic Impulse: Louis Owens' Use of Autobiography, Ethnology, and Blended Mythologies in *The Sharpest Sight*," *Studies in Native American Literatures* 10:2 (Summer 1998) 43–60.

"In Memoriam: Louis Owens," *UC Santa Cruz Currents Online*, http://www.ucsc.edu/curents/02-03/08-05/inmemoriam.html (accessed August 17, 2003).

LaLonde, Chris, "Discerning Connections, Revising the Master Narrative, and Interrogating Identity in Louis Owens's *The Sharpest Sight*," *American Indian Quarterly* 22:3 (Summer 1998) 305–325.

———, *Grave Concerns, Trickster Turns: The Novels of Louis Owens* (Norman: University of Oklahoma Press, 2002).

Owens, Louis, *Other Destinies: Understanding the American Indian Novel* (Norman: University of Oklahoma Press, 1992).

————, *The Sharpest Sight* (Norman: University of Oklahoma Press, 1992).

————, *Bone Game* (Norman: University of Oklahoma Press, 1994).

————, *Mixedblood Messages: Literature, Film, Family, Place* (Norman: University of Oklahoma Press, 1998).

————, *I Hear the Train: Reflections, Inventions, Refractions* (Norman: University of Oklahoma Press, 2001).

Purdy, John, "Clear Waters: A Conversation with Louis Owens," *SAIL* 10:2 (Summer 1998) 6–22.

Vizenor, Gerald and A. Robert Lee, *Postindian Conversations* (Lincoln: University of Nebraska Press, 1999).

Works Cited for Sherman Alexie

Alexie, Sherman,*The Lone Ranger and Tonto Fistfight in Heaven* (New York: HarperPerennial, 1993).

————, *Reservation Blues* (New York: Time Warner, 1995).

————, *Indian Killer* (New York: Time Warner, 1996).

Christie, Stuart, "Renaissance Man: The Tribal 'Schizophrenic' in Sherman Alexie's *Indian Killer*," *American Indian Culture and Research Journal* 25:4 (2001) 1–19.

Coulombe, Joseph L., "The Approximate Size of His Favorite Humor: Sherman Alexie's Comic Connections and Disconnections in *The Lone Ranger and Tonto Fistfight in Heaven*," *American Indian Quarterly* 26:1 (2002) 94–115.

Cook-Lynn, Elizabeth, "American Indian Intellectualism and the New Indian Story," in *Natives and Academics: Researching and Writing about American Indians*, Devon A. Mihesuah, ed. (Lincoln: University of Nebraska Press, 1998).

Evans, Stephen F., "'Open Containers': Sherman Alexie's Drunken Indians," *American Indian Quarterly* 25:1 (2001) 46–72.

Fanon, Frantz, "National Culture," repr. in *The Post-colonial Studies Reader*, Bill Ashcroft, Gareth Griffiths, and Helen Tiffin, eds. (London: Routledge, 1997).

Ford, Douglas, "Sherman Alexie's Indigenous Blues," *Melus* 27:3 (Fall 2002) 197–215.

Gilroy, John Warren, "Another Fine Example of the Oral Tradition? Identification and Subversion in Sherman Alexie's *Smoke Signals*," *SAIL* 13:1 (Spring 2001) 23–39.

Hafen, Jane P., "Rock and Roll, Redskins, and Blues in Sherman Alexie's Work," *SAIL* 9:4 (Winter 1997) 71–78.

Krupat, Arnold, *red matters* (Philadelphia: University of Pennsylvania Press, 2002).

Lourie, Dick, "Forgiving Our Fathers," http://www.paks.redacorn.org/ blog/archives/000005.html (accessed March 24, 2003).

McFarland, Ron, "Sherman Alexie," in *Dictionary of Literary Biography*, vol. 206, *Twentieth-Century American Western Writers, First Series*, Richard H. Cracroft, ed. (Detroit: Bruccoli Clark Layman, 1999) 3–10.

"Official Sherman Alexie Biography" http://www.fallsapart.com/ biography.html (accessed August 28, 2002).

Owens, Louis, *Mixedblood Messages* (Norman: University of Oklahoma Press, 1998).

Peterson, Scott, *Native American Prophecies* (New York: Paragon House, 1990).

Purdy, John, "Crossroads: A Conversation with Sherman Alexie," *SAIL* 9:4 (Winter 1997) 1–18.

Siskel, Gene and Roger Ebert, "Review of *Smoke Signals* June 28, 1998," http://www.fallsapart.com/rvw-ssse.html (accessed March 24, 2003).

Works Cited: Thomas King

Cook-Lynn, Elizabeth, "American Indian Intellectualism and the New Indian Story," in *Natives and Academics: Researching and Writing about American Indians*, Devon A. Mihesuah, ed. (Lincoln: University of Nebraska Press, 1998).

Goldman, Marlene, "Mapping and Dreaming: Native Resistance in *Green Grass, Running Water*," *Canadian Literature* 161/162 (Summer/Autumn 1999) 18–41.

King, Thomas, *Medicine River* (New York: Penguin, 1989).

———, *Green Grass, Running Water* (New York: Bantam, 1993).

———, *Truth and Bright Water* (New York: Atlantic Monthly, 1999).

Linton, Patricia, "'And Here's How it Happened': Trickster Discourse in Thomas King's *Green Grass, Running Water*," *Modern Fiction Studies* 45:1 (Spring, 1999) 212–234.

Mooney, James, *Myths of the Cherokee* (New York: Dover, 1995).

Owens, Louis, *Mixedblood Messages* (Norman: University of Oklahoma Press, 1998).

Wyile, Herb, "'Trust Tonto': Thomas King's Subversive Fictions and Politics of Cultural Literacy," *Canadian Literature* 161/162 (Summer/Autumn 1999) 105–224.

Chapter Five

Themes in Native American Literatures

White or Western thematic studies tend to jeopardize attempts to represent (re-present) the complexity of human experience—especially with regard to ethnic diversity. Reductive thought occurs when readers attempt to reduce the perceptions in a complex narrative, drama, or poem to a thesis statement, ethical assertion, or moral judgment. As a consequence, thematic studies tend to deny difference in favor of similarity. Russell Brown introduces an alternative type of "corpus thematics" he calls "cultural thematics—the reading of cultural themes out of national bodies of literature or out of the writing of ethnic or gender identified groups." Brown explains that because "cultural thematics joins literary studies with other disciplines such as history, sociology and anthropology, it has been common among critics interested in interdisciplinary approaches, and in fields such as American Studies" (645).

Two Overarching Themes: Indian Identity and Cultural Fragmentation

Often, in this chapter, examples of the topics at hand will be taken from poets, short story writers, and literary autoethnographers not referred to in Chapter Four but who are, nonetheless, prominent in Native literary circles. Certainly the complexity of speaking of themes in Native literatures can be demonstrated by the differing responses of two leading figures in Native literature and critical theory—full blood Simon Ortiz (Acoma Pueblo) and mixedblood

Paula Gunn Allen (Laguna Pueblo). One of the more enduring themes in Native literatures might more readily be posed as a question: Who is an Indian? In *Out There Somewhere*, Ortiz addresses the problem of "Indian" identity and the reductive nature of the term *Indian*. For example, in "Greatest Believers Greatest Disbelievers," Ortiz writes:

> To believe or not to believe,
> This was the question.
> And THE ANSWER.
> Asked and answered and believed
> by the greatest believers
> and disbelievers the world
> has ever known.
> Where are the Indians?
> Where are the real
> Indians?
> There are no Indians.
> There are no real Indians.
> There were never any
> Indians.
> There were never any
> Indians.
> There were never any real Indians.
> You mean . . . you mean, there were never any Indians?
> No real Indians?
> None.
> Never (48).

Indeed, there are no real *Indians*. The term *Indian* was imposed on numerous nations of indigenous peoples from the time of Columbus forward. In "'Indians' Wanted," Ortiz repeats this assertion: "Indians were what people in Europe wanted to believe. Indians were what / people in Europe wanted to believe. Indians were what people in Europe wanted to believe" (49). The last stanza of "Believing the Belief," continues the thoughts expressed in the first two poems with this augmentation: "Soon the Americans believed / since they were originally Europeans / and they yearned for 'the old country.'/ Oh my, they believed! / They absolutely believed!" (50) And in "Even 'the Indians' Believed," Ortiz adds, "Soon even 'the Indians' believed there were 'Indians'"(51). In "What We Know," Ortiz moves from belief to knowledge. "'Indians' who are our people / (The People, Human Beings, Hanoh, etc.) / knew themselves as people. Different from each other. Speaking / different and distinct and separate languages. They heard each others' / languages. Their people had different names. They wore different / clothes. They ate different foods. They danced different dances. They / celebrated their differences. Yes, they were different but they were all / the same: / The people, Human Beings, you, Me" (53).

Paula Gunn Allen reports that in her early years as a college instructor, she was "cautioned against grouping native peoples under the rubric 'Indian' because pan-Indianism was not popular among our various peoples." But "two decades" of further studies "suggested, indeed, confirmed, that while the distinctions among native communities are many and, linguistically at least, the differences are vast, the similarities are far greater and much more profound" (*Grandmothers of the Light* 205). Gunn Allen differs from Ortiz here in degree but not sentiment. Ortiz stresses the nonexistence of Indians, acknowledges the diversity of Native tribes, yet underscores the common humanity of Native peoples. Gunn Allen focuses on the profound conceptual similarities between peoples from diverse tribal and linguistic origins.

Perhaps a third author, Sherman Alexie (Spokane/Coeur d'Alene), will demonstrate the growing complexity of "Indian" identity. Nearly sixty percent of Native peoples in the United States live in urban areas. In *The Toughest Indian in the World* (2000) and *Ten Little Indians* (2003), Alexie explores the non-duplicatable nature of individual experience among Spokane-affiliated people living in Washington—most often off but related to Natives on the Spokane reservation. "One Good Man," for instance, is a story of a full-blood Spokane man who returns to the reservation to care for his father who has just had his feet amputated as a consequence of diabetes. "I'd left the reservation when I was eighteen years old, leaving with the full intention of coming back after I'd finished college," says the narrator. "I had never wanted to contribute to the brain drain, to be yet another of the best and brightest Indians to abandon his or her tribe to the Indian leaders who couldn't spell the word *sovereignty*." Despite his "idealistic" intentions, the narrator never does return.

"I left the reservation," he explains," for the same reason a white kid leaves the cornfields of Iowa, or the coal mines of Pennsylvania, or the oil derricks of Texas: ambition. Don't get me wrong. I loved the reservation when I was a child and I suppose I love it now as an adult (I live only sixty-five miles away), but it's certainly a different sort of love" (220–221).

"One Good Man" actually poses the question "What is an Indian?" several times throughout the story. Flashbacks to his youth, college years, and failed marriage rehearse the various chances the narrator has had to consider what constitutes being a *real* Indian. "Is it the lead actor in a miracle or the witness who remembers the miracle?" he wonders (221). Now, as the narrator looks in upon his father who is recuperating from surgery, he poses: "Is it a son who can stand in a doorway and watch his father sleep?" (222). One memory the narrator deliberates about is an episode when his father went to a college class with him to confront a particularly arrogant Native college professor. "*What is an Indian?*" the storyteller asks. "Is it a son who brings his father to school as show-and-tell?" Professor Crowell (he crows/brags well) interrogates the father: "'Excuse me sir. . . . Are you in my class?" To which the father responds: "You're in my class now." A verbal altercation ensues—Indian father challenging Native professor. At the end of his reverie, the narrator records this interchange—a conversation between political versus familial definitions of what it means to be an Indian male:

> 'What about Wounded Knee?' Crowell asked my father. 'I was at Wounded Knee. Where were you?'
>
> 'I was teaching my son here how to ride his bike. Took forever. And when he finally did it, man, I cried like a baby, I was so proud.'
>
> 'What kind of Indian are you? You weren't part of the revolution.'
>
> 'I'm a man who keeps promises.'
>
> It was mostly true. My father had kept most of his promises, or had tried to keep all of his promises, except this one: he never stopped eating sugar (*The Toughest Indian in the World* 229).

As the story progresses, the reader comes to realize that the title of the story applies to both father and son—they are both men of integrity and compassion.

"Lawyer's League," in *Ten Little Indians*, begins:

> My father is an African American giant who played defensive end for the University of Washington Huskies, and my mother is a petite Spokane Indian ballerina who majored in dance at U-Dub, so genetically speaking, I'm a graceful monster. But my father spent more time reading Frantz Fanon and Angela Davis than pumping iron in the weight room, and my mother played supernatural point guard for an all-Native women's barnstorming basketball team, so culturally speaking, I'm a biracial revolutionary leftist magician with a twenty-foot jumper encoded in my DNA (53).

In other words, in this story identity is a matter of genetic inheritance as well as a multiplicity of other culturally inherited patterns— identity by consent (choice), gender, ethnicity, historical circumstance, economic viability, geographic location, and so forth. The title "Lawyer's League" is a reference to a basketball league made up of mostly Anglo lawyers who can't accept this Afro/Indian athlete into their *league*; he can outplay the best of them. Even though these lawyers feel superior by reason of their profession, they are made to feel athletically inferior. This biracial man, however, also makes choices that limit his happiness. In actuality, he has a "limited range of [social/emotional/professional] motion" imposed on him as well as determined by him (68).

In a story about a mother/son relationship, "The Life and Times of Estelle Walks Above," the son says of himself:

> To this day, I rarely look in the mirror and think, I'm an Indian. I don't necessarily know what an Indian is supposed to be. After all, I don't speak my tribal language, and I'm allergic to the earth. If it grows, it makes me sneeze. In Salish, 'Spokane' means 'Children of the Sun,' but I'm slightly allergic to the sun. If I spend too much time outside, I get a nasty rash. I doubt Crazy Horse needed talcum powder to get through a hot summer day. Can you imagine Sacajawea sniffling her way across the Continental Divide?

I'm hardly the poster boy for aboriginal pride. I don't even
think about my tribal heritage until some white person
reminds me of it. . . (134).

This poignant story is a raucous journey through a son's insights
into being raised solely by a wonderfully eccentric mother. He learns
about periods, vaginas, feminism, Anglo women, and what those
Anglo women discover they want from his Indian mother.

At one point, the narrator considers his mother's construction of
sexual expression: "it was my mother who first gave up on love, who,
since my childhood, has lived what I assume to be a chaste life. She
could not sleep with a man who made her feel dirty. So as far as I
can tell, and I believe she would tell me otherwise, she has simply
gone without." Estelle embarrasses her son time and again. He is
perplexed and even infuriated by her range of female-generated
responses to life. And yet he concludes, "As for me, as crazy as it
sounds, I want to become the kind of man my mother would sleep
with. . . . I don't want to be cherished by my mother (and I am
beloved) as much as I want to be respected by her" (143). The last
sentence in the story reflects the cumulative information gained
from reading the story: "My mother and I have loved and failed each
other, and we keep on loving and failing each other, and one of us
will eventually bury the other, and the survivor will burn down the
church with grief's hungry fire" (*Ten Little Indians* 149).

In Alexie's most recent short story collections, each story pays
attention to what it means to be a particular Indian human being
within complex contexts. This is especially relevant in a post-
Postmodern world that has taught readers to play with the interchange between the meanings of *difference* and *deference* on a
cultural scale. No telling (signs) can re-present reality (the signified).
No human experience can be retold in a story (the words are not
the things, events, or people). Each human has experiences that are
shaped by the various cultures they inhabit; but such habitation is
also particular, unique, different. What is more, Postmodern thought
is engaged in understanding what constitutes a *just* (ethical) human.
The questions generating Postmodern thought might be: how can
humans in Western cultures continue to justify violence? And how
might a different way of reading lead humankind into nonviolent

ways of being in the world? Alexie explores answers to such questions.

Ortiz, Gunn Allen, and Alexie delineate a composite of concerns among Native authors—a rejection of imposed Native identities (there are no Indians); a recognition of the diverse cultures and languages that make up Native America; an understanding that commonalities exist despite that diversity; a recognition of the particular nature of individual Native experience; an acknowledgment of the basic humanity of Native peoples; and a conscious exploration of the meaning of place (reservation/urban) in shaping identity. This range of concerns, coupled with the ethics involved in such determinations, demonstrates the difficulties surrounding thematics.

Readers inevitably want to know what authors are talking about despite these complexities. Different readers, however, often arrive at different conceptions of what authors mean; nonetheless their common intent is to interpret. None of the themes indicated by a particular reading of an individual text may be the themes that diverse critics emphasize when they see literary texts as a part of a larger body of works. Brown, for example, cautions that critics "who emphasize individual texts have sometimes complained that comparative and corpus thematics produce results that are circular; [critics] find what they go looking for" (645). Nonetheless, cultures are identified by unifying approaches to life. Brown admits that "cultural criticism has valued thematics as a tool, especially for making comparisons between cultures, where analyses of contrasting themes or of contrasting ways of deploying the same theme may reveal a great deal about larger cultural patterns" (645). It is in light of "cultural criticism" then, that the themes in Native American literatures ought to be considered, not so much in the sense of various theses, but in terms of attitudes or approaches to Native American experiences as reflected by various authors from the vantage point of their particular tribal affiliations.

Attitudes and approaches to common concerns in Native American literary texts are interactional. As is evident from the discussion in Chapter Four, authors share a common concern with the **fragmentation** that has resulted from the incessant disruption of Native life-ways through the violent dislocations imposed on tribal peoples by colonizers. Fragmentation is often discussed in terms of genocide and ethnocide—physical and cultural death. Authors do not assert that Native communities were living in perfect harmony prior to the coming of immigrant peoples and ideologies. However, they do demonstrate that the loss of self-determination, lands, and life-ways has been and continues to be detrimental to the ongoing psychic life of five hundred nations of North American peoples. In order to survive or overcome virtually insurmountable trauma or obstacles, Native authors posit the need to either maintain or reclaim particular ethnic identities—identities, however, that are dynamic or in constant flux. Native characters must overcome the complex of influences that have produced *Indians* in favor of a restoration to specific tribal ancestries and inheritances as well as ancestral homelands —Hopi, Navajo, Sioux, Chippewa, Iroquois, and so forth. Or at least, they must position themselves in relationship to certain geographic, genealogical, psychological, and philosophic frames of reference in order to have a sense of well-being.

Such reformation projects are fraught with difficulty. Many Native authors are of mixed bloodlines—Native and European. For numerous reasons—primarily economic—many tribal people also live in the diaspora and attempt to accommodate their lives to the tenets of democratic individualism—competition, ascendance, the acquisition of private property, and adaptation to the sociality of urban life. Most of the successful Native authors are college graduates whose understanding of both Western and Native approaches to life enable them to offer unique insights into conflicts between cultures. Often, however, experiments with living in cities have met with further fragmentation and the need either for social programs or assimilation. Alcoholism; addictions to drugs, sex, and other self-defeating behaviors; disintegration of families; poverty—joblessness, despair, hunger, isolation; and humiliation plague the lives of urban Native Americans.

On reservations, says Scott B. Vickers, "Despair, poverty, alcoholism ('17.0 percent to 19.0 percent of all Indian deaths are probably alcohol-related,' as compared with the general U.S. average of 4.7 percent . . .), fetal alcohol syndrome, suicide, fractious tribal governments, AIDS, diabetes, land and resource management, tribal gaming operations and other problematic situations" abound. And yet, such situations "are increasingly being addressed within Indian communities themselves, without the intervention of the federal government," claims Vickers. "Each success brings tribes closer to sovereignty and closer to each other, as intertribal solutions are being worked out in increasing numbers" (161).

Many Native authors contend that the deracinating conditions or behaviors resulting from colonization needn't define Native people. Therefore, *Native literary themes pivot around various descriptions and confrontations with the causes and effects of Native fragmentation while at the same time imagining how healing from such debilitating fragmentation might occur.* Consequently, Native writers share a common approach to: (1) the **power of words and storytelling** as instruments of survival—including Trickster discourse; (2) the **inseparable connection between identity and a sense of place**—including the natural environment; (3) **the importance of bloodlines** (ancestry and posterity)—mixed or pure; (4) the perpetuation of powerful, often traditional, **gender identities**; (5) **sexual expression** used either to pervert (as a metaphor for cultural degradation) or enhance human relatedness; and (6) the possibility of **healing through reconciliation.**

The Power of Words and Storytelling as Instruments of Survival

> God made man because He loves stories.
> —Momaday, "Forward"

A Mythic Approach

Of singular importance in shaping conceptions of the power of words among Native communities is N. Scott Momaday's various works published under the title, "The Man Made of Words." In 1970, for example, Momaday addressed the First Convocation of American Indian Scholars held at Princeton University using as the title of his address, "The Man Made of Words." In 1972, Momaday spoke at the International Congress of Learned Societies in the Field of Religion in Los Angeles using the same title. The proceedings of that conference were later published in *Religion and the Humanizing of Man.* And in 1997, Momaday published a collection of his essays in the book, *Man Made of Words*. As can be noted, the audiences for these various compositions varied; Momaday adapted his remarks (as good storytellers often do) to the needs of those to whom he spoke/wrote—a convocation of Native scholars; a congregation of theologians; and a national audience interested in Momaday's approaches to language and place.

In Momaday's Princeton address, he says that the questions that "interest" him "most" are: "Who is the storyteller? Of whom is the story told? What is there in the darkness to imagine into being? What is there to dream and to relate? What happens when I or anyone exerts the force of language upon the unknown?" (103) For Momaday, "We are what we imagine. Our very existence consists in our imagination of ourselves. Our best destiny is to imagine, at least, completely, who and what, and *that* we are. The greatest tragedy that can befall us is to go unimagined." In other words, behavior stems from one's conception of self—an individual can't become what he can't imagine. Imagination is the mental capacity to create images, to interpret events, and to attribute meaning to human relationships and places. Language and literatures—orally transmitted tales or written texts—are the ways through which meaning is shared. Momaday suggests that:

> Storytelling is imaginative and creative in nature. It is an act by which man strives to realize his capacity for wonder, meaning and delight. It is also a process in which man invests and preserves himself in the context of ideas. Man tells stories in order to understand his experience, whatever it may be. The possibilities of storytelling are precisely those of understanding the human experience (104).

Furthermore, Momaday asserts that there is a "relationship between what a man is and what he says." Although this relationship is complex, says Momaday, "man has consummate being in language, and there only. The state of human being is an idea, an idea which man has of himself. Only when he is embodied in an idea, and the idea is realized in language, can man take possession of himself" ("The Man Made of Words" 104; also in *Nothing But the Truth* edited by John L. Purdy and James Ruppert, 82–93).

For Momaday, "the fullest realization of . . . humanity" comes through the "art and product of the imagination as literature." Here Momaday uses the term *literature* to apply to orally transmitted, as well as written, tales. Momaday believes that: "Language is the means by which words proceed to the formulation of meaning and emotional effect." Furthermore, to move to Momaday's Los Angeles speech, "This comprehension of the earth and air in language is a matter of morality, I believe, for it brings into account not only Man's instinctive reaction to his environment but the full realization of his humanity as well, the achievement of his intellectual and spiritual development as an individual and as a race" (192). In this speech to scholars of comparative religion, Momaday includes the "perceptive commentary upon the prose and poetry of the American Indian" by ethnographer Margot Astrov:

> The singing of songs and the telling of tales, with the American Indian, is but seldom a means of mere spontaneous self-expression. More often than not, the singer aims with the chanted word to exert a strong influence and to bring about a change, either in himself or in nature or in his fellow beings. By narrating the story of origin, he endeavors to influence the universe and to strengthen the failing powers of the supernatural beings. He relates the myth of creation, ceremonially, in order to save the world from death and destruction and to keep alive the primeval spirit of the sacred beginning. Above all, it seems that the word, both in song and in tale, was meant to maintain and to prolong the individual life in some way or other—that is, to cure, to heal, to ward off evil, and to frustrate death (*Religion and the Humanizing of Man* 193).

Certainly such assertions can be seen flooding through the works of Momaday, Silko, Welch, Vizenor, Erdrich, and Hogan. For example, Abel, in Momaday's *House Made of Dawn*, moves toward recovery from his disorientation and destructive behavior when he regains both the memories of his grandfather and discovers the healing power of the Navajo *Night Chant*. Tayo, in Leslie Marmon Silko's *Ceremony*, overcomes the evil designs of the "witchery" when he discovers that his "sickness was only part of something larger, and his cure would be found only in something great and inclusive of everything" (125–126). When Tayo finally sees "the way all the stories fit together—the old stories, the war stories, their stories—to become a story that was still being told," he realizes he has not seen the world as it always has been with "no boundaries, only transitions through all distances and time" (246). If Tayo can keep the destroyers from infiltrating his story then the "witchery would turn . . . upon itself . . ." (247). He does this through "making new ceremonies" that thwart "the destroyers" (249).

Fools Crow, in James Welch's *Fools Crow*, receives a powerful, disheartening, vision from Feather Woman about the future of his people. However, Feather Woman also imparts to Fools Crow that his people will endure through their tribulations if they keep their traditional stories alive. "The stories will be handed down, and they will see that their people were proud and lived in accordance with the Below Ones, the Underwater people—and the Above Ones," Feather Woman counsels (359–360). In *Heirs of Columbus*, Gerald Vizenor plays Trickster with the various "legitimate" and varied scholarly claims about who and what Columbus was/is. Five centuries after Columbus, his "crossblood descendants" declare "a new tribal nation." They do so by asserting that "the great explorer was tribal and he carried [Native] stories in his blood"(4). When Naanabozho, the Chippewa "compassionate tribal trickster . . . created the earth," he also "invented meditation with trickster stories and liberated his mind over his own excrement." The "Heirs of Christopher Columbus" therefore, "created one more New World in their stories and overturned the tribal prophecies that their avian time would end with the arrival of the white man"(5). Vizenor's various novels are "trickster stories of liberation" from victimization and defeat.

In Louise Erdrich's *Tracks*, Nanapush (also a play on the Chippewa Trickster), saves lives through storytelling—his own, Lulu's, Fleur's, and eventually his ancestors and their posterity. "I shouldn't have been caused to live so long, shown so much of death, had to squeeze so many stories in the corners of my brain," says Nanapush. "They're all attached, and once I start there is no end to telling because they're hooked from one side to the other, mouth to tail. During the year of sickness, when I was the last one left, I saved myself by starting a story" (46).

Linda Hogan's "To Light" explores the theme of storytelling through poetry:

> At the spring
> we hear the great seas traveling
> underground
> giving themselves up
> with tongues of water
> that sing the earth open.
> They have journeyed through the graveyards
> of our loved ones,
> turning in their graves
> to carry the stories of life to air.
> Even the trees with their rings
> have kept track
> of the crimes that live within
> and against us.
> We remember it all.
> We remember, though we are just skeletons
> whose organs and flesh
> hold us in.
> We have stories
> as old as the great seas
> breaking through the chest
> flying out the mouth,
> noisy tongues that once were silenced,
> all oceans we contain
> coming to light (*Harpers Anthology* 197).

In 1994, Brian Swann used a verse from Hogan's poem as a prologue and the last line of the poem as the main part of the title of his book *Coming to Light: Contemporary Translations of the Native Literatures of North America*. This 801-page book is a testament to Hogan's assertion that Natives "have stories / as old as the great seas / breaking through the chest / flying out the mouth, / . . . coming to light." Fifty-eight scholars contribute their works to this volume covering stories from Alaska, the Yukon, the Subarctic, the North Pacific Coast, the Great Basin and Plateau, the Plains, the Eastern Woodlands, the Southwest, the Southeast, and California—each region representing complex geographical and cultural diversity. Swann says his book "presents a *sampling* of the magnificence and diversity of the many different Native American cultures that have existed for thousands of years and continue to exist today, despite efforts to repress, suppress, and even extirpate them" (emphasis added; xiii).

The Healing Aspects of Artistic Expression

Carter Revard (Osage) addresses the healing nature of words. Poet, short story writer, and autoethnographer, Revard is considered one of the grandfathers of Native American Literatures. His contributions to the field of literature have been considerable; the board of *SAIL: Studies in American Indian Literature* devoted a special issue of their journal in honor of Revard in spring 2003. Born in Pawhuska, Oklahoma, among the Osage and Ponca in 1931, Revard went on to study at Oxford, received a doctorate in English from Yale, and taught English at Amherst (five years) and Washington University in St. Louis (thirty-nine years). Included in the *SAIL* issue on Revard is an address that Revard delivered at the Mystic Lake Symposium on Native American Literature held at Prior Lake in Minnesota in April 2002. His essay, "Some Notes on Native American Literature," bespeaks the wisdom and wit of his many years as a professor of English. Revard, in his stories and poems, shapes attitudes toward what good writers do with words. Revard claims that most people seem to "hate to read great literature—which is so much easier to read if the reader HAS developed this sense of wonder and awe and delight in things which people with their minds not yet open understand are so perfectly ordinary" (5).

Revard feels that most readers only come to understand the power of great literature when there is a need to make sense of human experience:

> Of course the death of a grandparent sometimes opens a young mind remarkably well, and quite a few of you may have had the good fortune to lose a mother or father or even a sibling you did not utterly hate. This loss might have led some of you to turn and read, say, the Twenty-third Psalm, or some verses of the New Testament, or the Koran,

or a little Old English Poetry—or maybe even some newer poetry in English. If you HAVE been so lucky in losing what you love, you may already be old enough to have felt the need for words that evoke a wonder and awe and delight that might help ease some of the grief you endured. Those who have had a rib broken, and lived to heal, may later notice how wonderful it is to breathe without pain— and may come to value 'simple breathing' a bit more highly when they think about it: each breath you can succeed in taking helps the rib to heal, *and so it is with a consoling set of words the breath may carry. What you breathe in helps heal you; what a good writer breathes out may help heal others* (emphasis added; 5).

Artistic expression can be used to find a voice, to survive loss, and to name experience for the sake of self and for others. Certainly Revard's *Family Matters, Tribal Affairs* (1998) and *Winning the Dust Bowl* (2001) attest to the efficacy of Revard's ability to accomplish these ends.

Six years before Revard taught at Amherst, he discovered he was going deaf. He writes, "I had otosclerosis, a kind of hereditary arthritis of the ear's little bones—the prognosis being that in a few years I would be as deaf as my mother and my Uncle Arthur" (*Winning the Dust Bowl* 4). One evening, while teaching at Amherst and as Revard thought about his gradual hearing loss, he remembered "an Oklahoma thunderstorm" (5)—a "slashing and swashing downpour" (6) in which he and his siblings were once caught. They retreated into a den where Revard imagined coyotes once lived. "I suddenly remembered there in my Amherst bed, and I said in surprise: suppose there *was* a den of coyotes there, and the pups were just opening their eyes, what would that thunderstorm have sounded like to them, given the wonderful ears a coyote has?" (6). The next morning "before dawn I woke up to the sound of rain on the roof," and composed a sonnet about "finding a voice" called "Coyote Tells Why He Sings." Revard writes from a coyote pup's point of view: "When I was born. One night in late August, it rained—/ the Thunder waked us." Revard recreates the sound of thunder as thunder is joined by the sounds of torrential rains hitting and running roughshod over the landscape. "And the rain came in a pelting rush down over the hill, / Wind blew wet into our cave as I heard the sounds / Of leaf-drip, rustling of soggy branches in gusts of wind." The rain cut "new ripples" in the surface of the earth around the coyote pups' den. "Where the new ripples were, I drank, next morning, / Fresh muddy water that set my teeth on edge. / I thought how delicate that rock's poise was and how / *The storm made music, when it changed my world*" (Revard's emphasis; 3).

In this poem, Thunder plays multiple roles. When Joseph Bruchac (Abenaki) interviewed Revard for *Survival This Way* (1987), he reminded Revard of the correspondence between Thunder in this poem and the fact that during Revard's naming ceremony he "had been brought into the Thunder clan" (Revard 6). Indeed, the thunder waked him; his genetic and clan heritage tricked him into a sense of the power of hearing and saying. Listening, naming, place, loss, and recovery are interwoven through words in this poem that tells why Coyote (Revard) sings.

A Symbolic Approach to the Power of Language

The last work in *Winning the Dust Bowl*, "A Song That We Still Sing," is a narrative poem that rehearses an August journey that Revard and his Ponca cousins took "from Oklahoma up to the Sun Dance / at Crow Dog's Paradise on the Rosebud Sioux Reservation." On their way, the group passed the ruins of a fort from which they could hear songs in the Ponca language. They were somewhat mystified by the sound of Ponca songs because they were outside traditional Ponca lands. "So they walked / through the dry short grass / towards the raised earth walls / and up on them, and looked / inside that wide compound, and there / was not a soul in sight." And yet, they clearly heard "*a Victory Song*," a familiar song still sung by contemporary Ponca.

At this point in the poem, Revard's cousins remember White Antelope, an old Ponca man who was caught in the massacre at Sand Creek. White Antelope composed his "death-song" for such an occasion. Revard contends that, "Once we can word ourselves in a world, we have to find how to stay alive in song" (25). "A Song That

We Still Sing," keeps alive the voices of those who witnessed the unimaginably brutal massacre at Sand Creek—rendering personalities and details alive through poetry:

> After Sand Creek it was,
> that time the news got out of what
> had been done to Black Kettle and
> his people there beneath
> that big American flag which they'd been given
> in token that this peaceful band
> Was not to be attacked,
> and then at dawn the Reverend Colonel
> Chivington and his men attacked and massacred
> some hundreds who could not escape—
> one small boy, running
> for refuge, was shot down at a hundred yards,
> because, as Chivington had told his troops,
> *Nits make lice.* The women's breasts,
> sliced off, were made into
> tobacco pouches, as were the scrotums
> of men. George Bent, a half-Cheyenne who was there,
> who'd been a Confederate soldier and
> both wrote and spoke English and Cheyenne
> has told about it in his letters—
> he saw White Antelope come out
> unarmed from his tepee, pointing up . . . (202–203)

Notice how Revard, while narrating a horrible event, also locates each character in relationship to place—between Oklahoma and a destination on the Rosebud Sioux Reservation made unusual through their visit to an old ruin mound near Sand Creek. Even though this poem might be read as a poem developing the power of story and song, certainly place also plays a significant role.

The Power of Words as Symbols

The name of Sand Creek has become more than a place name in Native literatures, as has Wounded Knee, among other places. Sand Creek has become *a cultural symbol* for various atrocities suffered by Natives. In his collection of poetry *From Sand Creek*, Ortiz explains the origin of the continuous concern with the meaning of Sand Creek:

> November 29, 1864: On that cold dawn, about 600 Southern Cheyenne and Arapaho People, two-thirds of them women and children, were camped on a bend of Sand Creek in southeastern Colorado. The People were at peace. This was expressed two months before by Black Kettle, one of the principal elders of the Cheyennes, in Denver to Governor John Evans and Colonel John W. Chivington, head of the Colorado Volunteers. 'I want you to give all these chiefs of the soldiers here to understand that we are for peace, and that we have made peace, that we may not be mistaken for enemies.' The reverend Colonel Chivington and his Volunteers and Fort Lyon troops, numbering more than 700 heavily armed men, slaughtered 105 women and children and 28 men (8).

President Lincoln gave Black Kettle a U.S. flag in 1863. This flag was to be a memento of the peace shared between the Cheyenne and Arapaho People and the United States. Ortiz's Sand Creek poems are about men in Veterans' hospitals, Native men killed in Vietnam, Indian lands exploited by Anglos, Buffalo herds before extermination, and so forth. In the first poem in the collection, however, Ortiz also uses Sand Creek as an image of hope: "This America / has been a burden / of steel and mad / death, but, look now, / there are flowers / and new grass / and a spring wind / rising / from Sand Creek" (9).

The Inseparable Connection Between Identity and a Sense of Place

In his introduction to *Between Earth And Sky: Legends of Native American Sacred Places*, Joseph Bruchac (Abenaki) orients his readers to a Native approach to place: "Native American cultures throughout the continent recognize seven [directions]. There are the cardinal directions of East, South, West, and North, directions that correspond to our life cycle of birth, youth, adulthood, and the time of being an elder, respectively. Then there are the directions of Earth and Sky"—which form a sphere. "These Six Directions are easy to locate," Burchac continues. "The Seventh Direction, however, is harder to see. It is the direction within us all, the place that helps us see right and wrong and maintain the balance by choosing to live in a good way"(i).

A Mythic Approach to Place: Sacred Place

"The events of one's life take place, *take place*. How often have I used this expression, and how often have I stopped to think what it means?" asks N. Scott Momaday in *Names*. Indeed what is the interaction between the events in a person's life and the place in which those events *take place*? "Events do indeed take place; they have meaning in relation to the things around them. And a part of my life happened to take place at Jemez. I existed in that landscape, and then my existence was indivisible with it," Momaday maintains (142). In *Man Made of Words*, Momaday proposes the interaction between language, storytelling, and place: "And the storyteller's place within the context of his language must include both a geographical and mythic frame of reference. Within that frame of reference is the freedom of infinite possibility. The place of infinite possibility is where the storyteller belongs" (112). The "geographical and mythic frame of reference" Momaday mentions here refers to another conception of place: sacred places. Says Momaday:

> Sacred places are the truest definitions of the earth; they stand for the earth immediately and forever; they are its flags and shields. If you would know the earth for what it really is, learn it through its sacred places. At Devil's Tower or Canyon de Chelly or the Cahokia Mounds you touch the pulse of the living planet; you feel its breath upon you. You become one with a spirit that pervades geologic time, that indeed confounds time and space. When I stand on the edge of Monument Valley and behold the great red and blue and purple monoliths floating in the distance, I have the certain sense that I see beyond time. There the earth lies in eternity (114).

The earth, in this mythic conception of place, becomes a "repository of the spirit" (N. Scott Momaday). Furthermore, "Sacred ground is in some way earned," claims Momaday. "It is consecrated, made holy with offerings—song and ceremony, joy and sorrow, the dedication of the mind and heart, offerings of life and death. The words 'sacred' and 'sacrifice' are related" (*Man Made of Words* 114).

When Abel, in Momaday's *House Made of Dawn*, returns to Walatowa to attend his grandfather's death and become a dawn runner, he is participating in this conception of place. Furthermore, Abel participates in the recreation of the earth, at dawn, as he chases away the night and any harmful forces that might be about in the landscape; and it does not matter if he lives or dies because he is in the process of rediscovering his voice—in a sacred landscape, among his people, and as a whole human being. Fools Crow, in Welch's *Fools Crow*, orients himself in kinship with the world around him. The Montana mountain range is the Backbone of the World. The sun is Sun Chief and the author of the Sun Dance. The moon is Night Red Light, the wife of the Sun and so forth. Indeed, as Bruchac insists: "The native people of North America speak of their relationship to the Earth in terms of family. The Earth is not something to be bought and sold, something to be used and mistreated. It is, quite simply, the source of our lives—our Mother. The rest of Creation, all around us, shares in that family relationship" (*Native American Stories Told by Joseph Bruchac* iii). Who could read Momaday's works, for example, without attention to his characters' relationship to bears? Certainly Fools Crow's development is dependant on Raven and Wolverine. Most Indian novels contain the close association of central characters to their natural environment.

Any study of Native American storytelling would be remiss without reference to Joseph Bruchac (Abenaki), born in 1942 in Saratoga Springs, New York. To date (2004), Bruchac has published over sixty books and has contributed to five hundred other literary journals and critical works. Even though many of Bruchac's works are primarily written for children and young adults, his contributions to the field of Native American Literatures is unparalleled. Bruchac has collected tales from Native American tribes concerning the creation of the earth, fire, wind, weather, water, sky, seasons, plants and animals, death, and so forth. He has also authored numerous books about Native youth successfully confronting or overcoming peer pressure, racism, and family dysfunction. As mentioned, Bruchac collected interviews from Native poets for *Survival This Way* (1987), a standard text in Native studies. Bruchac is also the director of the Greenfield Review Literary Center in Greenfield Center, New York. He tirelessly promotes the voices of other Native poets, short story writers, and novelists. Bruchac's *Between Earth and Sky: Legends of Native American Sacred Places*, while intended for youth, would be of particular interest in coming to an understanding of sacred space. *Sacred Lands of Indian America*, edited by Jake Page, also helps readers understand the political and ecological implications of Native sacred lands throughout the United States.

In Erdrich's *Tracks*, the land around Fleur Pillager's cabin near Matchimanito Lake is sacred space. When Fleur loses her lands to greedy lumber companies, she attempts to rob them of their bounty by preempting their violence against her woods. Nanapush goes to protect Fleur against this invasion of her space. As he enters the woods near Fleur's cabin, he can hear "the hum of a thousand conversations. Not only the birds and small animals, but the spirits in the western stands had been forced together. The shadows of the trees were crowded with their forms. The twigs spun independently of wind, vibrating like small voices. I stopped," says Nanapush, and "stood among these trees whose flesh was so much older than ours, and it was then that my relatives and friends [who have died] took final leave, abandoned me to the living" (220). Whenever Fleur re-enters Erdrich's novels, she gambles to get her lands back for her posterity—lands that aren't just real estate. In *The Bingo Palace*, Fleur calls the area around Matchimanito Lake, "a spirit place, good if you are good and bad if you have done bad things" (133). In the same novel, Fleur tells Lipsha, *"Land is the only thing that lasts life to life. Money burns like tinder, flows off like water, and as for the government's promises, the wind is steadier"* (148). The italics in this quote are Erdrich's—used to emphasize the visionary quality of this information as well as the philosophical import.

Linda Hogan's novels are dramatic examples of what happens to individuals when they are forcibly separated from the earth. Hannah Wing, in *Solar Storms*, is and excellent example of "ontogenetic crippling"—the failure to mature. The world in which Hannah must grow up has been deforested. The beaver and wolves have been trapped out. And the people around her are thrust into an environment that can no longer sustain them. Hannah's insanity is created when the earth's resources are depleted through the actions of ignorant and arrogant men and she is abused like the earth. The earth can no longer be experienced as a secondary womb. To fill her emptiness, Hannah abandons herself to sexual exploitation, alcoholism, and child abuse—her own and others'. "Hannah Wing . . . stood at the bottomless passage to an underworld. She was wounded. She was dangerous. And there was no thawing for her heart," writes Hogan (13). Hannah cannot be reclaimed. But her abused daughter can. And the novel is about such a process. Angela, through the kind tutelage of her grandmothers, develops the ability to communicate with the earth, her grandmothers (in life and in death), and her beloved Tommy that brings her a new name: Maniki, which means "a true human being" (347).

There are many conceptions of the relationships between people, time, space, and the natural world among the religions of the world. Muslims take pilgrimages to Mecca as one of the pillars of their faith. Muslims and Jews war over their place in the land of promise: Jerusalem. Hindus sanctify space with temples or understand various rivers to be holy and their waters to be healing. Considered a classic by scholars of Native American literatures, Vine Deloria, Jr.'s *God is Red* discusses Native religions within the context of Western history, religious systems, and scientific understandings. Deloria clearly explores how conceptions of history, time, space, and the natural world shape human personality. While Rome, or Jerusalem, or Mecca can be cited as places with special religious significance and influence for Christians, Jews, and Muslims, Deloria believes Native peoples are differently rooted to their sacred lands. Says Deloria:

> It is quite possible . . . that as we look for the origin of peoples, we must discover religious experiences; as we look for the origins of religions, we must discover nations of people, and whichever way we look, it is to the lands on which the people reside and in which the religions arise that is important. This possibility is what has dominated the concerns of American Indian's peoples from the very beginnings. The chance that lands would be lost meant that religious communities would be destroyed and individual identities forsaken. As sacred mountains became secularized, as tribal burial grounds became cornfields, as tribes no longer lived

on the dust of their ancestors' bones, the people knew that
they could not survive (145).

Christianity is portable, as is Islam. This means converts can be gathered in, from wherever they reside (Native tribes do not seek converts). A permanent connection to any region of the earth is not
necessary in either system. As Deloria suggests, "The physical world
is not often seen as a positive place in Near Eastern religions. It is a
vale of tears filled with unexplained human tragedies." Furthermore,
"religious ceremonies seek to purge nature from participation in the
rituals, rather than acknowledge the existence of the material world.
In many ways the human body is seen as evil. The goal of life is to
win eternal life where followers receive imperishable bodies. . . .
This condition is known as salvation" (153–154).
    On the other hand:

> The Indian format is precisely the opposite. Not only the
> natural physical world is regarded as integral to human
> ambitions and activities, but also even the hypothetical geo-
> metrical structures of the world receive some form of reli-
> gious acknowledgment. Thus, Indians pray to the 'four
> directions,' lay out elaborate sandpaintings to represent the
> cosmos, and see in pipe bowls and sweat lodges a model of
> the larger cosmic whole (154).

Sin, repentance, salvation, redemption, and eternal life are terms
fundamental to Near Eastern religions. What Deloria notes is that
"Near Eastern religions seek and guarantee *salvation*, which is conceived as an escape from this planet to a place where loyal followers can enjoy eternal life filled with the delights that they were
denied during this lifetime." On the other hand, most "Indians see
themselves returning to nature, their bodies becoming the dust of
Mother Earth, and their souls journeying to another place across the
Milky Way or sometimes being reborn in a new generation of the
tribe" (155).
    Louise Erdrich's novels *Tracks, Tales of Burning Love,* and *The
Last Report on the Miracles at Little No Horse* can be read as dialogues
between these two mythic approaches to human experience—
Native and Christian (Catholic). *Tracks* is written in two voices:

Nanapush's and Pauline's. Nanapush represents the Ojibway approach to land and spirituality while Pauline (as in the apostle Paul's theology) represents a perverse interpretation of Christ and Christianity—full of excessive penances, sacred violence, and the agony of seeing self and sexuality as fallen and sinful. Not until after her death, in *Tales of Burning Love*, does Pauline (Sis. Leopolda) recognize the actual meaning of Christ's life—Christ's balancing trick on the cross (370). And *The Last Report on the Miracles at Little No Horse* brings into radical questioning traditional Catholic beliefs: original sin (sexual); that spiritual power is heightened through celibacy; that ritual must be officiated through male authority; that the Creator privileges men over women in dispensing forgiveness, and so forth. In *The Bingo Palace*, Lipsha gets "to wondering if the Son of Man had any mad-green love affairs. Unless He did, He could never understand us humans, I am sure" (154).

Often when Natives become Christians, they do so with the desire to modify Christianity, to correct what has been polluted. The notion of the Fall of man is just one of those pollutions—especially with regard to human nature and attitudes toward this earth. Native and Christian theologians Paul Schultz (Ojibwa) and George Tinker (Osage/Cherokee) suggest that Christianity is amiss with regard to human creation:

> Before the missionaries came, the Native Peoples had little theoretical sense of sin, no sense of fallen humanity, and no sense of basic inclination in every human being to do evil. To the contrary, the primary sense that our peoples had of themselves in those early days was not a sense of individual fallenness, but the sense of community belonging as a whole group who were in relationship to God as Creator, who together participated in and celebrated the balance and harmony of creation. God created harmony and balance. The people's response was to participate with the Creator in maintaining the harmony and balance of all things (58–59).

This does not mean that Native peoples do not acknowledge the existence of evil in the world. But sin is seen as any action that brings about "community imbalance and disharmony" (65).

Cherokee/Christian Diane Glancy's poetry and prose similarly explore what it means to be both Native and Christian. In *Claiming Breath* (1992), for example, Glancy calls: "Christ's wilderness experience . . . a vision quest" (95). As she investigates the similarities between Native and Christian beliefs, Hogan plays Trickster through language. Glancy calls writing "word-cloth over disembodied meaning" (8). One example of her Trickster "word-cloth" can be found in Glancy's prose/poem "A Hogan in Bethlehem." In this work, Glancy positions Christ's birth in Native American idioms and, therefore, on Native ground: "& so it was in a country across the water, she gave birth to a son & wrapped him in a buffalo robe. The raccoon & elk & deer gathered in the hogan-manger. & there were shepherds, or animal-watchers, in the field, & lo, an angel, a spirit-being with wings, a bird-person, appeared the way a coyote or tumbleweed crosses the headlights on a reservation road at night." In this text, the divine light attendant to Christ's birth becomes "the high-beam of Wakan Tanka, the Great Spirit." Angels tell shepherds not to fear because: "Unto *all people* this night is born a Chief who is Wovoka, Christ our Lord." Immediately following this announcement, the angelic chorus of scripture sings a "chant." "Meanwhile," writes Glancy, "3 scouts, 3 Medicine Men," make "their vision-quest under one star still burning like a yard-light on the prairie. As if the Great Spirit didn't want to leave the baby, or in case the baby wanted to migrate back from earth." These medicine men hurry "with their bundle-gifts to find a hogan in Bethlehem." They hurry "to find the Wovoka-child wrapped like a holy ear of corn" (93).

According to Theresa S. Smith, the cohesion between Native and Christian theologies in Glancy's poem participates in "the Indianization of Christianity." Glancy's work could also be called *syncretic*—a term closely associated with hybridity. In a multicultural society such as exists in the United States, religions often go through a reformation. Religions adapt to the needs of groups within specific cultural and geographic regions. Smith quotes George Tinker who contends that Native/Christian readings of the Gospels "represent a radical disjuncture from the theologies and histories of Western churches of Europe and America as we pay attention to our stories and memories instead of to theirs" (147).

A Cultural or Psycho-Social Approach to Place

In the preface to his collected short stories *Men on the Moon*, poet, short story writer, and Native activist Simon J. Ortiz (Acoma Pueblo) claims: "Story has its own power, and the language of story is of that power. We are within it, and we are that power. As human beings, we, as personal and social cultural entities, are conscious beings because of story, no other reason." However, Ortiz continues: "Cultural consciousness, whether personal and individual or social and collective, is determined by our awareness of the self within circumstance, experience, and event. Place and time and motion: something happening" (viii). To illustrate his conjecture, Ortiz says his "identity as a Native American is based on the knowledge of myself as a person from Acoma Pueblo, a cultural and geographical place, and this knowledge has its source in 'story'" (ix). Ortiz is the only full blood among the best known authors of Native literatures. Ortiz is the author of sixteen books of poetry and prose. He is a frequent contributor to scholarly journals; and his presence is sought at numerous conferences. Indeed, his work to both promote Native authors and advance Native rights is incommensurable. He is a beloved poet-shaman who has also suffered the ravages of alcohol.

Healing—Displacement

While Ortiz finds constancy in his identity with Acoma Pueblo, that constancy can be ruptured through *displacement*. Alcoholism creates a sense of dis-place-ment; it is a dis-ease that separates individuals from family, community, and a sense of a place in the world. "Not By Any Chance" is a poem by Ortiz about an alcoholic *residing* in a detox center (Hooper Memorial Center) in Portland, Oregon. The word "residing" is used in the preceding sentence instead of place. And yet the movement in this poem is from the difficulty of thinking "in the detox haze" (27) to the desire for Native ground. "In my life I've been barely alive once or / twice and I've been pretty damn close to my real last chance," writes Ortiz. "*The street outside is running with winey puke, sour sweat, bloody men and women. / I see this out the smudged window. I hear the mournful wail of a ghost hiding from the dense heart of the city. / And through the screened window drifts the smell of Indian woods and smoke*" (Ortiz's emphasis; 27–28).

Numerous characters in Native fiction suffer the ravages of alcoholism. Abel in *House Made of Dawn* is a stumbling drunk for much of the novel. Tayo and his war "buddies" in *Ceremony* are particularly disturbing in their dependence on drink. Silko asserts that many of the war veterans in *Ceremony* try to drink away their sense of dispossession—from themselves and from the land. "They tried to sink the loss in booze, and silence their grief with war stories about their courage, defending the land they had already lost" (169).

Characters in Sherman Alexie's *Reservation Blues* are disabled or emotionally crippled because of drunkenness. Victor Joseph and Junior Polatkin reside on the Spokane Reservation; but neither character can be at home there because of an intergenerational dependence on alcohol. "Victor had started to drink early in life, just after his real father moved to Phoenix, and he drank even harder after his stepfather moved into the house. Junior never drank until the night of his high school graduation. He'd sworn never to drink because of his parents' boozing" (57). Similarly, Thomas Builds-the-Fire, the leading character, "lost count of the number of times he'd saved his father, how many times he'd driven to some reservation tavern to pick up his dad, passed out in a back booth. Once a month, he bailed his father out of jail for drunk and disorderly behavior. That had become his father's Indian name: Drunk and Disorderly" (95). And Michael White Hawk, a minor character, suffers from Fetal Alcohol Syndrome. "Michael was conceived during some anonymous three-in-the-morning pow-wow encounter in South Dakota. His mother's drinking had done obvious damage to Michael in the womb," writes Alexie (39).

Junior ends up committing suicide. In a surreal life-after-death conversation, Victor asks Junior why he committed suicide. "Because when I closed my eyes like Thomas, I didn't see a damn thing. Nothing. Zilch. No stories, no songs. Nothing. . . . And,' Junior added, 'because I didn't want to be drunk no more'" (290). The fact remains that members of the Spokane tribe don't want Coyote Springs—their local rock band—to represent them at home or abroad. "First of all, they are drunks. Victor and Junior are such drunks that even Lester FallsApart thinks they drink too much" (175).

When Thomas and the two Flathead Indian women (in his now defunct band) leave the Spokane Indian Reservation at the end of

Reservation Blues, they are imitating one of the primary themes in mainstream American fiction: leaving home. William Bevis, in his essay "Native American Novels: Homing In," explains that many Native novels are not "'eccentric,' centrifugal, diverging, expanding, but 'incentric,' centripetal, converging, contracting. The hero comes home" (582). Bevis claims that this is not simply a "structuralist pattern." Many Native novels "suggest that 'identity,' for a Native American, is not a matter of finding 'one's self,' but of finding a 'self' that is transpersonal and includes a society, a past, and a place. To be separated from the transpersonal time and space is to lose identity." Furthermore, says Bevis, "These novels [*The Surounded* and *Wind From an Enemy Sky* by McNickle, *House Made of Dawn* by Momaday, *The Death of Jim Loney* and *Winter in the Blood* by Welch, *Ceremony* by Silko], are important, not only because they depict Indian individuals coming home while white individuals leave but also because they suggest—variously and subtly and by degrees— a tribal rather than an individual definition of 'being'" (585). Thomas's move from the reservation, therefore, can be read as a move toward urbanity and individualism.

This escape (albeit in death) from alcoholism, rage, and reservation life is poignantly dramatized in *Skins* (2002), a film adaptation of the novel *Skins* by poet and novelist Adrian C. Louis (Paiute). This film is a bold attempt to claim the humanity of those living in the grip of alcoholism. Filmed on the Pine Ridge Reservation (a place ghettoized by economic deprivation, alcoholism, and domestic violence), *Skins* chronicles the lives of two brothers—Rudy (a vigilante reservation policeman, played by Eric Schweig) and Mogie (an infamous reservation drunk, played by Graham Greene). Rudy, under the tutelage of Iktome (the Sioux Trickster), spends his nights trying ineffectually and violently to avenge the violence plaguing the reservation. One night, Rudy torches a local liquor store. Mogie happens to be on the roof, trying to break into the store for booze. Badly burned, Mogie is rushed to the local hospital. It is there that Rudy confesses his vigilante exploits to Mogie. Flashbacks to Rudy's and Mogie's troubled youth, scenes with Mogie's loving and accepting son, and references to historical violence against the Sioux contribute to a growing empathy for Mogie. Mogie, in this film, cannot simply be reduced to his disease. Nevertheless, Mogie's dependence on alcohol leads to cirrhosis of the liver and death. Before Mogie dies from this disease, however, Rudy recognizes his undiminished love for his brother. During the final scene of the film, after Rudy has defaced Mount Rushmore (with red paint) in honor of his dead brother, Rudy returns to the reservation only to see a young hitchhiker heading in the opposite direction. When the hitchhiker turns to wave, the audience recognizes Mogie as a youth. In death, Mogie has finally escaped the social poverty attendant to reservation life on Pine Ridge.

Ortiz also writes about the dis-place-ment one can feel professionally (also attended by alcohol). In "Seed," Ortiz writes about a forty-five-year-old poet who is teaching a graduate seminar on authors like Tennyson. In the midst of all the words he must teach, he decides "to give up poetry, / It was one o'clock in the afternoon. It was a Tuesday, and he stood in the middle of a corridor / trying to think of where to go, where he was to be. / Where? He wondered. Mighty big question, he decided" (24). In this poem, "seed" refers to the poet's capacity to see connections, "the seed he thought he carried with him all his life." And yet, the works of another author draw him to make connections between his own experience and somebody who said, "No one ever sees the river anymore" (25). For Ortiz, the duty or burden of the poet is to help others gain a sense of wonder, a sense of place—including rocks, trees, and rivers. Ortiz writes:

> He did not want to be a poet anymore.
> He did not want to be swayed by the lilt of a bird somewhere
> beyond his view as he reached his hand toward the current
> shifting everything away, and he did not want to know
> the seed that stood before his eyes as a tiny monument
> of new life, the beginning that would flower by his seeing
> (*Out There Somewhere* 26).

Identity oftentimes comes out of a given time, place, and cultural circumstance. Ortiz's characters in *Men on the Moon* each bespeak such awareness. Ortiz, through his writing, also gives vitality and meaning to obscure lives. The title narrative, "Men on the Moon," is the story of an old traditional, Faustin, who receives a TV on Father's Day from his daughter—just in time to watch the Apollo spaceship land on the moon. Between watching boxing matches, the moon landing, and his own dreams, Faustin becomes befuddled. His dreams are about the coming of corn to his people—a story facing back toward creation day. Within this context, "Faustin wondered if the men had run out of places to look for knowledge on the earth." He asks his grandson if the men on the moon brought something back. "They brought back some rocks," his grandson tells him. His grandson tells him that scientists want to know how everything began—they want "to learn more about the universe in which we live" (11). Faustin thinks his grandson is joking—an activity frequently engaged in by his grandchildren. The exchanges in this story are seemingly simple. And yet the search on the moon for the "tiniest bit of life" (14) is a fragile search for knowledge—a knowledge already revealed in the dreams of an old man. Why search the cosmos for the origins of life, when the earth's answers have yet to be exhausted?

Ortiz's characters are disarming: Eloise from "Home Country" who is offered a job at Keams Canyon at the Indian Boarding school; Kaiser, a simpleton who is sent to prison for not complying with the draft in "Kaiser and the War." (Kaiser is still imprisoned long after the war ends. He is finally released with just a suit of clothes to account for his long absence from home. He works the remainder of his life in that suit, asking those around him to return it to the U.S. government when he dies.) Or nine-year-old Jimmo in "Something's Going On" whose beloved father is accused of murder and flees to the mountains to forestall capture. Each character, although located in or around his/her home country, is caught in tensions between being or not being educated in Anglo systems, believing or not believing in Native ways, and being tugged between traditional and nontraditional economic and belief systems at particular moments in the history of the Southwest near the Acoma Pueblo.

Ortiz's story "To Change Life in a Good Way" is a particularly gentle story about two couples—Pete and Mary from the Acoma Pueblo and Ida and Bill from Oklahoma. Both husbands work for Kerr-McGee in New Mexico. They share family stories, travel together, and become friends. When Bill's brother Slick is killed in Vietnam, Pete gives him some Kasheshi—a dried ear of corn. "You can take it with you to Oklahoma or you can keep it here. You can plant it. It's to know that life will keep on, your life will keep on. Just like Slick will be planted again. He'll be like that, like a seed planted, like corn seed, the Indian corn," Bill explains. "You and Ida and Slick are not Indian, but it doesn't make any difference. It's for all of us, the kind of way, with corn and with this, Bill. You take these sticks and feathers and you put them somewhere you think you should, someplace important that you think might be good, maybe to change life in a good way, that you think Slick would be helping us with" (113).

Pete and Mary are the first Indians that Bill and Ida know. When they go home for Slick's funeral, the "folks" make sense of the loss of Slick through making a story—a false story. "Look at how much and what past folks had to put up with, living a hard life, fighting off Indians to build homes on new land so we can live the way we are right now. Advanced and saved from the Communist peril like the *Tulsa Tribune* said the other day, Sunday. That's what Slick died for, just like past folks." All this rhetoric bothers Bill. He knows that "the mine Slick stepped on was American, and that the fact he was in a dangerous place was because he was in an army that was American. And it wasn't the same thing as what they were saying about past folks fighting Indians for democracy, and it didn't seem right somehow" (115). Bill and Ida return to New Mexico. Bill believes in Pete's goodness. He knows the ear of corn was given to him and Ida to help them with their lives—"to maybe change things in a good way for a good life." Pete "couldn't figure it out. He'd grown up in Claremore all his life, Indians living all around him, folks and some schoolteachers said so, Cherokees in the Ozark hills, Creeks over to Muskogee" (113–114). But when Bill finally finds a place for the ear of corn, he admits "he didn't know exactly all the right Indian things to do anymore, but somehow I believe Indians are more righter than we've ever been led to believe" (115–116).

The Importance of Bloodlines (Ancestry and Posterity)—Mixed or Pure

A Mythic Approach to Bloodlines

"Coyote, do you understand the theory of relativity?" asks Peter Blue Cloud (Mohawk) in his poem "Relativity." "Yes, yes, I do. It's much easier that way. When I'm hungry / I just stop at anyone's place and get a meal. Yes, it's really good to / know that all creatures are related" (*Wounds Beneath the Flesh* 5). The pun on the meaning of the word "relativity" in Blue Cloud's poem is actually a significant assertion about the *relationship* between the laws that govern the physical universe and those that apply to relationships between family, clan, tribe, and the cosmos. The law of symmetry in physics asserts that physical laws remain the same through a transformation in time and place. Such ideas are often rendered into formulas that can be applied no matter where a practitioner resides. Kinship patterns in Native American communities are a testament to the idea that a natural harmony between peoples can be achieved if those peoples adhere to appropriate behaviors with regard to family matters—whether those systems are patriarchal or matriarchal.

Although mixedblood ancestry complicates matters, the yearning for intergenerational care remains. The possibility of such care is poignantly described at the end of Louise Erdrich's novel *Tales of Burning Love*:

> We are conjured voiceless out of nothing and must return to an unknowing state. What happens in between is an uncontrolled dance, and what we ask for in love is no more than a momentary chance to get the steps right, to move in harmony until the music stops (Erdrich's emphasis; 452).

Although many creation narratives would dispute the assertion that humans are "*conjured voiceless out of nothing*," certainly what "*happens in between*" is the stuff of great literature—the desire to "*get the steps right*" intimates the difficulty of human relationships, and the possibility of moving "*in harmony until the music stops*" is an apt description of the human desire for well-being. Getting the steps right, however, is not merely a happenstance.

Creation narratives often demonstrate why mortal experience is vexed with trouble. Gender anxiety, greed, envy, and lust are among the passions that distort the inherent harmony intended by the creators. Elaine Jahner, for example, tells us that the Lakota creation story "defines the purpose of life as a progression from unity, through existential encounters with the meaning of diversity, toward renewed experience of unity." Jahner explains that in Lakota mythology, "The physical universe flows from Inyan's need to exercise power, so Creation begins because the very nature of power requires relationship and sharing. The initial exercise of power reveals the contrast between materiality and spirituality and shows that power's mode of functioning is through reciprocity" (197). This pattern—creation, division, conflict, and recovery through reciprocity—can be found in numerous creation stories chronicling the lives of sacred families.

Sacred families have agency—members can choose chaos or harmony. However, fractured originary family relationships can also be healed through ritual reformation—the Sun Dance is just one example. Contemporary authors draw on sacred narratives and ritual to bring about family and tribal reformation. Such patterns can be found in James Welch's *Fools Crow*, in N. Scott Momaday's *The Way to Rainy Mountain* and *House Made of Dawn*, in Leslie Marmon Silko's *Ceremony* and Linda Hogan's *Solar Storms*, among others. In other words, the Creators often bless the lives of those on earth with ritual information that will help humans heal from ancestral wounds. The incursions of Euroamericans into family bloodlines, however, complicate family woundedness and require additional methods for healing.

A Psycho/Social Approach to Bloodlines

Janet Campbell Hale's (Coeur d'Alene) literary autoethnography *Bloodlines: Odyssey of a Native Daughter* (1993) is an exemplary model of the importance of bloodlines—ancestry and posterity (mixed or pure). On her father's side, Hale's ancestral name, Campbell, is derived from the Indian name Cole-man-née, which means "dust" (171). In this text, Hale articulates her "experiences growing up in a dysfunctional family." Her book, "is in part an effort to understand the pathology of the dysfunction, what made [her] family the way it was." Says Hale, "I examine my own life in part, but reach beyond what I personally know or could know . . . back along my bloodlines to imagine the people I came from in the context of their own lives and times" (xxii). Several tribal groups conjoin in Hale: Canadian Kootenay, Chippewa (on her mother's side), and Coeur d'Alene (on her father's side). Hale's mother was "Canadian and not a 'status Indian' (that is, an Indian recognized as

such by the government) because her father, to whom her mother
was legally married, was a white (in this case, Irish) man" (xvi).

Much of Hale's narrative reports the abusive relationship between Hale and her mother. Hale's life is full of instability. She is
the product of both her parents' second marriages; children from
her parents' first marriages were abandoned. Hale's father (whom
she loved) is an alcoholic and has a long history of binges and abusive encounters with Hale's mother. During her father's long alcoholic episodes, Hale and her mother disappear from the family
home—running from town to town and job to job, in order to survive. "I attended twenty-one schools in three states before I dropped
out of school after eighth grade," writes Hale. "No, I went a month
or two in tenth" (34).

Two narrative lines run through Hale's chapter "Daughter of
Winter"—the history of her own abusive childhood coupled with
the discovery of her mother's. Hale writes this chapter from the perspective of an older, educated, and successful woman. (Hale's novel
The Jailing of Cecelia Capture, for example, was nominated for a
Pulitzer.) During Hale's unimaginably difficult years as a university
student, Hale learns several theories that help her find causes for her
mother's behavior—profiles of depressed personalities and family
scapegoating are among them. Hale says of her mother:

> She'd never had a chance as a child. She'd had a loveless
> first marriage to a man who degraded her, who called her
> denigrating names . . . who would not allow music any-
> where near him. She'd abandoned two children in order to
> save her own life. She married for love and then became
> victim of her second husband, a battered woman (44).

Hale writes these things about her mother not to justify her
mother's abuse, but as a way of understanding how "dysfunction
gets passed down from one generation to the next" (xxxii). Hale also
marries abusive men. She likewise lives in poverty while attempting to raise children—this time as a single parent, and so forth. And
yet, *Bloodlines* is an important work about how Hale breaks the
cycle of abuse.

In 1987, Hale had a dream about a turtle. The dream takes on particular significance because Hale is a member of "the last family left of the Turtle clan." In her dream, she is

> *walking along the shore of a lake or a bay towards a house in the distance. I step on a small turtle I did not see lying among the rocks and think I've killed it. I am filled with grief. I leave it there and hurry away towards the house. I come back to that place on the shore later and see that the turtle is not only alive but is no longer the size of a small rock. It has grown to a hundred times its previous size. It's like a giant sea turtle and is very strong. I am filled with joy now. I watch as the great turtle walks into the water and swims away* (Hale's emphasis; xxxi).

Hale begins her book by asserting that she is one of the "broken-off pieces" of her family. And yet, in her chapter "The Only Good Indian," Hale outlines her investigations into her mixedblood genealogies. Hale's great-great-grandfather (on her mother's side), for example, was Dr. John McLoughlin—the founder of Oregon City (near Portland, Oregon—where there is a street named after him: McLoughlin Boulevard). Dr. McLoughlin was the head of the Hudson's Bay Company, the leader of the unofficial "government" in the early Northwest Territory. McLoughlin married a Chippewa woman named Margaret: "Doctor McLoughlin was not ashamed of her," Hale's mother had told her (114).

As Hale traces her Sullivan ancestors (her mother's genealogy), she notes that her "mother alone, of seven Sullivan children, married an Indian, went to live on a reservation, and had Indian kids" (115). The bloodlines are complex in this chapter—bits of history mingled with character sketches (fragments). And yet, discrimination against Native Americans can be taken as the subtext. Hale's history exemplifies why her mother (who could pass for White) tried to teach Hale (who was clearly Indian) to hate her Indianness. When she was six or seven, Hale remembers: "*I went home after school and filled a white enamel basin with water, then poured a cup of Purex bleach into it and soaked my hands. For a long time. As long as I could. My hateful brown hands. I hoped and prayed I could make them white. That I could make myself acceptable enough"* (Hale's emphasis; 140).

"Return to Bear Paw" and "Dust to Dust" are the final two chapters of the book. In "Return to Bear Paw," Hale records her visit to Bear Paw (Montana), the place where the Battle at the Bear Paw was fought between the Nez Percé (led by Chief Joseph) and the U.S. Calvary (led by General Howard). Although Hale's grandmother was Coeur d'Alene, she was among those who ran with Chief Joseph. Chief Joseph and his band eluded General Howard and the cavalry for several months. Joseph and his people simply wanted to escape into Canada so they would not have to be corralled onto reservations away from their Native lands. Just a few miles short of the Canadian border, General Howard overtook Chief Joseph.

"When the Battle at the Bear Paw ended, 419 Indians—88 men, 184 women and 147 children—lay dead on the frozen ground," Hale writes (158). Chief Joseph's surrender speech is one of the most famous examples of traditional Indian Oratory in existence:

Tell General Howard I know his heart. What he told me before I have in my heart. I am tired of fighting. Our chiefs are killed. Looking Glass is dead. Toolhoolzote is dead. The old men are all dead. It is cold and we have no blankets. The little children are freezing to death. My people, some of them, have run away to the hills and have no blankets, no food; no one knows where they are—perhaps freezing to death. I want to have time to look for my children and see how many of them I can find. Maybe I shall find them among the dead. Hear me, my chiefs! From where the sun now stands I will fight no more forever (Hale's emphasis;159).

More than a century later, Hale describes how she felt when she stood on the grounds of that battlefield in the dead of winter:

The cold reached my bones, yet I stood in the snow and felt myself being in that place, that sacred place. I saw how pitifully close lay the mountains of Canada. I felt the biting cold. I was with those people, was part of them. I felt the presence of my grandmother there as though two parts of her met each other that day: the ghost of the girl she was in 1877 (and the part of her will remain forever in that place) and the part of her that lives on in me, in inherited memories of her, in my blood and in my spirit (158).

In *Bloodlines*, Hale turns to the legacy of grandfathers and grandmothers to locate herself in time and space. True, she inherited dysfunction, but also the power to endure. She chooses to both belong and to adopt a healing attitude toward what that belonging means. In "Dust to Dust," Hale speaks of what she now has to pass on to her children—especially to her daughter. "I have so little to pass down to my daughter, it seems. *Just the stories,* the history, who we came from: we are of the Salish People, the Coeur d'Alene tribe, and this is our country. The first ancestor whose name we know was a man born in about 1820, and his name was Coelmannée, which translates as Dust" (emphasis added;186). Here, Janet Campbell (Colemannée) Hale downplays the power of her legacy from Dust (her ancestry) to Dust (her posterity).

Hale notes that it isn't "obvious that her daughter (whose father is of Anglo-Saxon descent) is Indian. But Indian blood shows itself, in her high cheekbones and straight, dark hair and in her dark, dark eyes that are so much like my own. My daughter can choose, as I never could, whether or not to be an Indian. She has always considered herself one." Hale tells us that her daughter "wants to work with disturbed children in either a Native American community or a community that includes Native American people" (186). The legacy is clear here—a legacy of several generations of people who have, in one way or another, survived unimaginable circumstances accompanied by the desire to help others do the same.

Other autoethnographies explore similar themes: Gerald Vizenor's *Interior Landscapes*, W. S. Penn's *All My Sins are Relatives* (Urban mixed-blood), Diane Glancy's *Claiming Breath* (Cherokee), and Louis Owens *I Hear the Train* (Choctaw) are among titles worthy of investigation and further study.

Placing Self within One's Ancestry and Posterity or Walking the Good Road

In *Black Elk Speaks*, Black Elk describes walking on the Good Road in his Great Vision. He declares that he could see behind him the "ghosts of people like a trailing fog as far as I could see—grandfathers of grandfathers and grandmothers of grandmothers without number." And before him, he could see his people, palms raised, looking "to the far sky yonder . . . and the sky ahead was filled with clouds of baby faces" (36). This image of the dead, the living, and the not-yet-born is that intergenerational connectedness that reverberates throughout Native fiction, poetry, and autoethnography in various guises. Carter Revard describes it in *Family Matters, Tribal Affairs*. Of particular relevance is Revard's poem "Dancing with Dinosaurs." The context of this poem is an Osage naming ceremony—a ceremony intended to bring "new children" into the cosmic circle:

> Now as we face the drum
> and dance, shaking the gourds, . . .
>   to honor on a sunbright day
> and in the moonbright night
>   the little girl being brought in,
>   becoming one of us,
>   as once was done for me,
>   for each of us who dance,
>   I have called them here
>   to set them into song
> who made their rainbow bodies long before
>   we came to earth,
>   *who learning song and flight became*
>   *beings for whom the infinite sky*
>   *and trackless ocean are a path to spring—*
> now they will sing, and we
>   are dancing with them, here (25).

In the naming of a child, the ancestors are called upon to attend —to participate in the ongoing cycle of life.

The Perpetuation of Powerful, Often Traditional, Gender Identities

Historically, gender studies are an offshoot of Feminism. As feminist critics have championed the rights, visibility, and contributions of over half the human population, they have written about how inequality has come about—often based on sacred texts (Old and

New Testaments, the Koran, and so forth). Feminists worth their salt have also realized that the supplanting of women has also meant damage to men. As a result, any healthy sense of futurity has also been threatened. Children, in gender-imbalanced societies, often suffer most; masses of children are being raised in single-parent homes relying on yearly salaries below the poverty line. Many Native scholars and artists assert that traditional mythic narratives are stories of how the gods struggled to find gender harmony. Many sacred narratives are cautionary in nature—exploring how this earth was created to exist in harmony out of the trials of their sacred progenitors. The loss of traditional life-ways have generated problems between Native men and women throughout North America.

A Mythic Approach

In explaining the meaning of the flowering tree (in the center of the sacred hoop of his vision), Black Elk says: "The woman is the life of the flowering tree, but the man must feed and care for it." Other gifts from the six grandfathers to Black Elk include a pipe (for peace), an herb (for healing), and an emblem of the sacred hoop (the power to integrate a nation). Black Elk explains that "all these powers together are woman's power" (210). Great appreciation for women is maintained throughout Black Elk's description of his sacred experiences. He says "for out of the woman the people grows" (209). The journey to the center is led by women, while men follow: "for the power of the man encircles and protects the power of the woman" (211). In Black Elk's vision of "the Other World," twelve men and twelve women instruct Black Elk about the power he is given to make his nation live (246).

In Navajo sandpaintings, male and female deities complement one another. The great *Night Chant* of the Navajo was given to them by Talking God to enable Navajo practitioners to restore beauty and harmony in the world. The *Night Chant* is performed for Estánatlehi (Changing Woman), who reestablished beauty and harmony in the world after gender strife had rendered the world sterile and inert. Abel learns the words to this ceremony in *House Made of Dawn*. Heavy Shield Woman in Welch's *Fools Crow* represents Feather Woman in the Sun Dance—a ceremony given to the Blackfoot by

Sun Chief to "restore their sick to health and cause the growing things and those that fed upon them to grow abundantly." Sun Chief also supplies an elkskin robe (once worn by Feather Woman) "to be worn by a virtuous medicine woman at the time of the ceremony" (112). Feather Woman's yearning to be rejoined with her husband will eventually bring about a restoration of the balance between heaven and earth.

Tayo, in Silko's *Ceremony*, is aided on his journey to health and well being by Ts'eh, an incarnation of a Keres goddess. "The terror of the dreaming he had done on his bed was gone, uprooted from his belly; and the woman had filled the hollow spaces with new dreams" (219). The love that Tayo feels for Ts'eh remains with him when she leaves him. But, she has left him with the knowledge that "He had lost nothing. . . . The mountain could not be lost to them, because it was in their bones; Josiah and Rocky [who are dead] were not far away. They were close; they had always been close. And he loved them then as he had always loved them, the feeling pulsing over him as strong as it had ever been" (219). Tayo's love for Ts'eh is not exclusive (isolating) but inclusive. From the love she gives to him, he realizes that Josiah and Rocky love him beyond death.

> They loved him that way; he could still feel the love they had for him. The damage that had been done had never reached this feeling. This feeling was their life, vitality locked deep in blood memory, and the people were strong, and the fifth world endured, and nothing was ever lost as long as the love remained (219–220).

Gender imbalance or harmony is the stuff of myth—it drives creation and renewal.

Gender Harmony and Kinship

In his hundredth year, Tom Johnson (Pomo) had this to say about gender and family life: "What is a man? A man is nothing. Without his family he is of less importance than that bug crossing the trail, of less importance than the sputum or exuviae. . . . A man must be with his family to amount to anything with us" (*Native Heritage* 7). Ella Deloria (Yankton Dakota) suggests:

All peoples who live communally must first find some way to get along together harmoniously and with a measure of decency and order. This is a universal problem. Each people, even the most primitive, has solved it in its own way. And that way, by whatever rules and controls it is achieved, is, for any people, the scheme of life that works. The Dakota people of the past found a way: it was through kinship (9).

Individualism—the stuff of democratic romances—exists counter to the above Native ideas about gender and kinship. Individualism coupled with patriarchy has led many in Western nations to view the experiences of men as generic—as representing humankind. In the *Encyclopedia of North American Indians*, Beatrice Medicine (Lakota) asserts that "Women have traditionally been the 'hidden' half in the voluminous ethnographic reporting on the native peoples of North America. The thrust of the reporting by early observers—traders, trappers, missionaries, and pioneering anthropologists—was decidedly male centered and therefore carries a deep androcentric bias." Furthermore, what was or has been reported about the lives of Native women in traditional communities has often been extreme. Women were either seen as "beasts of burden and as servants of their lazy husbands," or as Indian princesses: "squaws" or "maidens" (1).

To counteract the invisibility or misconceptions of Native women in American academia, Paula Gunn Allen wrote three works of critical acclaim: *The Sacred Hoop: Recovering the Feminine in American Indian Traditions* (1986), *Spider Woman's Granddaughters: Traditional Tales and Contemporary Writing by Native American Women* (1989), and *Grandmothers of Light: A Medicine Woman's Source Book* (1991). In her introduction to *Spider Woman's Granddaughters*, Gunn Allen says: "if in the public and private mind of America Indians as a group are invisible in America, then Indian women are nonexistent." What is more, most Natives "are ever aware that we are occupied peoples who have no military power on earth ready to liberate us (as the Allies liberated France, say, or Greece or Lebanon earlier in this century). Against that backdrop, ever aware of our situation, we tell the tales of love, death, separation, and continuance" (8).

Gunn Allen's poem "Dear World" is a metaphor for being a mixedblood woman—doubly removed from a healthy gender identity. And yet, the real consequence of this poem lies in the insight into what it means to a culture if the mothers are sick, invisible, or dying. In this poem, the mother has lupus—"a disease of self-attack." Here, lupus is also symbolic of the disintegrating consequences of being born Native. Gunn Allen writes: "A half-breed woman / can hardly do anything else / but attack herself. / There are historical reasons/ for this."

> I know you can't make peace
> being Indian and white.
> They cancel each other out.
> Leaving no one in the place.
> And somebody's gotta be there,
> to take care of the house,
> to provide the food.
> And that's gotta be the mother.
> But if she's gone to war.
> If she's beaten and robbed.
> If she's attacked by everyone.
> Conquered, occupied, destroyed
> by her own blood's diverse strains,
> its conflicting stains? (121–122)

Gunn Allen's poem "Womanwork" can be read as a complement to "Dear World." In "Womanwork," Gunn Allen asks that readers "celebrate" women's work: "webs and making / out of own flesh / earth / bowl and urn / to hold water / and ground corn / balanced on heads / and springs lifted / and rivers in our eyes." In other words, women create, out of their own flesh, much that lives and brings life. Women feed, give drink, and shape vessels that hold life-giving substances. Women even make new pots from "castaway," "broken / fragments" of "old pots." New pots made from fragments of old pots, "mixed with clay," are stronger, more enduring. For such nurturance and endurance, "thank Her" (2), writes Gunn Allen.

Poet, short story writer, and autoethnographer Luci Tapahonso (Navajo) also writes about the lives of Native women. Several of her works address the various experiences a woman has in loving a man, giving birth, raising children, and sharing life within a supportive kinship complex. In *Sáanii Dahataal: The Women Are Singing*,

Tapahanso describes a baby's birth in her poem, "Blue Horses Rush In." The female infant, Chamisa Bah, arrives attended by her father who is "stunned" because his daughter arrives "amid a herd of horses, / horses of different colors" from the four directions—a symbol of blessedness. "White horses from the west / where plants of golden chamisa shimmer in the moonlight." "Yellow horses enter from the east / bringing the scent of prairie grasses from the small hills outside. . . . Blue horses rush in, snorting from the desert in the south" from where her "grandmothers went to war long ago." And "Black horses came from the north, / They are the lush summers of Montana and still white winters of Idaho." This daughter will "grow strong like the horses of [her] birth" (1–2).

However, for Tapahonso, motherhood is four parts: sacrifice, deep love, endurance, and prayer. In "Starlore," included in *Blue Horses Rush In*, Tapahonso explains the anguish of parenting:

> No one could have told me that growing older could be this way: that children would turn on parents and disappear into gritty border towns, or run the abandoned downtown streets of Denver or Phoenix; that families could split into hardened circles over one sentence uttered in anger; that sons and daughters would leave with friends for Europe or New York; that they would leave for boot camp, or a college where they are one of five Indian students, and that parents would not know all they endured. Yet through these instances and many more, we address our fears in ways that have never changed (15).

In the next paragraph, separated by white space, Tapahonso describes one particular response of parents who suffer similar anxieties. They gather, on a June night, "and leave in a caravan of nine cars, a string of headlights across the flat desert to the home of the man who will listen and help us. It is almost midnight when we park outside his hooghan [sic], the round ceremonial house." These parents enter in a clockwise pattern and sit on the cold ground. (A hogan recreates the cosmos.) They converse while they await the coming of "the one who knows the precise songs, the long, rhythmic prayers that will restore the world for us." In this sketch, Tapahonso writes in prose and poetry—altering voices and content with the use of different fonts. This ceremonial behavior places the parents in a good relationship with their surroundings: in the four sacred directions plus the earth and sky. And the narrator feels attended to: *"Because of this, I understand that I am valued. / Because of the years I have lived, I am valued. / Yes, I am pitied by the huge sky, / the bright moon, and glittering stars. / We consist of long, breathless songs of healing. / We are made of prayers that have no end"* (Tapahonso's emphasis; 15–16).

In another piece, "White Bead Girl," Tapahonso writes of a mother whose daughter, Sonny, runs away from home—without cause, without warning, without a clue as to where she might have gone. The police are called in. The search is fierce and painful. As the time passes, the mother remembers all the spiritual training her daughter has received throughout her life. For example, when her daughter was going on a trip with a group from school, her parents "arranged to have a Hózhóójí, a blessing ceremony, for her." The medicine man conducted the ceremony in both English and Navajo, explaining to Sonny how such ceremonies began. "This is how the holy people know us," he said, "by the songs and prayers they gave us. They'll say, 'Look, there is a Navajo away from her people. We can tell that person is a Navajo.'" Then he "showed her sacred stones and ears of corn." He explained that these items represent "Changing Woman. This represents you. It shows us that young girls like yourself are strong because you're Navajo." He handed the girl a basket "and instructed her to lift it four times—to the east, to the south, to the west, and to the north." When the day-long ceremony ended, Sonny "carried pollen to everyone in the room so that they could offer their prayers as well." This ceremony endowed the girl with "the blessings and strength of the holy people." All in attendance were likewise strengthened (69–70).

The mother reviews her daughter's life many times over as she waits for any word. When Sonny returns home, sad-faced and disheveled, her mother hopes that she has remembered her sacred promises. "I look at the moon and cry," says the mother, "out of gratitude, relief, and fear. This night I offer prayers for the pain a family endures, I offer prayers for the strength that springs from unknown places, and finely, I pray for the future that, at this moment, in the pure glow of the moon, shines on all of us like nothing I've ever seen" (71).

Many Native women authors address a wide range of female experiences—from rape and incest and other violence against women to the vision that is offered them of the sacred feminine. Tapahonso, for example, says that because of Changing Woman, Navajo women "think and create," "make songs," receive the designs that they weave, "tell stories and laugh," and "believe in old values and new ideas" (*Blue Horses Rush In* 39).

While Leslie Marmon Silko also addresses the sacred feminine in her works, many of her short stories report the darker experiences Native women share. Silko's autoethnography *Storyteller* contains several of her short stories. The story "Lullaby" is among them. Certainly the title is ironic. Ayah, the central character, loses her son Jimmie during a war. "A man in a khaki uniform trimmed in gold gave them a yellow piece of paper and told them that Jimmie was dead" (44). Because Ayah doesn't speak English, she must depend on her husband Chato to translate for her—to translate between her traditional world and the encroaching Anglo society. Chato works for a White rancher; when Chato breaks his leg on the job, the White rancher tells him he won't be paid until he can work again. Family problems abound—illness, poverty, and isolation. One day, when her husband is away, social workers come and take Ayah's other children, Danny and Ella. They have contracted T.B. from their grandmother and are taken away to a Denver hospital. Because Ayah can't read English, she signs her name to some government forms, unknowingly consenting to her children's removal. "It was worse than if they had died: to lose the children and to know that somewhere, in a place called Colorado, in a place full of sick and dying strangers, her children were without her" (47). Danny and Ella never return home for more than a few awkward visits. Despite the fact that Chato has been a loyal worker for his boss most of his adult life, he is quickly forgotten when he can no longer work. He turns to alcohol. In a blinding snow storm, Ayah attempts to take her husband home from the bar in which he numbs his life away. The story ends with Ayah singing a lullaby to her drunk husband as he stumbles and falls down, to sleep in the freezing snow.

Sexual Expression Used to Pervert (as a Metaphor for Cultural Degradation) or to Enhance Human Relatedness

Silko's short story "Storyteller" is far more grizzly in approaching what Native women endure in difficult circumstances. In this story, sexual intercourse is anything but a connection between two loving adults. The story takes place in Alaska—on the frozen tundra where White men, the Gussucks, have come to drill for oil. The central character is known only as "she." She is an Indian girl whose parents were killed by a local merchant who sold them alcohol not intended for human consumption. "She" lives with her grandmother and a licentious old man. The old man molests "she" on a continual basis. But he also tells her a story about a bear and a hunter that takes most of his remaining years to unfold. As the story expands, "she" comes to see how the bear outsmarts the hunter. And so, "she" plots revenge for her parent's death. She boldly goes to the store where the local merchant clearly intends that no Indians enter. But because "she" befriends a paying customer (a redheaded rigger), the merchant lets her stay. "She" has sex with the Gussuck. (This behavior is typical of abused young women; they use their bodies wantonly.) She knows the tundra fully—where the ice is thin beneath new snow. When the store keeper chases after her in a lustful frenzy, she leads him to a place where he falls through and freezes to death. Witnesses call it an accident; but "she" calls it murder. Her attorney clears her of all charges. He claims that she is "confused." In actuality, the bear has turned on human predators.

Silko's *Almanac of the Dead* is clearly a treatise on perverse sexuality as a metaphor for cultural degradation. The setting of the novel is far-reaching—to the four quarters of the continent; and yet the hub of activity is Tucson, Arizona. In the front piece, Silko says that Tucson, Arizona is "Home to an assortment of speculators, confidence men, embezzlers, lawyers, judges, police and other criminals, as well as addicts and pushers, since the 1880s and the Apache wars." The novel is ostensibly about ancient Native American prophecies—Mayan, Aztecan, Incan—that foretell the coming of Europeans to the Americas as well as the ultimate purging of European influence from this continent. Materialism, drug trafficking, sexual avarice, disrespect for the earth, and a failure of belief characterize the underbelly of American culture. At root of the problem is land theft, identity theft, and the subjugation of brown/black-skinned peoples. And the earth responds to such pollution. Silko writes, "The time had come when people were beginning to sense impending disaster and to see signs all around them— great upheavals of the earth that cracked open mountains and crushed man-made walls. Great winds would flatten houses, and floods driven by great winds would drown thousands. All man's computers and 'high technology' could do nothing in the face of the earth's power" (422–425).

Several assertions drive this novel. "Illness, dope, and hunger" are "the white man's allies." If those in control can keep minority groups doped up, then they will be prevented from rising up against oppressors. In a liberation address supposedly delivered by Clinton (to the music of Bob Marley, Jimmy Cliff, and Aretha Franklin), several warnings are established at the heart of this novel. There are thirteen items all together; but the first three are especially relevant to this thesis:

1. Slavery is any continuing relationship between people and systems that results in human degradation and human suffering.

2. Women and children are the most frequently enslaved because slavery relies on violence and systematic terrorism to maintain control.

3. Terrorism takes many forms, but most often the violence is sexual, to convince victims suffering is part of their very identity, as unchangeable as their sex or skin color (427).

Numerous characters, plots, and events inhabit this 763-page novel. The intricate webs of relationships therein have garnered lengthy critical analyses.

One caution adheres, however: this novel is not a Native versus Anglo text. Writes Silko: "The so-called conquerors merely aligned themselves with forces already in power or forces already gathered to strip power from rivals. The tribes in Mexico had been drifting toward political disaster for hundreds of years before the Europeans had ever appeared" (220). Silko suggests that prophecies also included pollutions among Native nations. "Hundreds of years earlier, the people who hated sorcery and bloodshed had fled north to escape the cataclysm prophesied when the 'blood worshipers' of Europe met the 'blood worshipers' of the Americas. Montezuma and Cortéz had been meant for one another" (570). And yet, over the past five hundred years, Anglos have been the major perpetrators. Silko has done her research; and that research informs every page. And yet what is abundantly clear in this work is that addictions—to alcohol, drugs, sex, wealth, technology—become impossible to satiate. And sexual violence delineates each addiction. Note the sexual images in the following quote, for example: "Ferro says the needle slips in like a lover's prick and shoots the dope in white and hot. That's why Lecha wants them all to watch her get off, Ferro says, but *he* doesn't watch junky orgasms not even for his *own* mother" (20). What Silko so graphically explains in this novel is that the self-gratifying nature of addictive behavior separates family members, social units, and humans from the natural world. When such behavior is orchestrated by sophisticated gangsters, global suffering ensues.

Healthy sexual relations—coupling—seems to be central to Native stability in numerous texts. For example, Belle and Moses Graycloud, and their home, are the constant center in Hogan's *Mean Spirit*. Locke Setman, in Momaday's *Ancient Child*, finds "endless wonder" in his relationship with his wife, Grey. "The greatest thing about it was that it had no definition; it was boundless. He had been moderate in his life, he believed, but in his love he could not be so. He could not account for his years. They were catalogs of loneliness, hurt, acquisition, and accomplishment, but they were not real as compared to this reality" (303). Most of Erdrich's novels chronicle the fumbling attempts of characters trying to find a kind of healing intimacy that will steady them against the contingencies of human existence. Louis Owens's novels are full of violent, failed, or hallowed relationships. The violent crimes in *Bone Game* are sexual. The madness in *The Sharpest Sight* is sex-linked. Will, in *Nightland*, almost loses his life through the entrapment of a sophisticated drug queen. What Will longs for in this novel is reconcilia-

tion with his estranged wife. And he manages to begin such reconciliation as the novel ends. Limitless examples could be given but
with two disclaimers: first, coupled love is inclusive—of siblings,
parents, grandparents, uncles, aunts, and cousins along multiple
bloodlines and among clan and tribal complexities. And second,
Victorian or Puritan notions of human sexuality aren't applicable to
traditional Native ideas of human intimacy. Homosexuality is also
not seen as aberrant among numerous tribes.

Linda Hogan has several poems which celebrate coupled love.
"Two" is especially applicable to this discussion:

> The weight of a man on a woman
> is like falling into the river without drowning.
> Above, the world is burning and fighting.
> Lost worlds flow through others.
> But down here beneath water's skin,
> river floor, sand, everything
> is floating, rocking.
> Water falls through our hands as we fall through it.
> And when a woman and a man come up from water
> they stand at the elemental edge of difference.
> Mirrored on water's skin,
> they are fired clay, water evaporating into air.
> They are where water turns away from land
> and goes back to enter a larger sea.
> A man and a woman are like those rivers,
> entering a larger sea
> greater than the sum of all its parts (*The Book of
> Medicines* 75).

The lines of this poem are in couplets. The last line, however, is singular: it unifies the coupling with an oceanic experience: large and
inclusive, "greater than the sum of all its parts."

In "Other, Sister, Twin," Hogan speaks of childbirth in an ever-
inclusive manner. The first two lines are: "She began with two lovers
/ on the swept floor of earth." These lines are followed by a single
sentence: "She was what passed between them." A birthing image
follows: "She was a gourd too heavy for the vine / and full of her
own wet seed." This line is an allusion to the biological fact that a
female child is born with all the eggs she will carry—eggs that will,

through similar coupling, produce children and grandchildren. Attending this birth is the grandmother who "kept the red bag / that held her stem / so she would not forget / the other women she lived inside / before this ruined time."

"Other, Sister, Twin," expands to include much of the ongoing creative universe—including the ceremonial world:

> Above is the betrayed world
> where our children are the children of strangers
> along the lost road
> in the land where barns are red
> because they are painted with the blood and milk
> of mothers
> of what they hold.
> The closed bundles of healing
> are beginning to open (83).

Hogan explains that "The first stem is growing like a vine. / It holds the cure / where you can reach through time / and find the bare earth / within your living hand." Each new birth is the possibility of healing or reconnecting with the elemental earth that is constantly re-producing. Hogan says, "I say her name. / It is earth calling land, / Mother" (84).

The Possibility of Healing Through Reconciliation

Author of more than ten books of poetry, Wendy Rose (Hopi, Miwok/Anglo) vents, "I hate it when other people write about my alienation and anger. Even if it's true, I'm not proud of it. It has crippled me, made me sick, made me out of balance. It has also been the source of my poetry" (253). In her youth, Rose was thrown away by her parents. "More than respect, I have needed to be claimed by someone as their own, someone who is wanted," writes Rose (253–254).

In her brief autobiographical sketch, "Neon Scars," Rose has a one-word paragraph that reads: "Healing" (255). As this study testifies, the wounds suffered by Native peoples over the past centuries have indeed been grievous. Rage, hatred, self-defeating behavior, despair, loneliness, degradation, betrayal, and humiliation are words that come to mind. Rose, notwithstanding, has used her alienation and anger to creative ends, as have numerous other Native authors. However, alienation and rage frequently revisit her. And yet, as the one-word paragraph belies, *healing* can be read as noun, verb, or adjective. Rose writes about healing; she is healing from her wounds; she is going through the healing process.

In her autobiographical sketch, "Ordinary Spirit," Joy Harjo (Muskogee/Creek) writes "I walk in and out of many worlds. I used to see being born of this mixed-blood/mixed-vision a curse, and hated myself for it. It was too confusing and destructive when I saw the world through that focus." However, Harjo says, "I have since decided that being familiar with more than one world, more than one vision, is a blessing, and know that I make my own choices." What is more, Harjo recognizes "that it is only an illusion that any of the worlds are separate" (266). Indeed, a human being inherits mixed identities but is one being—with both red and white blood cells. Harjo's poem "Transformations" is about the process of changing hatred into love. The poem begins: "This poem is a letter to tell you that I / have smelled the hatred you have tried / to find me with; you would like to destroy me." Harjo discusses the many forms memory takes—creative or destructive. She says her "poem could be a bear treading the far northern / tundra, smelling the air for sweet alive meat. Or a piece / of seaweed stumbling in the sea." But what she really means through her images "is that hatred can be turned into something / else, if you have the right words, the right meanings / buried in that tender place in your heart where / the most precious animals live" ("Ordinary Spirit" 266).

As "Transformations" unfolds, the poet notices that "Down the street / an ambulance has come to rescue an old man who is slowly / losing his life. Not many can see that he is already / becoming the backyard tree he has tendered for years." This man, however, "is not sad, but compassionate / for the fears moving around him." And this Creek/Muskogee poet takes this moment of the old man's dying to say:

> That's what I mean to tell you. On the other side
> of the place you live stands a dark woman.
> She has been trying to talk to you for years.

You have called the same name in the middle of a
nightmare,
from the center of miracles. She is beautiful.
This is your hatred back. She loves you (268–269).

Harjo says that "Transformations" is about "the process of the 'hater'
becoming one who is loved, and who ultimately loves. The 'I' is also
involved in the process" (269). In other words, both parties suffer a
transformation of being toward the other; there is reciprocity.

How is such healing possible? Certainly many Indian authors
write about the healing nature of tribal ritual. They also extol intergenerational connections, a healthy respect for the earth and her
creatures, and Indian sovereignty. However, with so many mixedblood Natives, how can the Anglo part of their genetic inheritance
be ignored? Furthermore, there are many good and worthy Euroamericans whose roots run deep into their adopted environments.
Is there a reconciliation, like the one described in "Transformations,"
possible in a such a complex multi-cultural society such as the
United States?

Harjo suggests that some rethinking needs to take place. This is
especially true about the divisions felt between urban and reservation Indians. Sherman Alexie's *Indian Killer* (1996) is a dismal
assessment of the impact of urban life on American Indians. *Grand
Avenue* (1994) and *Watermelon Nights* (1998) by Greg Sarris
(Miwok/Pomo), on the other hand, clearly show that community
life can be painstakingly developed among urban Indians. Sarris's
life story is a testament to the possibility of healing and his works
reveal his insights. Sarris is an adopted son. His birth mother
(Jewish/Irish) died during Sarris's birth. His biological father
(Miwok/Pomo/Filipino) left Sarris and became a drunk who finally
killed himself. Sarris was adopted by Mary and George Sarris (also
an alcoholic) after his birth, but lived a rather ragged life until he
met Mabel McKay, a Pomo elder who taught Sarris the traditions of
his people.

One biography of Sarris succinctly outlines Sarris's rise to prominence: "from a childhood that was spent roaming from household
to household, running with gangs, and held back by poverty, Sarris
has overcome challenges to become a noted scholar at the University of California, Los Angeles (UCLA), as well as an award-

winning author." Sarris is successful on two fronts: as an urban academic and reservation Indian. Indeed, in California, the borders and boundaries between such spaces is often obscured. "Sarris's political activities include having been elected as chairman, or chief, of the Federated Coast Miwok Tribes, an office he held for three straight terms" (6–7). Nearly three thousand California Indians claim Miwok ancestry. Sarris has been actively engaged in gaining political recognition for his people as an Indian nation. A conflict arises here—in praise of Sarris's private and professional life. Is it fair to collapse the boundaries between private and public life— between the life of Sarris as an example for other Native youth and his excellence as a scholar, novelist, critic, and short story writer? So many dualities are being reconfigured in contemporary Native literatures: between writer and text; men and women, individualism and community, tradition and progress, urban and reservation life and so forth.

David Hollinger, in *Postethnic America: Beyond Multiculturalism*, submits that indigenous people are continually becoming more fluent in cosmopolitan affairs. They are "rooted cosmopolitans," Hollinger claims (5). This oxymoron—a cosmopolitan with roots— is played out in Gerald Vizenor's *Dead Voices*. Vizenor offers a comic, mind-liberating, perspective on *perspective* in *Dead Voices*: "We heard the voices of creation at the airport, the stories that transformed the waste and garbage into dinner. We saw the end, the dead voices in the headlines, and we heard the origin stories of animals and birds in the cities" (138). *Dead Voices* is about living with a Native consciousness in cities. This collection of stories is a wild romp through the city as a player of the *wanaki* game. Wanaki (a game given to Nanabozho in the time of the beginnings) means "to live somewhere in peace, a chance at peace" (17). The wanaki game is a "war with loneliness and with human separations from the natural world" (29). For seven days, a player draws a card each day and lives that day as though he/she were living in the city as a bear, beaver, squirrel, crow, flea, praying mantis, or Trickster (28)—some traditional clan names, some comic inventions. This is a particularly difficult game to play in a "chemical civilization."

Vizenor's *Dead Voices* is a complex Postmodern treatise. But perhaps one example of his humorous treatment of the paradigms being brought into question will entice readers to want to read more. Vizenor's story "Tricksters" plays with the ironies of the evolutionary model of human development. Split Thumbs, for example, "created his own stories in the city. He was a crossblood elder from the reservation who came to town as a refrigerator repairman and founded the Harmless Abusement and Appliance Bondage Center." Split Thumbs's advertising slogan is: "Machines are no friend of man, woman, or beast, and sometimes they want to rule our worlds." Certainly any audience realizes that "petulant machines and rude appliances, toasters that burn the toast, automobiles that hesitate in traffic, automatic washers that overflow and spread soap on the floor, refrigerators that freeze the milk, hazy television sets, and automatic coffee makers that start in the middle of the night can be disciplined and trained to mind their owner." Split Thumbs's advice on abusement, to would-be clients, is "Remember, learn to abuse your machines and not your families, take charge of the machines, dominate machines." To force machines to obey, Split Thumbs advises trashing disobedient machines, like toasters, and buying new ones (127–130).

What comes from this comic diatribe is the hope that readers will become conscious of the control that technology exerts over most of our lives. Technology has overwhelmed our access to the natural world, to community with others, and to our own potential. If the thumb is that appendage that enables us to use tools, then it is also the cause of our split consciousness—our separation from our selves. We have become dependent on the extensions of our bodies: the ear (telephones, radios), the eye (telescopes, microscopes, televisions, computers), our legs and feet (cars, buses, trains, elevators), and our hands (all kinds of machines that do work for us like toasters, washing machines, and the like). Our hands typically work to sustain our lives and to extend care to others. Split Thumbs? We also tend to measure our success by the number of machines we have or can afford rather than on our capacity to relate. What is more, we spend more time "inside" buildings, protected from the environment, than we do outside. In actuality we are "outside" of the world. And certainly we are seldom aware of the amount of waste that is produced in our advanced "civilized" state. Vizenor's game is a way of rethinking such issues within an urban setting. And yet, if the game is played wisely, there is a chance of peace.

In *The Woman Who Fell From the Sky*, Harjo includes her poem, "RECONCILIATION: A Prayer," written for the Audre Lorde Memorial in 1993. This poem addresses many of the themes in this chapter on *themes*. This poem is a fitting conclusion to a section on reconciliation, or for the entire chapter for that matter. Written in four sections (perhaps to reflect the four cardinal directions), Harjo attempts her ceremonial prayer of healing:

I.
We gather at the shore of all knowledge as peoples who were put here by a god who wanted relatives.

This god was lonely for touch, and imagined herself as a woman, with children to suckle, to sing with—to continue the web of the terrifyingly beautiful cosmos of her womb.

This god became a father who wished for others to walk beside him in the belly of creation.

This god laughed and cried with us as a sister at the sweet tragedy of our predicament—foolish humans—

Or built a fire, as our brother to keep us warm.

This god who grew to love us became our lover, sharing tables of food enough for everyone in this whole world.

II.
Oh sun, moon, stars, our other relatives peering at us from the inside of god's house walk with us as we climb into the next century naked but for the stories we have of each other. Keep us from giving up in this land of nightmares which is also the land of miracles.

We sing our song which we've been promised has no beginning or end.

III.
All acts of kindness are lights in the war for justice.

IV.

We gather up these strands broken from the web of life. They shiver with our love, as we call them the names of our relatives and carry them to our home made of the four directions and sing:

Of the south, where we feasted and were given new clothes.

Of the west, where we gave up the best of us to the stars as food for the battle.

Of the north, where we cried because we were forsaken by our dreams.

Of the east because returned to us is the spirit of all that we love (i).

Certainly, Harjo's poem tells a story that positions the reader within the complex web of life—with attention to an equitable reconciliation between myth, kinship, gender, and place.

Works Cited

Alexie, Sherman, *Reservation Blues* (New York: Time Warner, 1996).

———, *The Toughest Indian in the World* (New York: Grove Press, 2000).

———, *Ten Little Indians* (New York: Grove Press, 2003).

Allen, Paula Gunn, "Womanwork," in *Wounds Beneath the Flesh*, Maurice Kenny, ed. (Fredonia, New York: White Pine, 1987).

———, "Dear World," in *Harper's Anthology of 20th Century Native American Poetry*, Duane Niatum, ed. (New York: HarperSanFrancisco, 1988).

———, *Grandmothers of Light*, (Boston: Beacon Press, 1991).

Bevis, William, "Native American Novels: Homing In," in *Recovering the Word*, Brian Swann and Arnold Krupat, eds. (Berkeley: University of California Press, 1987).

Blue Cloud, Peter, "Relativity," in *Wounds Beneath the Flesh* (Fredonia, New York: White Pine, 1987).

Brown, Russell, "Theme," in *Encyclopedia of Contemporary Literary Theory*, Irena R. Makaryk, ed. (Toronto: University of Toronto Press, 1993) 642–646.

Bruchac, Joseph, *Native American Stories Told by Joseph Bruchac* (Golden, CO: Fulcrum, 1991).

———, *Between Earth & Sky* (New York: Voyager Books, 1996).

Deloria, Ella, "Kinship was the All-important Matter," *Native Heritage*, Arlene Hirschfelder, ed. (New York: Macmillan, 1995).

Deloria Jr., Vine, *God is Red* (Golden, CO: Fulcrum Publishing, 1994).

Erdrich, Louise, *Tracks* (New York: Harper and Row, 1988).

———, *Bingo Palace* (New York: HarperCollins, 1994).

———, *Tales of Burning Love* (New York: HarperCollins, 1996).

Glancy, Diane, *Claiming Breath* (Lincoln: University of Nebraska Press, 1992).

"Greg Sarris," excerpts from *Contemporary Authors Online* (The Gale Group, 2000) http://www.embusa.es/irc/gregsarris (accessed April 5, 2004).

Hale, Janet Campbell, *Bloodlines* (New York: HarperPerennial, 1993).

Harjo, Joy, "Ordinary Spirit," in *I Tell You Now*, Brian Swann and Arnold Krupat, eds. (Lincoln: University of Nebraska Press, 1987).

———, *The Woman Who Fell From the Sky* (New York: Norton, 1994).

Hogan, Linda, "To Light," in *Harper's Anthology of 20th Century Native American Poetry*, Duane Niatum, ed. (New York: HarperSanFrancisco, 1988).

———, *The Book of Medicines* (Minneapolis: Coffee House Press, 1993).

———, *Solar Storms* (New York: Simon & Schuster, 1995).

Jahner, Elaine, "The Spiritual Landscape," in *I Become Part of It*, D. M. Dooling and Paul Jordan-Smith, eds. (New York: Parabola, 1989).

Johnson, Tom, "Without the Family We are Nothing," in *Native Heritage*, Arlene Hirschfelder, ed. (New York: Macmillan, 1995).

Medicine, Beatrice, "Women," in *Encyclopedia of North American Indians* (Houghton Mifflin) http://college.hmco.com/history/readerscomp/naind/html/na_043400_women.htm (accessed March 26, 2004).

Momaday, N. Scott, "The Man Made of Words," in *Religion and the Humanizing of Man*, James M. Robinson, ed. (Waterloo, Ontario: Riverside Color, 1973).

———, "The Man Made of Words," in *Literature of the American Indians: Views and Interpretations*, Abraham Chapman, ed. (New York: New American Library, 1975).

———, *Names* (Tucson: University of Arizona Press, 1976).

———, *Ancient Child* (New York: Harper Perennial, 1989).

———, "Forward," in *Native American Stories Told by Joseph Bruchac* (Golden, CO: Fulcrum, 1991).

———, *The Man Made of Words* (New York: St. Martin's Griffin, 1997).

N. Scott Momaday (Princeton, NJ: Films for the Sciences and Humanities; 1995), video.

Neihardt, John G., *Black Elk Speaks* (Lincoln: University of Nebraska Press, 1988).

Ortiz, Simon J., *Sand Creek* (Tucson: University of Arizona Press, 1981).

————, *Men on the Moon: Collected Short Stories* (Tucson: University of Arizona Press, 1999).

————, *Out There Somewhere* (Tucson: University of Arizona Press, 2002).

Revard, Carter, *Family Matters, Tribal Affairs* (Tucson: University of Arizona Press, 1998).

————, *Winning the Dust Bowl* (Tucson: University of Arizona Press, 2001).

————, "Some Notes on Native American Literature," *SAIL* 15:1 (Spring 2003) 1–15.

Rose, Wendy, "Neon Scars," in *I Tell You Now*, Brian Swann and Arnold Krupat, eds. (Lincoln: University of Nebraska Press, 1987).

Schultz, Paul and George Tinker, "Rivers of Life: Native Spirituality for Native Churches," in *Native and Christian*, James Treat, ed. (New York: Routledge, 1996).

Silko, Leslie Marmon, *Ceremony* (New York: Penguin, 1977).

————, *Storyteller* (New York: Seaver, 1981).

————, *Almanac of the Dead* (New York: Simon & Schuster, 1991).

Smith, Teresa, "The Church of the Immaculate Conception: Inculturation and Identity among the Anishnaabeg of Manitoulin Island," in *Native American Spirituality*, Lee Irwin, ed. (Lincoln: University of Nebraska Press, 2000).

Swann, Brian, "Introduction," in *Coming to Light*, Brian Swann, ed. (New York: Random House, 1994).

Tapahonso, Luci, *Sáani Dahataal: The Women Are Singing* (Tucson: University of Arizona Press, 1993).

————, *Blue Horses Rush In* (Tucson: University of Arizona Press, 1998).

Vickers, Scott B., *Native American Identities: From Stereotype to Archetype in Art and Literature* (Albuquerque: University of New Mexico Press, 1998).

Vizenor, Gerald, *Heirs of Columbus* (Hanover, NH: Wesleyan University Press, 1991).

————, *Dead Voices* (Norman: University of Oklahoma Press, 1992).

Welch, James, *Fools Crow* (New York: Penguin, 1986).

Chapter Six

Key Questions

Two questions direct the discussion in this chapter: What are the *key* critical and cultural questions generated by reading Native American Literatures? And, what questions might broaden the discussion of Native American literatures and point the way toward further study? Six interrelated questions will be posed. The questions raised in this chapter are difficult; they emerge from the moral reasoning of scholars and students who study Native American Literatures within the United States.

What Is the Relationship between Democracy, Native Literatures, and Ethics?

In *Other Destinies* (1992), Louis Owens writes that many Native American authors are "redefining American Indian identity, and they are doing so in the face of often stunning ignorance of American Indian cultures on the part of the rest of the world" (7). Overcoming this "stunning ignorance of American Indian cultures" is not merely of matter of reconfiguring the American Literary Canon. Nor is it necessarily a matter of exploring what constitutes Native American identity in a "post-Indian" era, though both of these issues continue to generate conversations in the field of Native American studies.

The "stunning ignorance" that Owens describes is an ignorance of the violent foundations of the democratic experiment in the United States. Not only are the foundations of the American experience flawed, but the ongoing tragic lives of a vast majority of Native peoples speak to the unresolved identity crises indigenous peoples continue to suffer in the United States. Surmounting this "ignorance" will require more focused explorations into the relationships between politics, aesthetics, and ethics. What is being called for in such an interdisciplinary inquiry is a paradigm shift (a rethinking of the basic tenets of belief). Consider, for example, the implications of the following statement: "The emergence of the indigenous voice in academia in the last several decades has been recognized as a huge breakthrough for the right to speak for oneself and one's people. It is thought by some to be [as] fundamental to the human condition as food and decent housing, an acknowledgment that men and women do not live by bread alone; they live by the creative arts, by storytelling and the intellect, all of which give vibrancy to culture and politics" (Cook-Lynn 197). A study of Native literatures is singular and crucial in understanding the creation and sharing of literatures as a basic human right.

Where Are We Now?

Strides have been made by national presses to advance public knowledge of Native cultures and texts. For example, *The Norton Anthology of American Literature* (2002) includes works by numerous Native authors throughout their discussion of American literary periods. Arnold Krupat served as a member of the editorial board for this anthology. Norton has also published an *Anthology of World Literatures* (2002) in six volumes with John Bierhorst as a member of the editorial board. St. Martin's Press recently published the six-volume *The Bedford Anthology of World Literatures* (2004), which includes Native perspectives. For example, the discovery unit on "The Americas: Aztec Empire and New Spain" is set alongside selected excerpts from Christopher Columbus, Hernan Cortes, and Bartolomé De Las Casas. The Facts On File Library of American History recently published an impressive *Encyclopedia of American Indian Contributions to the World* (2002). And several major university presses publish Native American texts as part of an ongoing series devoted to Native Americans, including the universities of Arizona, Nebraska, New Mexico, and Oklahoma. These series are edited by leading Native American scholars. Numerous professional journals also advance critical conversations about Native American Literatures and Cultures, including the *American*

Indian Culture and Research Journal, American Indian Quarterly, SAIL, and *Wicazo Sa Review.* Vast literatures, as this present volume suggests, by and about Native peoples are available to the reading public. In *Postindian Conversations* (1999), A. Robert Lee asks Gerald Vizenor, "What has become of multicultural programs at universities in the past decade? What is the future of native or ethnic studies?" To these questions, Vizenor answers:

> You might expect natives to find some solace for their visions, originary stories, and resistance to empire at universities and in ethnic studies departments, but that has not been the case in my experience. Regrettably, many natives have encountered anew the separatists in academic robes, and some of these ethnic separatists are in administrative positions. Natives, more often then not, are caught in the ethnic contests over budgets and academic positions and waived aside in the national ideologies of Asians and Chicanos. Natives are not the new immigrants, not the separatists, and not the ethnic simulations of cultural victimry. Natives are the diverse visionary sovereigns of this continent (179–180).

The point that Vizenor makes, over and over again in his works, is that "natives are the very start of any history of the United States. Not the absence of natives, not the myths of savagism and civilization, not mere museum natives, and not natives as eternal victims, but natives as a diverse continental presence" (178). Even when American history texts or anthologies of American literature do begin with an awareness of Native presence, such cognizance is often not contextualized. Such contextualization requires the study of Native issues to move from the margins to the center of academic concerns.

In *Critical Confrontations: Literary Theories in Dialogue* (1997), for example, Melli Steele claims: "The conflicts in contemporary critical theory are not just internal disputes about the correct model of interpretation but intensely political discussions that have consequences for the teaching of the humanities and the public understanding of the links between culture and democracy" (111).

Steele's focus is "on the conditions of democratic interpretation. *These conditions require us to recognize the differences and the atrocities of the past along with the resources [literatures and criticisms] that make this recognition possible and desirable*" (emphasis added). Steele believes that "without an account of the resources of democratic interpretation, we cannot give a satisfying justification of the study of the humanities" (114). In other words, the study of Native literatures requires a context—a context that demonstrates the interconnection between literary expressions, the diversities existing among multiple Native cultures within the United States, and the atrocities committed inside the American experiment with Democracy.

In 1916, John Dewey claimed: "Democracy has to be born anew every generation, and education is the midwife" ("The Need of an Industrial Education" 410). Certainly this present chapter attempts to explain why this is so. In her 2002 Pulitzer Prize winning work *"A Problem from Hell": America and the Age of Genocide*, Samantha Power clearly outlines the ongoing hesitation of U.S. officials to get involved with mass murders perpetrated against ethnic groups within the borders of foreign nations. Powers chronicles the unwavering attempts of Raphael Lemkin to name and establish laws against "race murder." Powers explains: "The word that Lemkin settled upon was a hybrid that combined the Greek derivative *geno*, meaning 'race' or 'tribe,' together with the Latin derivative *cide*, from *caedere*, meaning 'killing.'" Lemkin, a Polish Jew, hoped that the word would bring "lasting association with Hitler's horrors" (42).

Powers outlines the practices included within the parameters of *genocide*: "The perpetrators of genocide . . . attempt to destroy the political and social institutions, the culture, language, national feelings, religion, and economic existence of national groups. They . . . hope to eradicate the personal security, liberty, health, dignity, and lives of individual members of the targeted group" (43). In *Anti-Indianism in Modern America*, Elizabeth Cook-Lynn defines genocide as: "*the denial of basic human rights through the development of a nationalistic legal and social and intellectual system that makes it impossible for a domestic people or domestic nation to express itself collectively and historically in terms of continued self-determination*" (193). Cook-Lynn furthers the implications of genocide by including in her discussion the "concept of *ecocide*, the intentional destruction of the physical environment needed to sustain human health and life in a given geographical region" (195).

Lemkin, according to Powers, firmly believed that "The destruction of foreign national or ethnic identities would bring huge losses to the world's cultural heritage. All of humankind, even those who did not feel vulnerable to genocide, would suffer." Powers quotes Lemkin's assessment of the probable costs of genocide:

> We can best understand this when we realize how impoverished our culture would be if the peoples doomed by Germany, such as the Jews, had not been permitted to create the Bible, or to give birth to an Einstein, a Spinoza; if the Poles had not had the opportunity to give to the world a Copernicus, a Chopin, a Curie; the Czechs, a Huss, a Dvořák; the Greeks, a Plato and a Socrates; the Russians, a Tolstoy and a Shostakovich (53).

Certainly such logic implies that those peoples who have died as a result of genocidal practices include artists, scientists, and philosophers who could have produced another Shakespeare, the cure for cancer, or an ethics that would expand conceptions of justice across ethnic boundaries.

Similar lists of losses could be made from Native contributions to humanity. Among them would be included the contributions of the Iroquois Confederacy to the U.S. Constitution and the League of Nations (UN), the multiple contributions of Native nations to agriculture, medicine, sports, anthropology, sociology, and the arts—architecture, weaving, jewelry, music, movies, and literatures. Imagine, for example, a society without private property or classes. Friedrich Engels' book *The Origin of Family, Private Property and the State* (1884) became "the cornerstone of modern socialist theory" and was based largely on Engels' study of Iroquois culture (Keoke and Porterfield 243–244).

Lemkin spent a decade lobbying against genocide and for international laws that would both recognize genocide as a crime and outline appropriate punishments. In December 1948, the UN held a "Convention on the Prevention and Punishment of the Crime of Genocide" wherein nine articles were proposed for ratification.

Ironies abound here. For example, Keoke and Porterfield explicate the influence of the principles of the Iroquois Constitution on the formulation of the United Nations. Those who signed the Covenant of the League of Nations" agreed to "open, just, and honorable relations between nations" and to maintain justice and "scrupulous respect for all treaty obligations in dealings of organized people with one another" (157). Within this context, "Article 2" from the convention is of particular interest. It states:

> In the present Convention, genocide means any of the following acts committed with intent to destroy, in whole or in part, a national ethnical, racial or religious group, as such:
>
> (a) Killing members of the group;
>
> (b) Causing serious bodily or mental harm to members of the group;
>
> (c) Deliberately inflicting on the group conditions of life calculated to bring about its physical destruction in whole or in part;
>
> (d) Imposing measures intended to prevent births within the group;
>
> (e) Forcibly transferring children of the group to another group (Powers 62).

The convention on genocide "earned criticism for stipulating that a perpetrator could attempt to obliterate a group not only by killing its members but by causing serious bodily or mental harm, deliberately inflicting damaging conditions of life, preventing births, or forcibly removing children," Powers notes (66). Many of the novels talked about in Chapter Four discuss these practices. Of added interest concerning "transferring children of the group to another group," are the numerous accounts by Natives about forced attendance at boarding schools. Recent literary works on this subject include Laura Tohe's (Navajo) *No Parole Today* (1999) and Leslie Marmon Silko's (Laguna) *Gardens in the Dunes* (1999).

Other critics of the "Articles" on genocide, "suggested that U.S. ratification would license critics of the United States to investigate the eradication of Native American tribes in the nineteenth century." However, writes Powers, even though "reckoning with American brutality against native peoples was long overdue, . . . the convention, which was not retroactive, could not be used to press the matter" (67). Part of the "stunning ignorance" that Owens addresses in *Other Destinies* is the belief that brutality against Native Nations is primarily confined to the nineteenth century and, therefore, no longer a pressing issue. Furthermore, calling such brutalities "genocide" and "crimes against humanity" is a more recent phenomena and generally not associated with the treatment of Natives by the U.S. government. The U.S. general populace can more readily identify genocide with regard to activities in Cambodia, Iraq, Bosnia, Rwanda, and Kosovo than within its own borders. It is much easier to export an idealized Democracy to these nations than to recognize and examine the failures of Democracy for minority groups residing in America. Perhaps it is also easier to deny the state of Native America due to the fact that Native Nations exist as separate sovereign nations within the United States.

As Carol Ward, Elon Stander, and Yodit Solomon explain, American Indians "continue to experience the ramifications" of separatism as the "status of Indian peoples" has moved from that of "captive nations" to "internal colonies" (212). As internal colonies, Native communities tend to withdraw into social, intellectual, and economic isolation. As isolated groups, social fragmentation, poverty, and dependence on the U.S. government is often the rule rather than the exception. Furthermore, *differences* (tribal particularities) often perpetuate *separatism*—us/them, America/Native America, Anglo/Native, and so forth. These bipolarities, it must be noted, can be reversed, creating Native tribal entities as elite (superior) groups against mainstream America. Or particular tribal groups can legislate to define Native America at odds with the wishes of other Natives. Furthermore, members of tribal groups living in the diaspora (urban settings) are dependent on the very systems and programs that problematize their identity.

In current parlance, the above questions are concerned with *God* issues: issues confronting the fundamental *Truth* claims within American ideologies.

Why Can't Mainstream America See Its
Own Colonial Violence?

René Girard finds the *atrocities* of *separatism* in the foundations of cultures. In *The Scapegoat*, Girard concludes that: "human culture is predisposed to the permanent concealment of its origins in collective violence. Such a definition of culture enables us to understand the successive stages of an entire culture as well as the transition from one state to the next by means of a crisis" which is met with "periods of frequent persecutions" (100). Girard writes about the relationship between violence and the sacred. In Postmodern terms, Girard deconstructs cultures. Drawing on images and metaphors from various fields, Girard looks at a genealogy of ideologies; he performs an archeology of the ethical foundations of religious and political systems. Conceptions of the *sacred* are revealed in sacred and secular narratives that are accepted by cultures as being central to their identity—Bibles and Constitutions, for example. In his work *Things Hidden Since the Foundation of the World*, Girard explores what he calls "acquisitive mimesis." Girard generates a "complete theory" based on this principle. "We will see now that not only the prohibition [taboos] but also ritual and ultimately the whole structure of religion [and political systems grounded in religion] can be traced back to the mechanism of acquisitive mimesis" (18). Central to Girard's theory of acquisitive mimesis are sacrifice, victimage, and scapegoating.

Students of world literatures might well understand Girard's concerns when they pose questions about some of the great Greek tragedies. Why, for example, must Oedipus be banished or unknowingly suffer the violent consequences of an ancestral curse in order for Thebes to reclaim a semblance of social, political, and environmental stability? Or why do the Gods require that Agamemnon sacrifice his daughter in order for his military forces to move forward in battle?

Because the United States has been shaped by Judeo/Christian theologies, perhaps examples of separatism, sacrifice, victimage, or scapegoating taken from the Bible might more clearly illuminate the implication of Girard's theory for Native American cultures. Why, for example, is Abraham commanded to banish Ishmael (the progenitor of Islam) or to sacrifice Isaac (the progenitor of Judaism and Christianity)? And why do these cultures accept such unjust acts as being divinely sanctioned? What theological, philosophical, or ethical assumptions require the favoritism of one son—(Abel, Isaac, Jacob) at the expense or *sacrifice* of the other (Cain, Ishmael, Esau) —in order to guarantee the survival of a patriarchal family line or the establishment of Israel?

Winner of the 1986 Nobel Peace prize, Elie Wiesel, frames these issues with reference to the nature of God. "Why did God choose to commit the first act of discrimination [Cain and Abel] between men?" asks Wiesel.

> . . . did God wish to make the point—even then—that injustice is inherent in the human condition; that two human beings—no matter who they are or who their grandparents were—are never equal, since their duties and privileges are never the same? That therefore men could be brothers and still could not claim equal rights? How is one to understand God's arbitrary way of handling His creatures, playing one man against the other, turning them into irreconcilable enemies? (44)

In the United States, *democracy* is both a theological (attains to the status of the sacred) and political term—a God term. And therefore, to continue the logic of Girard and Wiesel, this question can be posed: why must whole Nations of Native Americans be dispossessed or separated out from immigrant America in order for a democracy to be established?

Vizenor claims:

> Natives have resisted the colonial separatists at every river, at every mountain, at every treeline, at every lake; and in every treaty natives have carried on their resistance in the company of animals, birds, tricksters, and visionary sovereignty. The separatists were treacherous, but natives have resisted their manifest manners and dominance. The separatists have tried to ruin nature, and even the memories of native survivance, but most natives resist the romance of victimry. This is a diverse native country, not a separatist nation (170).

In other words, is it possible for there to be a unity in the acceptance of such diversity? Can diverse peoples meet and dialogue with the intension of learning from one another's experiences, stories, and views of the world without trying to reduce the Other to the Same? Again, politically, Native peoples have been placed on reservations (separated out or banished) or have assimilated. How can Native people maintain unique historical, geographic, ethnographic, and ancestral genealogies within the borders of the existing United States without being consumed by assimilationist policies? How can mutually beneficial dialogues be maintained between Natives in the diaspora, reservation Natives, and mainstream Euroamerican political entities?

What Are the Ongoing Consequences of Colonial Oppression on Native Americans?

The creation of the Other—collective Indian, the "scapegoat" or "victim"—often results in (if not warfare), *humiliation, illness,* or *death.* Scholars of the Holocaust are intimately aware of the affects of violence against an entire people. Alan L. Berger, for example, speaks about the effects of the Holocaust on second- and third-generation survivors in his book *Second Generation Voices: Reflections by Children of Holocaust Survivors and Perpetrators (Religion, Theology, and the Holocaust).* In a personal interview, Berger reported that mental illnesses abound among holocaust survivors and their posterity. The lives of many Jewish people are witnesses to the long-range, inter-generational effects of the Holocaust. According to Berger, *severe trauma can be inherited* (personal interview). Sociologists Carol Ward and Karren Baird-Olson are attempting to give a clinical name to the effects of long-term oppression on members of many Native communities. To date, Ward and Baird-Olsen are calling the effects, "inherited oppression" (personal e-mail from Ward). Ward, Stander, and Solomon quote Maria Anna Jaimes Guerreo who claims: "The systematic displacement of native peoples from their land base, which was both their economic source of livelihood as well as their spiritual foundation, set up conditions for colonially induced despair" (213).

Inherited oppression or colonially induced despair manifests itself in joblessness, poverty, poor health, cultural malaise, family disintegration (spouse and child abuse), alcoholism, and other collective indicators of a failure to thrive. According to Ward, Stander, and Solomon, "One of the most serious conditions affecting reservation populations is substance abuse. Alarming rates of alcoholism have been and are currently reported among American Indian tribes: 80 to 90 percent are not uncommon rates" (213). Explanations for such high rates of alcoholism include an "adaptive view," a "medical model," a "sociobiological" theory, and substance abuse as a "valuable form of resistance or protest." The "adaptive view" has been debunked by sociologists but is still held by the public. The adaptive view maintains that alcoholism stems from "addiction to moral or psychological weakness" or a "lack of will power and strength of character"—even when such behavior "means loss of family, employment, and self-respect" (214). The "medical model views alcoholism as a disease and attributes the development of the disorder in part to a genetic dysfunction. Heredity is also implicated as a factor in development of alcoholism: one indication is the 4-to-1 odds of becoming alcoholic if a parent is alcoholic" (214). The "sociobiological" view posits that "social disorganization undermines the protective influence of neighborhood and community." Furthermore, the "weakening of old belief systems and hopes as well as disillusionment with religious beliefs predisposes [Native Americans] to substance use as an escape, as does loss of a sense of continuity, traditions and habits" (214). And, finally, substance abuse is seen as a "useful way of bringing attention to certain issues that may eventually lead to change and, at the very least, serves as a forum for expressing opposition" (214). The bottom line, however, is Native grief, "for the loss of cultural practices that integrated their communities socially and spiritually. Therefore, Indian drinking is one mechanism for adapting to the social disorganization (loss of culture and identity) that has resulted from acculturation" (214). Clearly portions of "Article 2" of the "Convention on the Prevention and Punishment of the Crime of Genocide" can be recognized in the above discussion.

Girard, however, would posit that such social disintegration stems from "acquisitive mimesis." In *Things Hidden From the*

Foundations of the World, Girard explains "acquisitive mimesis." "If *acquisitive mimesis* divides by leading two or more individuals to converge on one and the same object [i.e. lands] with a view to appropriating it, *conflictual mimesis* will inevitably unify by leading two or more individuals to converge on one and the same adversary that all wish to strike down." Girard asserts that acquisitive mimesis is "contagious." And "if the number of individuals polarized [us and them—Native and White] increases, other members of the community, as yet not implicated, will tend to follow the example of those who are." As "mimetic attraction multiples with the number of those polarized, it is inevitable that at one moment the entire community will find itself unified against a singe individual [or group]." Conflictual mimesis creates an "allegiance against a common enemy." Furthermore, "the conclusion of the crisis is nothing other than the reconciliation [or reestablishment] of the community"(26). In other words, can the United States exist without the construction of a common enemy—either within (minority groups) or without?

What can be inferred from Girard is that the unity of manifest destiny was/is predicated on creating the victim—Native Americans —who serve as scapegoats for real or imagined rivalries for the same desired goods. Moreover, the sacrifice is deemed necessary for the establishment of the laws that stem from such appropriation: laws that protect individualism, private property, ownership, capitalism, survival by competition, and so forth.

What Is the Unconscious Nature of the Immemorial Lie?

In *The Scapegoat,* Girard suggests that, "Persecutors always believe in the excellence of their cause, but in reality *they hate without a cause.* The absence of cause in the accusation . . . is never seen by the persecutors" (103). Girard demonstrates his theory with extracts from the Gospel of John in the New Testament (11: 47–53). In these verses, the High Priest Caiaphas argues: "'You don't seem to have grasped the situation at all; you fail to see that it is better for one man [Christ; think Native peoples] to die for the people [Jews or Americans] than for the whole nation to be destroyed.' He did not speak in his own person, it was as high priest that he made this prophecy that Jesus was to die for the nation—and not for the nation only, but to gather together in unity the scattered children of God. From that day they were determined to kill him" (112). Girard maintains, "Without using our terminology, . . . the Gospels reveal the scapegoat mechanism everywhere, even within us." Girard justifies such an audacious claim by suggesting the often "unconscious nature" of the scapegoat mechanism. In Luke, when Christ says, "Father, forgive them: they do not know what they are doing," Girard maintains that "we are given the first definition of the unconscious in human history" (110–111).

Perhaps many view colonial wars with Native American nations as part of the Revolutionary War. And yet, few can not avoid the irony of wars being fought against England in the name of liberty while military campaigns were simultaneously being fought to take away the liberty of Native Americans. In other words, while struggling against colonization by England, Euroamericans were colonizing Native Americans. When students become more aware about past and present-day condemnable treatment of Native Americans, they often retort that they have nothing to do with such practices. Here the "unconscious" nature of these events begins to formulate. Other students frequently realize that they are inadvertently the beneficiaries of immoral and illegal conduct. Many feel anxiety or guilt for being members of an American culture capable of malevolence. And yet, they also feel powerless in the face of their own and others' unintentional (unconscious) complicity.

Girard maintains that the scapegoat can not be incorporated into the dominant culture because of the "fate-filled idolatry to which the victim is subject, but also and especially [due to] the effects of the reconciliation created by the unanimous polarization" (*Things Hidden From the Foundations of the World* 27). This means that actual dialogue between the Self and the Other might disturb being at home with the Self. It is easier to maintain separatism than to entertain difference. The "fate-filled idolatry," therefore, must remain repressed (remain in the unconscious) or the entire project (the majority rules) will be found to be unjustified or unsupportable. In other words, the "fate" or "destiny" of such idolatry (worship of the self or one's people) will be discovered as "hate-filled." In *The*

Scapegoat, Girard argues the "human culture is predisposed to the permanent concealment of its origins in collective violence." Girard maintains that his model is "valid for our society." Girard admits the difficulty "persecutors" have in "decoding" their own "accounts of persecution." And he worries that their will to "occultation" will continually struggle against the "revelation of the immemorial lie." However, "during the periods of crisis and widespread violence there is always the threat of subversive knowledge spreading, but that very knowledge becomes one of the victims or quasi-victims of the convolutions of social disorder" (100). Native American Literatures and criticism are that "subversive knowledge." The question emerges: how does the richest, most powerful, most technologically advanced society in the modern world import Democracy as a solution to turmoil in foreign, troubled nations when that democracy is bound up in the "immemorial lie"?

What Are Some Political and Narrative Examples of the Theory in This Chapter?

Perhaps an application of the above theory might elucidate these ethical dilemmas. Scott B. Vickers, in *Native American Identities: From Stereotype to Archetype in Art and Literature*, writes in his "conclusion" that:

> . . . in the world of the modern Indian, issues of identity are becoming more flexible and less and less dependent on the bipolar opposition between black and white, or between white and red. The stereotypical sameness of the 'red man' as constructed by the racist ideology of white America appears to be giving way to new dimensions of Indian authenticity, as more and more Indians seek to rediscover their human complexities and potentialities and to redefine their identities in order to continue to live as *Indians*. Recognizing the perilous prospects of total assimilation into the white hegemony, modern Indians have insisted, for instance, on the teaching of their native language in reservations schools and are busily trying to recapitulate their traditional religions and customs in a process that Vine Deloria Jr. calls 'retribalization' (159).

Such movement toward "new dimensions of Indian authenticity" and the rediscovery of "human complexities and potentialities" is indeed affirming. And yet Native peoples must continuously fight against attempts to derail such advances. As Vickers points out:

> Recent developments suggest that the BIA, the Department of the Interior, and the U.S. Treasury have, over the last several decades, mismanaged and actually 'lost' or misappropriated unspecified millions of dollars (up to $2.4 billion) of Indian monies funneled through their offices. The Native American Rights Fund filed suit against the federal government in the spring of 1996, alleging 'illegal conduct in what is viewed as the largest and most shameful financial scandal ever involving the United States government' (161).

Are citizens of the United States aware of such fraudulent behaviors? Are such events masked so that acquisitive mimesis will remain in the realm of the unconscious?

Just what are the implications of the "largest and most shameful financial scandal ever involving the United States government"? One need not be a rocket scientist to realize the fundamental role economics plays in the survival of Native Nations. Vickers explains: "Neither fully sovereign nations nor fully entitled wards of the state, Indian societies exist in a power vacuum arbitrated by the authority of the federal government" (161).

In *Killing the White Man's Indian: Reinventing Native Americans at the End of the Twentieth Century* (1997), Fergus M. Bordewich further explains:

> We [Natives and non-Natives alike] are still haunted by John Marshall's brilliant, evasive compromise, whose definition of Indian tribes as 'domestic dependent nations' bequeathed a contradiction in terms that continues to confuse our thinking about Native Americans up to the present day. As the landscape of Indian Country becomes steadily more complex and ever more reflective of the vast diversity of tribes that always existed beneath the conforming grid of federal policy, it is increasingly essential to disentangle the contradictions with which the principle of

'sovereignty' has become freighted. To do so with enough finality to accommodate the rights of tribes as well as those of individual Indians and the other Americans *deserves, and may well require, an amendment to the United States Constitution* (emphasis added; 338).

Are the issues surrounding political power, Native American self-determination, and economic self-sufficiency so crucial that an amendment to the Constitution is required to address them? Certainly, if *internalized oppression* or *colonially induced despair* are maladies that continually plague Native peoples.

Bordewich, however, also debates the risks of sovereignty. "Since political autonomy must be contingent upon economic self-sufficiency, true tribal sovereignty has to mean cutting not only the apron strings of the federal government but its purse strings as well" (338). Bordewich continues, "As self-supporting states, tribes would have to accept responsibility for their own economic failures and social problems and face the possibility that bad investment or mismanagement could even lead to the liquidation of the tribes themselves." What is more, asks Bordewich, are tribal leaders (who don't want interference from the federal government) "willing to consider relinquishing the safety net of public services and federal protection of tribal assets, or to jeopardize in any fundamental way a relationship that provides them, collectively, with $3 billion per year in taxpayer's money, including free schools, health care, and technical assistance"? Bordewich admits, "Unfortunately, there is an irreducible conflict between the aspirations of many tribes for a self-sufficient homeland and their need for imported capital and industry in order to create even a minimum number of jobs" (339).

(As any self-respecting Trickster might chide: and yet, why couldn't such yearly expenditures be considered rent monies for the use of stolen lands—i.e., the "lands from sea to shining sea"? And why couldn't tribal elders, therefore, achieve some legislative status as de facto landlords—or at least representatives of foreign nations within the larger United States? Or could tribal leaders become members of the United Nations?)

Bordewich notes a federal study conducted in the 1980s which "discovered . . . that private investment is discouraged by jurisdictional disputes between tribal and state governments, by the frequent turnover of tribal regimes and their ineptness at business management, by unskilled and unreliable Indian labor forces, and by the cumbersome regulations of the BIA. It can scarcely be surprising," says Bordewich, "that communities far from airports, interstate highways, and cities, populated by ill-trained workers, and governed, in some cases, by politicians who do not abide by the most basic democratic rules are not prime locations for large-scale investment" (340).

Louis Owens, in typical Trickster fashion, addresses these issues in his novel *Dark River* (1999). Again, Owens uses the mystery genre to help readers become detectives—*re*-searchers into the complexities of economic survival on reservations. In *Dark River*, Owens demonstrates that economic stability is inseparably connected to ethics as well as to psychological and social well-being. Several characters in the novel hold distinct positions on how the Black Mountain Apache ought to become economically viable. Most comic, however, is Avrum Goldberg's. Goldberg is a Jewish anthropologist who knows more about Natives than the people he studies.

Following a visit by an investigative team from *National Geographic*, Xavier Two Bears, the corrupt tribal Chairman, holds an impromptu council meeting. He begins the meeting by thanking Goldberg for allowing the tribe to pawn him off as a "real Indian" for their *National Geographic* guests (70). Then he turns the meeting over to Goldberg who has a plan. "My idea is this," says Avrum. "The tribe is making a pretty good income from the casino and lodge and other things, like hunting." Council members murmur their "assent." "But there's a cultural cost involved in such enterprises," Avrum warns. "Gambling attracts the wrong kind of people. People who can have a bad influence especially on the young. And some might question the morality of selling our animals to rich hunters." Two-Bears interrupts Avrum with an "unheard-of rudeness," asking Avrum to: "Cut to the chase"—a White man's way of "rushing a council meeting" (71).

"My proposal," Goldberg asserts, "is that the tribe give up the casino and lodge and commercial hunting and instead become a traditional tribe again, living the way everyone lived before the white men came" (71). This proposal meets with "curious amusement" from the rest of the council. And Two-Bears claims, "That's nuts" (72). Shorty Luke tells the council that Goldberg's ideas are worth listening to. By converting their "whole reservation into a traditional 1800s tribal community," Shorty claims, "we can get a lot of grants" (72). Goldberg tells them that he has already "looked into it":

> If we lived entirely traditionally in every way, we could get grants from an incredible number of sources. Costner, Fonda and Turner, Paul Newman, The MacArthur Foundation, Guggenheim, National Endowment for the Humanities as well as the National Foundation for the Arts, not to mention at least a hundred other culturally and historically sensitive organizations (72).

Shorty adds *National Geographic* and Disney to the list. Avrum nods, "Both have expressed deep interest and more or less promised technological and financial support." The council asks how much money would be involved. The answer is "millions."

When Mrs. Martinez asks Avrum what he means by living "traditionally," Shorty buts in: "You know, the old ways. We'd tear down these government shacks and build authentic wickiups, eat venison and dried chokecherries and that sort of thing, dress like Avrum, tell stories, make arrows and bows in the old way, hunt, all the things our ancestors did. Avrum's an expert; he can teach us." The humor escalates. Another tribal member, dressed in up-to-the-minute Western attire, asks: "So we could make a lot of money living like that?" And then he poses an ironic contingency to the plan: "Only one problem then . . . How we going to spend it? We got to live in wickiups and make our own clothes and eat berries and walk everywhere, what're we going to do with all that money? I mean we can't have no satellite dish or color TV and no Land Cruiser, can we?" Another woman adds, "We couldn't even have electricity" (73).

The former chairman of the tribe holds up his hand and adds, "But the professor ain't said we got to live here all the time. If we could make all that money, we could all buy condominiums down there in Scottsdale on one of them golf courses. We could live down there where it's warm and just come up for weekends during tourist season" (74). Laughter begins to erupt. Especially when another old man adds: "Maybe we could hire some hippies to live here. There wouldn't be no tourists to speak of in winter anyway, and hippies like to dress and live like old-time Indians" (74). When Shorty tells them all funding would be lost if any lack of authenticity prevailed, Two-Bears tells Shorty and Goldberg to go home and "get some sense" (75). Owens plays with ideas of authenticity here. Essentially he is satirizing public expectations of authenticity as well as Native ideas of sovereignty.

Dark River, however, is a rather dark novel with comic irruptions. Two-Bears and other tribal officials are collecting illegal fortunes off of temporary permits to would-be warriors from suburbia who want to use the remote parts of the reservation for war games —war games that actually amount to a type of hunt-and-kill weekend sports vacation with "soldiers" fully equipped with the latest in combat strategies and weaponry. Jake Nashoba—the forest ranger, a Vietnam veteran with ghost sickness, and an estranged Choctaw on an Apache reservation—stumbles on these war games in search of his adopted granddaughter. He ends up the dead hero in the novel. His death, however, challenges notions of tribal sovereignty, the possibility of cross-tribal unity, and the ethics of independent Native nations within larger democratic systems. Nashoba's death is also tangled with narrative threads—of mystery plots, Native myths, modern war scenarios, and Western film clichés.

What Is to Be Done?

Dark River is a Postmodern text. It brings into question the project of liberty for Native communities. Such a project is inseparably connected with ethics—the demand for virtue on the part of every individual that makes up any community. Numerous institutions promote values in a democracy—universities, corporations, government agencies, religions. In *The Good Society*, Robert N. Bellah and a team of sociologists explain how institutions "mediate our ultimate moral (and religious) commitments. Not only are our moral and spiritual beliefs and attitudes learned in institutional contexts . . . but institutions themselves are premised on moral (and religious) understandings, what sociologists call ultimate values in terms of what is right and wrong, good and bad" (288). Such institutions, for this team of sociologists, "mediate the relations between self and world. Meeting another person with no institutional context is a situation of anxiety and, possibly, fear." Institutions provide "common ground" and create "a set of mutual expectations about what is appropriate" (285). Bellah's team believes that "America's social institutions are damaged and threatened by many of the same forces that threaten the natural environment." Furthermore, Bellah's group asserts that "we cannot repair the damaged environment unless we also repair our damaged social ecology" (292). For Bellah's team, the majority of Americans are still "spiritual immigrants" (293).

As so many Native American texts testify, tribal peoples have their own solutions to the mental and social illnesses they have suffered from overwhelming injustice. And yet so many forces align themselves against Native approaches to mental and spiritual health. Indeed, mainstream America must be educated to the possibility that Native American healing practices are not only valid, but might offer some insights into mental and communal health to the rest of humanity. There are numerous indigenous psychologies worthy of recognition and support. For example, while working among Northern Cheyenne and Fort Peck women, Karren Baird-Olson and Carol Ward found "women's spirituality" to be central "in their efforts to survive, heal, and grow." Baird-Olson and Ward found that:

> Native women are contributing to social and cultural changes through the creation of new forms of religious and spiritual expression. These new forms represent not only the results of their efforts to resolve personal problems or oppressive situations, but also the effects of particular generational experiences and historical eras that laid the foundation upon which new forms of spiritual renewal could be built (30).

Certainly, in a democratic society, such practices ought to be encouraged—even sought after. Writers like Momaday, Silko, Welch, Erdrich, Hogan, and Vizenor continually bear witness to the possibility of healing. They assert: Native peoples are or can be models of survivance; their narratives can be comic (demonstrate how to heal) rather than tragic (examples of the agony of defeat). Vizenor claims, "We the natives of this continent, are the storiers of presence, and we actuate the observance of natural reason and transmotion [adaptability, transformation, and change] in this constitutional democracy" (*Fugitive Poses* 199). What does democracy mean? Vizenor uses the term "constitutional democracy" to establish the legal or formal aspects of democracy rather than the actual practices of the members of citizens of that constitution. Is there an ethical democracy—a democracy of responsibility? "Democracy means paying attention," claims Bellah's company of sociologists. Until the present moment, the democratic experiment has not paid "sufficient attention to the whole. Its legacy is environmental damage, social neglect of the least advantaged, and restricted possibilities for all" (270). Bellah's group, however, does not confront the "atrocities" that Steele refers to.

Leaders of this nation have been aware of the need to be more inclusive in our understanding of democracy. However, William J. Clinton is "the only sitting U.S. President in history to travel to an Indian reservation for a 'nation-to-nation' meeting" (*We the People* 6n). Clinton also drafted a proclamation to Native America. In this proclamation, Clinton says that in 1994 he "met with the tribal leaders of more than 500 Indian nations at the White House," where he "saw the strength and determination that has enabled Native Americans to overcome extraordinary barriers and protect their hard-won civil and political rights." In his proclamation, Clinton also resolved: "While we cannot erase the tragedies of the past, we can create a future where all of our country's people share in America's great promise" (6). To this end, in November of 2000, Clinton issued "a revised Executive Order on Consultation and Coordination with Indian Tribal Governments" to insure that "agencies consult with Indian tribes and respect tribal sovereignty as the agencies consider policy initiatives that affect Indian communities" (Clinton 6). Is this a move toward the rediscovery of democracy that Dewey suggests must occur in every generation?

Will there be a literature of democracy that will help us deconstruct foundational violence and, at the same time, provide a narrative map for the future (for Natives and non-Natives alike)—a map that shows how mutual respect and a greater consciousness of what democracy means for minorities might be negotiated? These are indeed *key* questions.

Works Cited

Baird-Olson, Karren, and Carol Ward, "Recovery and Resistance: The Renewal of Traditional Spirituality among American Indian Women," *American Indian Culture and Research Journal* 24:4 (2000) 1–35.

Bellah, Robert N., Richard Madsen, William M. Sullivan, Ann Swidler, and Steven M. Tipton, *The Good Society* (New York: Knopf, 1991).

Berger, Alan L., interview with Suzanne Evertsen Lundquist, Jewish American Literature and Holocaust Conference, October 26, 2003.

Bordewich, Fergus M., *Killing the White Man's Indian* (New York: Anchor, 1996).

Chapman, Serle L., note in "Forward," in *We, the People of Earth and Elders—Volume II*, Serle L. Chapman, ed. (Missoula, MT: Mountain Press, 2001).

Clinton, William J., "Native America—a Proclamation," in *We, the People of Earth and Elders—Volume II*, Serle L. Chapman, ed. (Missoula, MT: Mountain Press, 2001).

Cook-Lynn, Elizabeth, *Anti-Indianism in Modern America* (Urbana: University of Illinois Press, 2001).

Dewey, John, "The Need of an Industrial Education in an Industrial Democracy," *Manual Training and Vocational Education* 17 (1916) 409–414.

Girard, Rene, *The Scapegoat* (Baltimore: The Johns Hopkins University Press, 1986).

———, *Things Hidden from the Foundations of the World* (Palo Alto, CA: University of Stanford Press, 1987).

Keoke, Emory Dean, and Kay Marie Porterfield, *Encyclopedia of American Indian Contributions to the World* (New York: Facts on File, Inc., 2002).

Owens, Louis, *Other Destinies: Understanding the American Indian Novel* (Norman: University of Oklahoma Press, 1992).

———, *Dark River* (Norman: University of Oklahoma Press., 1999).

Power, Samantha, *"A Problem From Hell": America and the Age of Genocide* (New York: HarperCollins, 2002).

Steele, Meili, *Critical Confrontations: Literary Theories in Dialogue* (Columbia: University of South Carolina Press, 1997).

Vickers, Scott B., *Native American Identities: From Stereotype to Archetype in Art and Literature* (Albuquerque: University of New Mexico Press, 1998).

Vizenor, Gerald, *Fugitive Poses* (Lincoln: University of Nebraska Press, 1998).

———, and A. Robert Lee, *Postindian Conversations* (Lincoln: University of Nebraska Press, 1999).

Wiesel, Elie, *Messengers of God* (New York: Simon and Schuster, 1985).

Ward, Carol, Elon Stander, and Yodit Solomon, "Resistance through Healing among American Indian Women," in *A World-Systems Reader: New Perspectives on Gender, Urbanism, Cultures, Indigenous Peoples, and Ecology,* Thomas D. Hall, ed. (Lanham, MD: Rowman & Littlefield, 2000).

Ward, Carol, e-mail to author, October 10, 2003.

Chapter Seven

Who Are the Major Critics in the Field, and What Are Their Arguments?

Late twentieth and early twenty-first century Native American literary theory is caught up with the relationship between individual authors, tribal politics, and global literary concerns. Critical issues involve *representation* (how Indians are represented politically, nationally, and by individual authors); *sovereignty* (how Native communities can actualize their rights as independent nations); *authenticity* (what constitutes *real* Indian identity and thought); *intellectual sovereignty* (what rights or responsibilities individual authors have to engage in theory formation); and *cosmopolitanism* (how or *if* tribal societies and individual authors ought to engage in multicultural/multinational deliberations).

Professor of American Indian Literature and Intellectual History at Stanford University, Robert Allen Warrior (Osage) discusses four historical literary periods in the movement of Native intellectuals toward a Native American aesthetic. The first two periods, the post-Wounded Knee era (1890–1925) and the Civil Rights era (1961–1973), are characterized as a time when Native writers "associated closely with one another." The next two periods, closely associated with Modernism (1925–1961) and Postmodernism (1973 to the present), are characterized as a time "marked by a lack of associative cohesion" (3). While these periods are interesting in themselves, perhaps a discussion of the critical aftermath of the Wounded Knee Massacre (1890) and Wounded Knee II (1973) will serve to demonstrate the inseparable tie between tragic historical events and the creation of literary theory.

On December 29, 1890, Sioux men, women, and children were massacred at Wounded Knee on the Lakota Sioux reservation. Many conditions conspired to cause what has been called "the last of the Indian Wars." Broken treaty promises, starvation due to poor food rationing, the murder of Sitting Bull, fear of the Ghost Dance revival, and the animosity of U.S. soldiers against the Sioux for the death of Custer and his Seventh Calvary at the Battle of the Little Bighorn (1876) led to heightened unrest. Tensions mounted, and the U.S. military fired on an unarmed Sioux camp. Paul M. Robertson (Oglala) tells us that the "Bodies of women and children were found scattered for three miles from the camp." Robertson continues: "On New Year's Day, a pit was dug . . . and the frozen bodies of 146 men, women, and children were thrown into the pit like cordwood until it was full." However, before these bodies were covered, the soldiers "stripped" many of them, "keeping as souvenirs the Ghost Shirts and other clothing and equipment the people had owned in life, or selling them later in the thriving trade over Ghost Dance relics that ensued" (696).

One of the first physicians to arrive on the scene was Dr. Charles Eastman (Sioux). In the decade following the massacre, Eastman, Carlos Montezuma (Yavapai), and Gertrude Simmons Bonnin (Sioux) joined with other Indian activists to form the Society of American Indians (SAI). According to Frederick E. Hoxie—from the Newberry Library in Chicago—these "red progressives" were "pledged to improving the lives of native people by opposing government paternalism and defending the legal right of tribesmen" (534). In order to broadcast their cause, these activists also established a journal, the *American Indian Magazine*—which Bonnin edited from 1918 to 1919. When the SAI dissolved, Bonnin established The National Congress of American Indians (NCAI). Her desire was to acquire both Indian rights and U. S. citizenship for Native peoples. (U.S. citizenship was granted to Native Americans in 1924.)

Eastman, Montezuma, and Bonnin were never idle spectators of historical occurrences. Each of them suffered unimaginable events in their own lives but went on to educate themselves, become professionals (doctors, lobbyists, and teachers), write about their experiences in essays, autobiographies, and fictions, as well as engage in proactive behavior. For example, when Montezuma was six, he was kidnapped by Pima Indians and sold for thirty dollars to a photographer, Carlos Gentile. Montezuma eventually ended up in the care of a Baptist minister who recognized Montezuma's intelligence and supported his education. Montezuma did graduate from Chicago Medical School (1889) and enter into a successful medical practice. But this does not compensate for the fact that Montezuma was unable to return to his Yavapai relatives before his parents died. When he did return, he found his people imprisoned on the Fort McDowell Reservation. Montezuma spent much of his means and time lobbying for better conditions for reservation Indians. All of the members of SAI filled their lives with social service. Warrior describes their writings and activities, however, as being "Christian and secular assimilationist" (4). Warrior feels they encouraged other Natives to survive, as they had, by entering into the dominant society.

Events leading up to the 1973 occupation of Wounded Knee and the Wounded Knee Takeover generated current literary criticism. In the fall of 1972, the Trail of Broken Treaties Caravan marched on Washington. One thousand AIM (American Indian Movement) members, led by Russell Means (Lakota) and Dennis Banks (Leech Lake Chippewa), intended to hold a demonstration prior to election week in November. The purpose of this rally was to draw attention to "twenty-two" points of redress for Indian people. However, advance teams failed to secure lodging for the group and they ended up taking over the BIA building. Due to hostile political response and negative press, this march became a failed event.

In February 1973, AIM leaders and local Oglalas took over several buildings near the site of the original Wounded Knee massacre. For seventy-one days, armed AIM activists held off armed U.S. Marshals and local law enforcement agencies. Wounded Knee II became an international event. Joseph M. Marshall III (Sicangu Lakota) tells us this event demonstrated "the courage and commitment that Indian men and women could bring to a cause, to the point of dying if necessary to bring about positive change for their people"(699). Background for such radical action comes from a long line of broken treaties made with the U.S. government. Eight hundred treaties were entered into between tribal societies and Federal government agencies. Less than four hundred of these treaties were ratified (approved by the U.S. government). And of those less than four hundred treaties, few were honored. Such neglect led to land loss, disgraceful legal treatment as well as loss of hunting and fishing rights; educational opportunities; passable health care; and mere survival provisions for thousands of people (Richard Monette "Treaties" 643–646).

One of the most influential Indian intellectuals, lawyer and theologian Vine Deloria, Jr. (Sioux) was both moved by the fervor of AIM activists and critical of their methods. However, Deloria was, according to Warrior, able to see two critical points emerge from Wounded Knee II:

> First, the various sectors of the grassroots Indian movement confronted the Native establishment with the fact that their reformist tactics did not speak to large numbers of American Indian people on reservations and in urban areas. Second, the militant gravitated with ease toward traditional spiritual leaders very early on, asserting that a truly liberative American Indian politics would have at its center an affirmation of culture, spirituality, and tradition (Warrior 90).

At this time, Deloria began to articulate the need for Indian nations to move toward *sovereignty* through recognition first, that their ancestors weren't "barbaric, pagan, and uncivilized," and second, that "tradition provides the critical constructive material upon which a community rebuilds itself" (Warrior 95). However, Deloria cautioned that gaining sovereignty must be recognized as a process requiring multiple acts of discovery rather than unreasoned and impassioned demands.

The reasons for Deloria's cautions are explained by Roger Dunsmore (University of Montana):

> Deloria's work seeks dimensions far beyond the surface realities of contemporary Indian affairs or the history of white-Indian encounters in North America. Deloria shows us the nature of the huge rift between the spiritual 'owners' of the land, the Indians, and the political owners of the land, the whites—a rift which creates obvious turbulence throughout the political, moral, and psychic life of the

nation. Deloria believes that until a reconciliation between the two is achieved, our society will be unstable and very dangerous (415).

Deloria's broad training in Western and Native intellectual traditions has prepared him to argue the intellectual and spiritual viability of Native traditions. In his seminal works—*Custer Died for Your Sins; We Talk, You Listen; God is Red; Red Earth, White Lies;* and *Behind the Trail of Broken Treaties,* among others—Deloria convincingly argues the merits of Indian philosophy, social science, education, religion, and science. Deloria's political tracts, legal activity, teaching positions, and publishing record are too vast to summarize here.

Two journals (among others) dealing with literary and cultural topics were established following Wounded Knee II: *American Indian Culture and Research Journal* (1974), at UCLA; and the *American Indian Quarterly* (1974), at UC Berkeley.

The seriousness of the current work engaged in by Native intellectuals can be further exemplified by an interview between Joseph Bruchac (Abenaki) and Carter Revard (Osage). In the consultation, Revard declares:

> I think, if we're lucky, we'll have writers come along who know the mythical dimensions and are very, very honest, fiercely, unflinchingly, almost meanly vivid about the tough parts of Indian life and will not neglect either dimension. Which really means I'd like to see American Indian writing be a standard for this country. I'd really like to see this country judged by its Indian people as a civilization and brought into the dock and given its good and bad marks. Until you do that you don't have an epic, and I'd like to see the Indian people do the epic for this part of the earth. It may not be just one person, it may be a bunch of people. That's what I'm looking for (*Smoke Rising* 378).

In other words, until non-Natives *and* Natives allow Native experiences to become a standard of measurement against which we judge our democratic experiment, the American experience will remain defective from its inception to the present moment.

How can Native authors create an "epic for this part of the earth" if their works aren't known or are inadequately represented? *Representation* is a complex political and literary term. Notions of representation are central in a democracy. And in a democracy, the majority often rules. According to Gregory S. Jay, most universities have, until recently, engaged in "whiteness" studies—studies of the works of White, Anglo-Saxon, protestant, Eurocentric males. In addition, Jay maintains, "Classic liberal theory begins with the individual as its primary unit, whereas current conflicts over representation stem from the claim that *groups* also have right to representation." Moreover, Jay asserts, "the language of recognition [of the dominant elite] tends to reinforce rather than investigate the privileged position of those who do the recognizing." What this means is that people of color, the poor, and women—since the creation of the U.S. Constitution and Bill of Rights—have struggled to gain equal representation under the law. They have historically been denied commensurate access to "life, liberty, and the pursuit of happiness."

Jay explains that *representation* likewise "refers both to systems of knowledge made out of signs and to material or economic arrangements for the (re)production of knowledge." In other words, people have access to information *depending on* which books get written, published, advertised, purchased, and taught. Representation is a term that furthermore "tends to bridge the gap between politics and culture, since it is a term often used in analyzing films, paintings, poems, and novels as well as political systems" (29).

Professor of English and Native American Studies at the University of California, Davis (until his death in 2002) Louis Owens (Choctaw/Cherokee) explores issues of representation as applied to Native texts and authors. In his essay "Native American Voices and Postcolonial Theory," Owens notes that the leading representatives of Postcolonial theory—Edward Said, Dipesh Chakrabarty, Toni Morrison, Homi Bahbha, and to a lesser degree, Trinh Minh-Ha—either dismiss or don't acknowledge Native American writers in their published works (*I Hear the Train* 207–215). Owens asks, for example, how can Homi Bhabah, "a student of postcoloniality, difference, liminality, and what he terms 'culture as a strategy of survival' be utterly ignorant or indifferent to such writers as N. Scott Momaday, James Welch, Leslie Silko, Louise Erdrich, Simon Ortiz . . . or Gerald Vizenor?" Owens further laments the almost "complete erasure of Native American voices" in general works of literary criticism (209).

Owens likewise discusses the "reproduction of knowledge." Owens is critical about where and how Native works are taught and disseminated. Owens contends that "Books that appeal to the metropolitan center's desire for the exotic, the colorful fringes of itself . . . will continue to be produced." But "the voices that tell stories too disturbing or too alien will be kept silenced or at best on the publishing margins represented by small presses and, more than ever today, university presses" (212). A quick perusal of the bibliographies of Native authors would validate Owens' assertions. Gerald Vizenor (Ojibwa), professor of American Studies at the University of California, Berkeley, has published thirty five books to date. Of those thirty five, twenty one are published by university presses and the rest by a small press in Minnesota.

The toughest agitator triggering contemporary critical debates is Elizabeth Cook-Lynn (Crow Creek Sioux). Cook-Lynn is a poet, novelist, storyteller, retired college professor, and founder and editor of *Wicazo Sa Review*—an Indian Studies journal. In Cook-Lynn's estimation, "there can be no doubt, despite recent disclaimers in the media, about the power of intellectuals at universities to direct the course of American life and thought" ("American Indian Intellectualism and the New Indian Story" 130). Cook-Lynn believes that changes in the American imagination with regard to Native peoples will come primarily through education. And yet, even though several big name Native American authors are taught in literature courses at major universities, they are often taught in isolation, as examples of marginalized voices, or because they maintain desired images of "vanishing" Indians—drunks, misfits, socially misguided or morally corrupt humans. Cook Lynn argues:

> the American Indian writers who have achieved successful readership in mainstream America seem to . . . present Indian populations as simply gatherings of exiles, emigrants, and refugees, strangers to themselves and their lands, pawns in the control of white manipulators, mixed-bloods searching for identity—giving support, finally, to the idea of

nationalistic/tribal culture as a contradiction in terms ("The American Indian Fiction Writers" 29–30).

Cook-Lynn is also anxious about Louise Erdrich's "Christian-oriented apocalyptic vision" in her abundant prose; James Welch's "dismissal of nationhood of the Blackfeet" in his novels; N. Scott Momaday's "mythic self-absorption"; and Gerald Vizenor's "whoever wants to be tribal can join the tribe" ("The American Indian Fiction Writers" 29–30). In other words, Cook-Lynn feels that many of the major Native authors aren't accountable enough to their tribal heritages. Cook-Lynn would agree with Revard, then, that Native writers must keep mythic dimensions open *while* being frankly honest about the "tough parts" of Indian lives.

Owens acknowledges Cook-Lynn's concerns with the following qualifications: "Because poverty and hopelessness are such unavoidable realities of Indian existence, it is natural that poverty would be a part of such fiction. To ignore the painful would be to falsify the picture." Furthermore, Owens contends that "Poverty and an inability to imagine a future different from the intolerable present lead to despair, and despair leads to abuse of self and others as well as the natural desire for temporary escape"—through alcohol, drug abuse, sexual avarice, violence, and other antisocial behaviors. However, "such portraits not only represent just one side of Indian existence, but more unfortunately conform readily to Euramerican readers' expectations that the American Indians are doomed by firewater." Owens does not want White readers' "stereotypes comfortably reinforced by sensationalized alcoholism and cultural impotence" (*Mixedblood Messages* 27). Owen's work *Other Destinies: Understanding the American Indian Novel* is a text dedicated to the proposition that the above lifestyles do not need to be the destiny of Native peoples. And to demonstrate his thesis, he explicates the works of numerous novelists who create characters who not only survive abusive contexts but return to tribal kinship or mythic tales to heal.

In an offhanded way, Owens does take into consideration what readers might imagine about reservation life from the writings of Louise Erdrich and Sherman Alexie. In Erdrich's nine *North Dakota* novels, "the reservation seems to be little more than a place where people live in cheap federal housing while drinking, making complicated love, feuding with one another, building casinos, and dying self-destructive and often violent deaths." In a comic play on his own assessment of Erdrich's reservation Indians, Owens continues: in Alexie's "stories and novels the reservation is a vaguely defined place where people live in cheap federal housing while drinking, playing basketball, feuding with one another, and dying self-destructive and often violent deaths." Both authors use Trickster discourse techniques in their fiction. In fact, many of their characters are self-critical as a way of pointing out the consequences of certain behaviors. However, Owens believes that "self-destructive, self-deprecatory humor provides an essential matrix for this fiction because such humor deflects any 'lesson in morality' from the non-Native reader and allows authors to maintain an aggressive posture regarding an essential 'authentic' Indianness while simultaneously giving the commercial market and reader exactly what they want and expect" (76). Owens worries that "Such fiction tells the reader that the Indian is a helpless, romantic victim still in the process of vanishing just as he is supposed to do" (*Mixedblood Messages* 77). That is, readers are amused and charmed, even threatened, by the behaviors of Erdrich's and Alexie's characters without understanding their underlying compassion and moral vision.

Leslie Marmon Silko (Laguna) also criticizes Erdrich's novel *The Beet Queen* for not being ethnic enough. Susan Perez Castillo believes that the "vehemence" of Silko's critique of Erdrich is "rooted in a restrictive view of ethnicity and an essentialist, logocentric concept of textual representation" (15). In other words, Silko is imposing notions of "authenticity" and pure "representation" onto Erdrich's text. Is there a true, real, uncorrupted, unchanged Native community? Furthermore, have tribal peoples experienced colonization similarly? Castillo suggests that tribal affiliation makes a difference in how Native authors create their imaginary landscapes. Silko is Laguna; Erdrich is Ojibwa. The Ojibwa for "historical and geographical reasons has suffered the effects of acculturation on a far greater scale." Furthermore, Castillo asserts that "*The Beet Queen* may be mimetic in character, mirroring the fragmented ontological landscape in which many Native Americans exist today, shuttling between radically diverse realities" (18).

It is not that Cook-Lynn, Owens, Silko and others are looking for didactic fiction. And yet they share a belief that the literary imagination can transform consciousness. Poet, novelist, theorist, autoethnographer, and former professor of English at UCLA, Paula Gunn Allen (Laguna) further complicates this discussion by noting that authors, in dealing with the mythic dimensions, must do so with care. Gunn Allen criticizes Leslie Marmon Silko (Laguna), for example, for breaching tribal protocols in her novel *Ceremony*. The Laguna story that underscores the protagonist's activities "is a clan story, and is not to be told outside the clan," says Gunn Allen. Perhaps "no one ever told her why the Lagunas and other Pueblos are so closed about their spiritual activities and the allied oral tradition," states Gunn Allen ("Problems in Teaching Silko's *Ceremony*" 60–61). Many critics have attempted to decode the mythic components of *Ceremony*, and yet they have often done so like detectives trying to solve mysteries or spiritual voyeurs trying to gain uninitiated access to tribal secrets. Two questions emerge out of this discussion: How do Native American writers explicate tribal situations without reducing characters to pathetic, fake artifacts, however wondrously funny or tragic? And how do these same writers gain a semblance of *authenticity* without violating tribal authority?

In current Native discourse, *authenticity* is inextricably connected to *sovereignty*. There are two kinds of sovereignty being discussed in contemporary circles—one is land-based and nationalistic, the other is concerned with intellectual rights. Intellectual rights entertain ideas about who should possess, define, study, or write about Native individuals and cultures. Oren Lyons, one of the traditional chiefs of the Onondaga nation, defines sovereignty as "Self recognition. . . . Self-determination, the ability and right to govern oneself, exercising national powers in the interest of the nation and its peoples, is fundamental to sovereignty. This along with the jurisdiction over the lands and territories that we live and exist on, is sovereignty." Furthermore, Lyons argues that sovereignty is "a state of mind and the will of the people" (Udall 266). Under treaty obligations, individual tribal nations have the right to be recognized as separate nations within the boundaries of the United States. Cook-Lynn adds: "the very origins of a people are specifically tribal (nationalistic) and rooted in a specific geography (place), that mythology (soul) and geography (land) are inseparable, that even language is rooted in a specific place" ("The American Indian Fiction Writers" 33). What is more, sovereignty includes kinship relations—bloodlines.

Just who is an Indian? Eva Marie Garroutte answers, "Many people are surprised to discover that each tribe sets its *own* legal criteria for citizenship." Garroutte explains that about "two-thirds of all federally recognized tribes of the coterminous United States specify a minimum blood quantum in their legal criteria, with one-quarter blood degree being the most frequent requirement" (224). However, the blood quantum is generally "calculated on the basis of the immediacy of one's genetic relationship to ancestors whose bloodlines were (supposedly) unmixed" (225). Some tribal affiliations are also determined through either matrilineal or patrilineal descent. Often, residency is a requirement as well. If being a "real" Indian is determined by the above factors, legitimacy issues are not only complicated but also precarious. Imagine the dilemma of a child whose father is full-blooded Navajo and whose mother is White with some degree of Hopi ancestry. Hostilities between Navajo and Hopi nations are legendary as well. Imagine also that this child lives in New York City. The Navajo are matrilineal—and so the complications mount. Another question arises: Who is inside a culture and who is outside? If you are one-eighth Indian but attend all ritual activity held on tribal lands, are you more Indian than the full-blood living in Los Angeles who never attends tribal rites? Questions raised by "mixedblood" distinction are also at the center of theoretical discourse.

The within/without debate hinges on notions of land-based communities where elders of the community can converge with other generations in order to pass on tribal wisdom and life-ways. Historically, reservations were "reserved" portions of land held back from more massive traditional homelands for the use of tribal peoples. In addition, reservations were also areas of confinement where Natives could be controlled or more readily acculturated. Since the reservation era, however, these homelands have become havens of continuity understandably protected from further incursions from the outside. Why not, however, view traditional lands as home base and those living in the diaspora as members who are "out" there, not relocating but reclaiming—taking back, piece by piece, lost territory?

Cook-Lynn, however, feels that literary theory and productivity must be generated from "within" tribal cultures and not from "without." "It is evident that the mixed-blood literary phenomenon is not generated from the inside of tribal culture since many of the practitioners admit they have been removed from cultural influence through urbanization and academic professionalization or even, they suggest, through biology and intermarriage," Cook-Lynn remarks ("Intellectualism and the New Indian Story" 129). In *Mixedblood Messages*, Owens responds to Cook-Lynn's insinuations. "Leading Cook-Lynn's list of what appears to be a kind of mixed-blood hall of shame are the names of Gerald Vizenor, Louis Owens, Wendy Rose, Maurice Kenny, Diane Glancy, Thomas King, Joseph Bruchac, Michael Dorris, and a few others" (151). In fact, in her book *Anti-Indianism in Modern America*, Cook-Lynn dismisses Michael Dorris entirely because his ancestors' names cannot be found on tribal roles. Furthermore, Cook-Lynn exposes charges of child abuse made against Dorris as a way of indicating that anyone of contestable reputation cannot be recognized from "within."

Owens feels that the mixedblood writer is especially qualified to discuss the Postmodern condition. In *Mixedblood Messages*, Owens contends:

> given the fact that almost all of the more than sixty novels by Native American authors are by writers of mixed Native and European descent—mixedbloods who embody the frontier, transcultural experience—I would suggest that the Native American novel is the quintessential postmodern frontier text, and the problem of identity at the center of virtually every Native American novel is the problem of internalized transculturation (46).

Mixedblood identity is morally problematic here. The ethics of making children responsible for the presumed illegitimacy of their parents' status is at best curious. The history of mixedblood identity places mixed-bloods at the margins of the marginalized. And, finally, if mixedblood status is an urban phenomenon, this places vast numbers of people with some Native ancestry in a condition of invisibility to both "insiders" (Native Nationalists) and "outsiders" (those who formulate government policies).

An editorial by Jason Begay in the August 29, 2002 edition of *The New York Times* begins: "The City with the largest American Indian population, according to the 2000 Census, is not Phoenix, not Los Angeles. It is New York City." Begay goes on to note that the "census counted 41,289 American Indians and Alaska natives living in the city." Furthermore, the 2000 census "allowed people to claim more than one race." And "those people who claimed only some American Indian or Alaska native heritage" brought the numbers of people claiming some Native birthright to 87,241 (B1). Begay writes that the Natives in New York come from numerous tribal ancestries and want to preserve their heritages (B4).

Gunn Allen speaks frankly of hyphenated identities in her essay, "The Autobiography of Confluence." Gunn Allen was born in New Mexico, a state which is often called "the triculture state." But New Mexico is more than three cultured, says Gunn Allen; it is

> Pueblo, Navajo and Apache, Chicano, Spanish, Spanish-American, Mexican-American; it is Anglo and that includes everything that is not Indian or Hispanic—in my case, Lebanese and Lebanese-American, Mexican-American, German-Jewish, Italian-Catholic, German-Luthern, Scotch-Irish-American Presbyterian, halfbreed (that is, people raised white-and-Indian), and Irish-Catholic; there are more, though these are the main ones that influenced me in childhood, and their influence was literary and aesthetic as well as social and personal (145).

Joseph Bruchac calls himself a *metis*. "In English it becomes 'Translator's Son,'" says Bruchac. "It means that you are able to understand the language of both sides, to help them understand each other" ("Notes of a Translator's Son" 203). Linda Hogan (Chickasaw) says: "I come from two different people, from white pioneers who crossed the plains and from Chickasaw Indian people from south central Oklahoma" ("Two Hands" 233). Gerald Vizenor (Ojibwa) mocks the impetus toward an invented blood purity. He writes about himself in third person:

> The mixedblood is a new metaphor, he proposed, a transitive contradancer between communal tribal cultures and those material and urban pretensions that counter conserva-

tive traditions. The mixedblood wavers in autobiographies; he moves between mythic reservations where tricksters roamed and the cities where his father was murdered ("Crows Written on the Poplars: Autocritical Autobiographies" 101).

Vizenor's "autocritical"—self critical—approach to literature and identity is based in Trickster discourse—a type of self-reflexive, comic wordplay that calls ideologies into question.

The politics of mixedblood identity is worth noting. Patricia Riley explains that early in American history "intermarriage between whites and Indians was advocated as a means of achieving a 'bloodless' conquest, one that could be arrived at not by the spilling of blood, but by the mixing of it." Riley cites Thomas Jefferson who, in 1803, maintained that "the ultimate point of rest and happiness for them is to let our settlement and theirs meet and blend together, to intermix, and to become one people . . . and it will be better to promote than retard it" (230). Riley reports that Christian missionaries often felt intermarriage was the solution to civilizing and Christianizing the Indians. "In the 1830s, Alexis de Tocqueville held that 'the half-blood forms the natural link between civilization and barbarism,'" explains Riley (231). Actual Native words for crossing bloods are equally important to this discussion. Cook-Lynn might be chagrined, for example, to note that in her own Native tongue, "the word used to describe a mixed blood is *iyeske*"—meaning "one who not only interprets between the red and white worlds, but between the world of spirits and the human beings as well" (Riley 231).

The moral implications of mixedblood identities are further raised by Deloria, who teaches that "Nothing has incidental meaning and there are no coincidences. . . . Every bit of information must be related to the general framework of moral interpretation." Deloria believes that "every entity" has a responsibility "to enjoy life, fulfill itself, and increase in wisdom and the spiritual development of personality" ("If You Think About It, You Will See That It Is True" 47). Deloria contends that current critical debates about tribal sovereignty and Indian identity must be "in process" because there is so much to consider. Mixedblood identities are revelatory and ask that humans become humble before such composite expressions of human life.

Critics who align themselves as *nationalists, indigenists,* or *cosmopolitans* are currently attempting to define the direction Native aesthetics should take. Arnold Krupat is one of the leading non-Native scholars on these issues. He is a professor of Literature on the Global Studies Faculty at Sarah Lawrence College. Krupat has formulated an entire system of literary theory based on his life-long study of Native American literatures and cultures—a system he calls *Ethnocriticsm* (1992). In his book *red matters* (2002), Krupat defines the key approaches in the advancement of Native aesthetics. Krupat's title plays off of Craig Womack's (Cherokee) book *Red on Red, Native American Literary Separatism* (1999)—one of the first books by a Native intellectual devoted to Native separatism. Krupat is a *cosmopolitan* and Womack is a *nationalist.* A nationalist believes that it is time for Native people to exclude any European or Euroamerican influence from a developing Native aesthetics. This is a necessary tactic because tribal views of the world are incomparable, worthy of independent investigation, and therefore must, at this point in time, be exclusionist. In other words, Nationalists are tired of, even enraged by, outsiders' incessant need to define Native experience. Says Womack:

> The postmodernists might laugh at claims of prioritizing insider status, questioning the very nature of what constitutes an insider and pointing out that no pure Creek, or Native, viewpoint exists, that Native and non-Native are constantly deconstructing each other. In terms of a reality check, however, we might remind ourselves that authenticity and insider and outsider status are, in fact often discussed in Native communities, especially given the historical reality that outsiders have so often been the ones interpreting things Indian. Further it seems foolhardy to me to abandon a search for the affirmation of a national literary identity simply to fall in line with the latest literary trend. The construction of such an identity reaffirms the real truth about our place in history—we are not mere victims but active agents in history, innovators of new ways, Indian ways, of thinking and being and

speaking and authoring in this world created by colonial contact (5–6).

Furthermore, Womack claims there can be no canon of American literature without Native literatures because such literatures are originary. "I say that tribal literatures are not some branch waiting to be grafted onto the main trunk. Tribal literatures are the *tree*, the oldest literatures in the Americas, the most American of American literatures" (6–7).

Krupat feels that "national positions also need other positions, those of indigenists (as persons with different bodies of systematic knowledge) and cosmopolitans (as persons who can translate between different bodies of knowledge), for their anticolonial projects to succeed (for them not to replicate colonialism under another name or to become 'neurotic' entitites)" (*red matters* 7).

Postmodern thought is insistent that consciousness is more ethically formulated based on *difference* rather than on bipolarity. This means that meaning begetting paradigms are based on multiplicity (cross-cultural and dialogic experiences with reality) rather than on dualities (us and them; male and female; black and white; good guys and bad guys; civilized and uncivilized constructions of reality). Such considerations inform the concerns of cosmopolitans. Nationalists, however, believe that the multiplicity of Native cultures can serve the ends of difference.

The majority of Vizenor's literary productivity is informed by tribal aesthetics—particularly in his Trickster approach to various ideologies. However, Vizenor's theory is embodied in the behaviors of his characters who often represent the foolish excesses of ideologies whether Anglo or Native. Vizenor's style is *dialogic*, a term important to contemporary cross-cultural conversations. Another influential scholar of Native American Studies, David L. Moore defines the importance of the dialogic by showing how dualistic and dialectic approaches to Indian/White deliberations are terminal—static, fixed, deadly. Further, Moore demonstrates how significant Native authors are actually more dialogic than dualistic (bipolar). "A dialogic emphasizes, however, the changeability of meaning in 'both' participants, the colonized and the colonizer, the text and the author, the text and the reader, by showing how they are not aligned dualistically but rather are surrounded by influences in a multiple field." What Moore so clearly demonstrates in his essay is how the dualistic, dialectic, and dialogic approaches to thought and behavior each generate "different epistemological expectations and perceptions" (105). In other words, the dialogic processes found in many Native works constitute a "relationality" that is cutting edge.

And yet, the merits of separatism are more readily understandable from an experiential perspective. In her essay, "The Great Pretenders," poet and university professor Wendy Rose (Hopi) chronicles numerous events she has undergone with "outside" experts. For example, while wearing long shells, "dentalia," given to her by a Yurok woman "as payment for a painting," a "famous" anthropologist commented that it was sad "northwestern California Indians were no longer familiar with their ancient form of money, long shells called 'dentalia.'" On another occasion, a "basket specialist" told Rose that California Indian women no longer wear "basket-hats." And yet "nearly every weekend such women attended the same social functions as I, wearing basket-hats that had been passed down through their families and, more importantly, were still being made." Another famous anthropologist and art collector told Rose that "pottery was no longer produced by Laguna Pueblo." Rose writes that the art collector "continued to insist on this, even after I told her the names of the women who produce it there." A noted linguist asked Rose to "escort a group of Yuki elders around the [university anthropology] museum, and then confided to me that it was a shame no one spoke Yuki anymore." The irony was, "the elders spoke to one another in Yuki the entire time they were there." One final exasperating example will serve to illustrate Rose's frustrations. *The* expert on "Laguna Pueblo pottery said to me, face to face, that Indians only *think* they know more about themselves than anthropologists" (406). Few Native authors could not cite similar experiences. And there comes a time when it is enough.

Several points arise out of the above anecdotes: Traditional artistic expression is dynamic and ongoing. And Natives are tired of the ignorance of "experts" who attempt to define Native people. Each tribe possesses complex understandings about the creation and maintenance of beauty. Consider the belief among the Navajo, for example, that a poor man is one who has no song. This means that the creation of beauty is not for collectors to hang on their walls, to file in libraries, or gather into museums, but for the health and well being of individuals in their open and ongoing participation with life. Native approaches to the articulation of beauty exist in abundance. However, the coming decade will see such articulation become more available to wider audiences through the efforts of Native authors and critics.

Works Cited

Allen, Paula Gunn, "The Autobiography of Confluence," in *I Tell You Now*, Brian Swann and Arnold Krupat, eds. (Lincoln: University of Nebraska Press, 1987).

———, "Special Problems in Teaching Leslie Marmon Silko's *Ceremony*," in *Natives and Academics*, Devon A. Mihesuah, ed. (Lincoln: University of Nebraska Press, 1998).

Begay, Jason, "Native New Yorkers (The Original Kind)," editorial, *New York Times* sec. B, August 9, 2002.

Bruchac, Joseph, "Translator's Son," in *I Tell You Now*, Brian Swann and Arnold Krupat, eds. (Lincoln: University of Nebraska Press 1987).

Cook-Lynn, Elizabeth, "American Indian Intellectualism and the New Indian Story," *Natives and Academics*, Devon A. Mihesuah, ed. (Lincoln: University of Nebraska Press, 1998).

———, "The American Indian Fiction Writers," in *Nothing But the Truth: An Anthology of Native American Literature*, John Purdy and James Ruppert, eds. (Upper Saddle River, NJ: Prentice Hall, 2001).

Deloria Jr., Vine, *Spirit and Reason: The Vine Deloria, Jr. Reader* (Golden, Colorado: Fulcrum, 1999).

Dunsmore, Roger, "Vine Deloria, Jr. (March 26, 1933–)," in *Handbook of Native American Literature*, Andrew Wiget, ed. (New York: Garland, 1996).

Garroutte, Eva Marie, "The Racial Formation of American Indians," *American Indian Quarterly* 25:2 (Spring 2001).

Hogan, Linda, "Two Hands," in *I Tell You Now*, Brian Swann and Arnold Krupat, eds. (Lincoln: University of Nebraska Press 1987).

Jay, Gregory S., *American Literature and the Culture Wars* (Ithaca, NY: Cornell University Press, 1997).

Krupat, Arnold, *red matters* (Philadelphia: University of Pennsylvania Press, 2002).

Lyons, Oren, "In Jack Utter," in *American Indians: Answers to Today's Questions* (Norman: University of Oklahoma Press, 1993).

Marshall, Joseph M., III, "Wounded Knee Takeover, 1973," in *Encyclopedia of North American Indians*, Frederick E. Hoxie, ed. (New York: Houghton Mifflin, 1996).

Monette, Richard, "Treaties," in *Encyclopedia of North American Indians*, Frederick E. Hoxie, ed. (New York: Houghton Mifflin Company, 1996).

Moore, David L., "Decolonializing Criticism: Reading Dialectics and Dialogics in Native American Literatures," in *Nothing But the Truth*, John L Purdy and James Ruppert, eds. (Upper Saddle River, NJ: 2001).

Owens, Louis, *Mixedblood Messages* (Norman: University of Oklahoma Press, 1998).

———, *I Hear the Train* (Norman: University of Oklahoma Press, 2001).

Revard, Carter, in *Smoke Rising*, Janet Witalec, ed. (Detroit: Visible Ink, 1996).

Riley, Patricia, "The Mixed Blood Writer as Interpreter and Mythmaker," in *Understanding Others*, Joseph Trimmer and Tilly Warnock, eds. (Urbana, IL: National Council of English, 1992).

Rose, Wendy, "The Great Pretenders: Further Reflections on Whiteshamanism," in *The State of Native America: Genocide, Colonization, and Resistance*, M. Annette Jaimes, ed. (Boston: South End Press, 1992).

Vizenor, Gerald, "Crows Written on the Poplars: Autocritical Autobiographies," in *I Tell You Now*, Brian Swann and Arnold Krupat, eds. (Lincoln: University of Nebraska Press, 1987).

Womack, Craig S., *Red on Red* (Minneapolis: University of Minnesota Press, 1999).

Warrior, Robert Allen, *Tribal Secrets* (Minneapolis: University of Minnesota Press, 1995).

Chapter Eight

Selected Further Readings, Reference Works, and Research Tools

General Reference Materials

Hirschfelder, Arlene and Paulette Molin. *Encyclopedia of Native American Religions.* New York: Checkmark, 2001.

"The entries in this book cover the spiritual traditions of Native peoples in the United States and Canada before contact with Europeans and Americans, the consequences of this contact on sacred traditions, and contemporary religious forms" (vii–viii). References to sacred sites, famous religious practitioners, significant rituals, influential Catholic and Protestant missionaries, and ideas of spiritual well-being and illness are included in this work. The work provides respectful and carefully researched information about the nature of the sacred—a topic frequently referenced in Native literatures.

Hoxie, Frederick E., ed. *Encyclopedia of North American Indians.* Boston: Houghton Mifflin, 1996.

Frederick E. Hoxie amassed the expertise of two hundred seventy tribal and nontribal scholars to combat massive ignorance about Native peoples. Four kinds of entries appear in this work: (1) descriptions of one hundred major tribes, five major languages, and four major language families; (2) one hundred biographies of famous Natives; (3) one hundred "interpretive entries" on "significant topics"—from "African Americans and American Indians," to "Bible Translations," "Dreams," "Treaties," and "Diseases," among others; and (4) "definitions for terms and events that are frequently mentioned

and often misunderstood" (ix). This work is an excellent tool for readers who need to understand allusions to historical events, personalities,
and key political issues found in Native literature.

Keoke, Emory Dean and Kay Marie Porterfield. *Encyclopedia of
American Indian Contributions to the World.* New York: Facts on
File, 2002.

"American Indians, from the Arctic Circle to the tip of South America,
donated many gifts to the world's common fund of knowledge in the
areas of agriculture, science and technology, medicine, transportation,
architecture, psychology, military strategy, government, and language.
These contributions take the form of inventions, processes, philosophies, and political, or social systems" (ix). Native Literature is often
about the reclamation or adaptation of traditional medical, psychological, social, political and religious practices referenced by articles contained in this encyclopedia.

Online Resources about Native American Authors

These online resources will open up the field of Native American
Literatures to students interested in understanding the vast com-
plexity and abundant reading possibilities available in the field of
Native American Literatures.

ABELL (Annual Bibliography of English Language and Literature)
http://lion.chadwyck.com/lion_ref_abell/search (This is a sub-
set of Literature Online)

This is a database of English literature. It contains everything from
periodical articles, to book reviews, to essays and dissertations from
around the world, all dealing with English literature. The database
includes full-text versions of 120 journals, and covers work published
between 1920 and the present.

Humanities Full Text (Wilson Web) (This website is usually
accessed through a university library system)

This database "indexes and abstracts over 500 periodicals in art,
archaeology, classical studies, communications, film, theatre, literature,
folklore, etc." It deals with work from 1984 to the present, is updated

four times a week, and includes full text versions of over 180 publications since 1995.

Native American Authors on the Web dizzy.library.arizona.edu

This site includes biographies and information about North American Indian Authors arranged either by author, the title of a work, or by authors who have particular tribal affiliations. This site also includes links to the Internet Public Library as well as other relevant sites. Sites for each author include fairly up-to-date biographic and bibliographic information—including each author's major works of literature as well as contributions to major research journals and the like. Literary awards granted to each author are also noted.

Storytellers: Native American Authors Online www.hanksville.org

This site includes alphabetical listings of authors, tribal listing of authors, and links to traditional storytelling events and relevant tribal information from throughout Native America. Special series are also included—especially those related to Native women's literary contributions.

Handbooks and Dictionaries

Wiget, Andrew, ed. *Handbook of Native American Literature*. New York: Garland, 1996.

Sixty-four scholars contribute their expertise to this volume under the categories of "Native American Oral Literatures," "The Historical Emergence of Native American Writing," and "A Native American Renaissance: 1967 to the Present." This is an authoritative work by the best-known academics in the field of Native American Literatures. Historical contexts, overviews, genre studies, and biographical sketches of major authors are contained therein.

Dictionary of Literary Biography. Published by A. Bruccoli Clark Layman. Gale Research.

The *Dictionary of Literary Biography* is made up of 256 volumes to date. Each volume is devoted to a particular region, culture, genre, author, or group of authors. Several volumes are of particular interest to students of Native American Literature: Volume 175, *Native*

American Writers of the United States, edited by Kenneth M. Roemer (1997); Volume 206, *Twentieth-Century American Western Writers, First Series*, edited by Richard H. Cracroft (1999); Volume 212, *Twentieth-Century American Western Writers, Second Series*, edited by Richard H. Cracroft (1999); Volume 227, *American Novelists Since World War II, Sixth Series*, edited by James R. Giles and Wanda H. Giles (2002); and Volume 256, *Twentieth-Century Western Writers, Third Series*, edited by Richard H. Cracroft (2002). Editors of *The Dictionary of Literary Biography* are noted for their efforts to select experts in the field who will compile correct and complete examinations of the lives and works of the authors contained in each volume. Each text also contains an introductory essay acquainting students with relevant historical, theoretical, and literary contexts for the authors, era, or area being discussed.

Autobiographical Essays and Interviews

Swann, Brian and Arnold Krupat, eds. *I Tell You Now*. Lincoln: University of Nebraska Press, 1987.

This accumulation of literary autobiographies gives insights into how/why each author developed a literary voice. Eighteen authors—including Mary TallMountain, Elizabeth Cook-Lynn, Maurice Kenny, Carter Revard, Duane Niatum, Simon Ortiz, Linda Hogan, Wendy Rose, and Joy Harjo, among others—write about the generation of their creative voice. In each instance, these autobiographical essays attain the status of art.

Bruchac, Joseph. *Survival this Way: Interviews with American Indian Poets* (Sun Tracks Books, No. 15). Tucson: University of Arizona Press, 1990.

In this much-used collection of interviews, Bruchac asks questions of leading Native American poets about what constitutes a uniquely Indian work. Time-worn questions are debated. Should the ethnic or gender status of an author make a difference in the critical analysis of his/her work? And if ethnic differences contribute to the reason for the excellence of a particular work, why is that so?

Coltelli, Laura. *Winged Words: American Indian Writers Speak.* Lincoln: University of Nebraska Press, 1990.

Winged Words contains interviews with eleven Native American authors. In each interview, Laura Coltelli asks particular questions relative to each author's life and works. For example, Coltelli asks Linda Hogan how urban tribalism works. She asks N. Scott Momaday how the written word might reflect oral traditions. Cotelli asks Simon Ortiz how his storytelling is related to place. She asks Gerald Vizenor how he likes being labeled a Postmodern novelist and what this means in terms of Postmodern themes. Because of the nature of Cotelli's questions, this text remains timely.

Noted Anthologies

Bierhorst, John, ed. *Four Masterworks of American Indian Literature.* Tucson: University of Arizona Press, 1974.

Four timeless classics of ancient Native American literature are contained in this volume—including the Aztec hero Myth of *Quetzalcoatl* (a savior figure); the Iroquois restoration ceremony, *The Ritual of Condolence* (a grand healing ritual based on the lives of the founders of the Iroquois Confederacy—Deganawida and Hiawatha); the Maya prophecy *Cuceb* (which explains the causes for the destruction of the world); and *The Night Chant,* one of the great restoration rituals of the Navajo. N. Scott Momaday based his novel *House Made of Dawn* on verses from the Navajo *Night Chant.* These works are equivalent to ancient Greek classics like *The Iliad* and *The Odyssey.* However, these Native texts are also considered great mythic works equivalent to various genres found in the Old and New Testaments.

Niatum, Duane, ed. *Harper's Anthology of 20th Century Native American Poetry.* New York: HarperSanFrancisco, 1988.

In this anthology, Duane Niatum (Klallam) brings together poetry by thirty-six of "the most widely read and respected Native American writers as well as a generous selection of poems by new and young writers who are publishing American art and literature in new directions" (ix). Readers interested in becoming acquainted with the best known Native poets will enjoy this anthology. Mary TallMountain

(Athabaskan-Russian), Maurice Kenny (Mohawk), Peter Blue Cloud (Mohawk), Duane Niatum (Klallam), Lance Henson (Cheyenne), Barney Bush (Shawnee/Cayuga), Roberta Hill Whiteman (Oneida), Wendy Rose (Hopi/'Me-wuk), and Nia Francisco (Navajo) are included. Among the more familiar Native authors already addressed in this study of Native Literatures included in this anthology are Louise Erdrich, N. Scott Momaday, Simon Ortiz, Linda Hogan, Carter Revard, and James Welch. Brian Swann's introduction is informative and foundational to a study of what makes the poetry in this volume Native poetry.

Ortiz, Simon J., ed. *Earth Power Coming: Short Fiction in Native American Literature.* Tsaile, AZ: Navajo Community College Press, 1983.

In his introduction to this collection of thirty authors' short stories, Simon Ortiz says these stories are more than literature; they are creations that make "sure . . . the voice keeps singing forth so that the earth power will not cease, and [so] that the people [will] remain fully aware of their social, economic, political, cultural, and spiritual relationships and responsibilities to all things" (vii-viii). This collection contains stories by high profile writers like Leslie Marmon Silko, Linda Hogan, Louise Erdrich, Joseph Bruchac, Carter Revard, and Gerald Vizenor as well as authors well known among Native circles—Peter Blue Cloud (Mohawk), Geary Hobson (Cherokee/Quapaw/Chickasaw), Maurice Kenny (Mohawk), Ralph Salisbury (Cherokee), Luci Tapahonso (Navajo), Mary TallMountain (Athabascan/Russian), Anna L. Walters (Pawnee/Otoe/Missouria), and others. Carter Revard's "Report To The Nation: Claiming Europe," is frequently anthologized due to Revard's ironic presumption of claiming Europe for the Osage people.

Purdy, John L. and James Ruppert, eds. *Nothing But The Truth: An Anthology of Native American Literature.* New York: Prentice Hall, 2001.

This highly acclaimed anthology contains twelve essays by leading critics of Native American literature as well as fiction, poetry, and drama by forty-three of the best known Native American authors, from A to

W—from Sherman Alexie through Gerald Vizenor to James Welch. The combination of classic critical essays with creative works makes this anthology enormously useful to students interested in literature and literary criticism.

Quantic, Diane D. and P. Jane Hafen, eds. *A Great Plains Reader.* Lincoln: University of Nebraska Press, 2003.

This reader is a collection of creative texts by diverse authors whose works reflect the rich North American landscape known as the Great Plains. This work is not made up of exclusively Native authors. While it does include works by Louise Erdrich (Ojibwe), Diane Glancy (Cherokee), and James Welch (Blackfeet), it also includes the contributions of such notable writers as Willa Cather, Loren Eiseley, Langston Hughes, Garrison Keillor, and Mark Twain among others. Readers can study excerpts from tribal histories as well as essays on ecology amidst creative expressions of living in this unique landscape. This reader acquaints students with the vast social and creative contexts needed to understand the American experience as a complex possibility of conversations across disciplines and within larger historical as well as social fields.

Journals

American Indian Culture and Research Journal (AICRJ)

A leading journal in American Indian Studies, AICRJ is published four times a year by the UCLA American Indian Studies Center. Critical essays on a wide variety of Native subjects, contemporary literature, and book reviews are contained in each issue. All entries are peer reviewed. This means that works are accepted based on their sound scholarship and timely contribution to Native American Studies.

American Indian Quarterly (AIQ)

An interdisciplinary journal containing articles on the anthropology, literature, religion, and arts of Native Americans. This journal encourages dialogue on recent developments on theories and methods attendant to Native studies.

Leading Native scholars—Devon A. Mihesuah, Geary Hobson, Vine Deloria, Jr., and Jack D. Forbes, among others—are on the editorial board of this journal published by the University of Nebraska Press.

Studies in American Indian Literatures (SAIL)

SAIL is the only journal in the United States devoted entirely to American Indian Literatures. Also published by the University of Nebraska Press, this journal has special issues devoted to special topics as well as leading Native Authors like Carter Revard, Leslie Marmon Silko, and Sherman Alexie. SAIL also contains creative works and reviews of pertinent books. Articles in SAIL are also peer reviewed.

Wicazo Sa Review

A journal that supports research on Native cultural, religious, legal, and historical issues. The goal of this journal is to help indigenous peoples come to an interdisciplinary understanding of the forces at work in determining their sovereignty in creative, legal, intellectual, and cultural arenas. Every issue contains critical essays, interviews, book reviews, literary criticism, and scholarly articles on Native studies. Numerous Native authors have contributed to this journal—including such notables as Vine Deloria, Jr., Joy Harjo, Gerald Vizenor, Thomas King, and Simon Ortiz.

Chapter Nine

Glossary

Authenticity   What constitutes *real* or tribally recognized Indian identity and thought.

Autobiography   A genre which has traditionally focused on the uniqueness of a significant person's life-experiences; tribal peoples, however, do not see the story of an individual life as an authentic or ethical mode of expression because autobiography is another form of democratic individualism—focusing on separatism rather than communalism.

Biomedical reductionism   According to Theodore Roszak, "the normally functioning ego [who falsely assumes to be] an isolated atom of self-regarding consciousness that has no relational continuity with the physical world around it."

Cosmopolitanism   The awareness and ability to act on multicultural/multinational deliberations for the mutual benefit of urban and tribal peoples—with attention to issues of cross-fertilization.

Cosmopolitans   Persons who can translate between different bodies of systematic knowledge—ethnic/immigrant/American/regional—and Western intellectual, literary, critical, and social histories.

Cultural expression   According to Ethnologist Charles David Kleymeyer "the representation in language, symbols, and actions of a particular group's collective heritage—its history, aesthetic values, beliefs, observations, desires, knowledge, wisdom, and opinions."

Dialogic   A cross-cultural conversation which, according to David L. Moore, "emphasizes the changeability of meaning in 'both' participants . . . by showing how they are not aligned dualistically (us/them) but rather are surrounded by influences" from multiple fields.

Dualistic   A type of bipolar thinking that divides conceptions of the world into us and them, male and female, white and black, civilized and uncivilized constructions of reality, etc.

Ecocide   According to Elizabeth Cook-Lynn, "the intentional destruction of the physical environment needed to sustain human health and life in a given geographical region."

Ecological groundedness   According to William Cahlahan, a term used by Gestalt therapists to describe "a dynamic state of the person that includes the sense of confidence, pleasure, and wonder resulting from progressively deepening contact with the wild and domesticated natural community. . . ."

Ethos   Personal evaluation of the meaning or value of a topic often based on one's ethnic identity.

Fragmentation   On a personal/cultural level, fragmentation occurs when a colonial power insists that indigenous people adapt to mainstream ideologies; the result of such incursions into the life-ways of traditional peoples can be recognized in personal despair, family and cultural dysfunction, alcoholism, joblessness, and other kinds of personal/cultural disorientation.

Hybridization   A term used to denote the combining or cross-fertilization of multicultural threads into a new, more viable way of being in the world; such adaptation does not absorb the contributions of ethnic minorities into dominant cultural norms but rather creates revitalized or hybrid biological, social, political, and cultural forms of survival.

Indigenists   Persons with local or original bodies of systematic knowledge as opposed to colonially imposed systems.

Indian oratory   Individual verbal and/or tribal leaders' oral expressions concerning tribal values, political concerns, community squabbles, and the tragic consequences of Euroamerican incursions; also includes speeches to outsiders.

Intellectual sovereignty   The rights or responsibilities of individual authors to engage in theory formation based on tribal histories and literary expressions independent from Western influence.

Liminal A space where individuals from two cultures meet and realize their views of the world are constructed by the culture into which they are born; or a space in ritual practice where an initiate is thrust into unknown psychological/religious spheres.

Literary autoethnography An emerging new literary genre characterized by Native authors who perform an anthropology of their own experience—often demonstrating how ethnicity, race, ancestry, gender, historical moment, and geographical location shape each author's identity, an identity that is inseparable from communal contexts.

Logos Scientific, factual, or historical description of a concept or event.

Memoir Usually concerned with personalities and actions other than those of the writer during a particularly memorable era in cultural history.

Meta-narrative Sacred stories that presume to narrate and explain how and why the world was created and how humans ought to act while they occupy their role in society.

Metis One who is mixedblood. According to Joseph Bruchac, it means "translator's son. . . . It means that you are able to understand the language of both sides, to help them understand each other."

Mystery In Owens's works, analogous to the French *mystère* plays, early medieval dramas based on sacred narratives and rituals.

Mysticism The belief that reason and logic are not the only means of gaining knowledge.

Mythologies Sacred, timeless stories considered true, living, and exemplary; such stories are most often about creation as well as the intervention of the divine into human affairs to establish cultures, lands of inheritance, laws of behavior, and callings for shaman (healers and prophets).

Mythos A mythological orientation to the world, often revealed in stories.

Nationalist One who believes that Native people should exclude any European or Euroamerican influence from a developing Native sovereignty or aesthetic.

Native Christian narrative discourse   Narrative works by tribal members who are also Christians; these works often testify about how tribal experiences with the divine can correct conceptions of Christ proffered by other world religions; these works also tend to emphasize personal and collective experience in developing religious insight.

Ontogenetic crippling   According to Paul Shepard, the arrested development experienced by most adults in the modern era because they can't position themselves within their natural environment.

Original trauma   According to Chellis Glendinning, "the disconnection from the earth" as the origin of subsequent traumas.

Postcolonial   The movement away from colonial domination toward a recovery of Native life-ways and Native cultural contributions to personal and communal well-being as well as a recuperation and publication of Native contributions to American culture.

Postmodern   The movement in cultural theory which challenges or provides evidence against those narratives that have, historically, viewed indigenous peoples as existing on the lowest ranks of the evolutionary chain toward civilization, scientific inquiry, religious thought, and creative achievement.

Reductive thought   Reducing the ideas in a complex narrative, drama, or poem to a thesis statement, ethical assertion, or moral judgement; or reducing a culture to simple characterizations of Indian or tribal identities.

Representation   How Indians are represented politically, nationally, and by individual authors.

Ritual language   The language used during ritual performance; ritual language is passed on from one generation to the next and is intended to remain stable or unaltered through time.

Sacred texts   Those texts which deal with ultimate human concerns including: the creation of all life forms, time, the causes of suffering, loss, the power of language, the human ability to imagine, and the reorienting intent of ritual.

Signified   Those realities to which words, gestures, actions, or things refer.

Signifier A word, gesture, action, or thing used as a symbol for a referent.

Signs Words, symbols, acts, or creeds used to convey meaning.

Simulations Poses, inventions, and false images manufactured to sell what audiences expect or want (i.e. the images of the noble savage or vanishing Indian).

Sovereignty The right of Native communities to actualize their status as independent nations.

Species arrogance According to John E. Mack, "a prevailing attitude, conscious and unconscious, toward the Earth" as a thing to be owned and used; species arrogance also applies to those who deem their race superior to all others as well as to animal and plant domains.

Spirituality According to Lee Irwin, "that connectedness to core values and deep beliefs."

Survivance In Vizenor, a term describing survival and endurance in a comic mode.

Syncretic A recombination or re-formation of disparate Native and non-Native cultural forms; Nanapush, in Louise Erdrich's novels, is able to recombine immigrant and Native social values to meet the needs of those around him.

Terminal creeds In Vizenor, fixed religious, cultural, anthropological, scientific, and government constructions of human society which result in misunderstanding, misappropriation, violence, and death; philosophies and policies that terminated Native ways of life.

Totalization The desire for complete understanding and total control.

Wa-bano In Louise Erdrich's novels, the term applies to evil shamanism.

Windigo An Ojibwa person with a psychic disorder who projects her own maladies onto others and then proceeds to vindicate herself through various forms of violence.

Index

Native Christian narrative
  discourse, 308
Navaho Symbols of Healing, 56
Nightland, 4, 135
Nussbaum, Martha C., 32, 37–38

O

"Of Cannibals," 18
online resources, 298–299
ontogenetic crippling, 123, 308
orality, 4
original trauma, 121, 308
Ortega y Gassett, Jose, 31
Ortiz, Simon J., 6, 196–197, 220
Other Destinies, 253
Owens, Louis, 4, 41, 71, 134–151,
  253, 269

P

Peyer, Bernd D., 46–47
place, cultural approach to, 220
Pokagon, Simon, 39
postcolonial, 308
posterity, 225–231
Postindian Conversations, 255
postmodern, 308
Postmodern Explained, The, 54
Power, 134
power of words theme, 203–212
psycho/social approach to
  bloodlines, 227–231

R

reconciliation, 244–250
reductionism, biomedical,
  120, 305
reductive thought, 308
representation, 277, 282, 308
Reservation Blues, 151, 157–164,
  221
Revard, Carter, 208–210
Riley, Patricia, 290
ritual language, 308

Roemer, Kenneth M., 53, 64–65
Rose, Wendy, 244

S

sacred texts, 308
salvation, 217
Sands, Kathleen M., 104
Scapegoat, The, 264
sexual expression, 240–244
Shakespeare, William, 18
Sharpest Sight, The, 135, 137–142
Shepard, Paul, 123–124
signified, 308
signifier, 309
signs, 309
Silko, Leslie Marmon, 71–80, 239,
  285–286
simulations, 32, 309
*Singing Spirit: Early Short
  Stories by North American
  Indians*, 46
Skins, 222
Smith, Theresa S., 219
Smoke Signals, 151, 153–157
Solar Storms, 130–134, 215
Soul of the Indian, The, 49
sovereignty, 277, 286, 309
species arrogance, 122–123, 309
spirituality, 309
Steele, Melli, 255
Steinbeck, John, 136–137
Stiffarm, Lenore A., 21
storytelling theme, 203–212
Sundown, 40
Surrounded, The, 41
survivance, 91, 309
Swann, Brian, 6, 207
symbols, 62–63
syncretic, 309

T

Tales of Burning Love, 101,
  108–109, 113–114, 226
Tempest, The, 18

Continuum Publishing is committed to preserving ancient forests and natural resources. We have elected to print this title on 30% postconsumer waste recycled paper. As a result, this book has saved:

7 trees

330 lbs of solid waste

2,997 gallons of water

5 kw hours of electricity

649 lbs of air pollution

Continuum is a member of Green Press Initiative, a nonprofit program dedicated to supporting publishers in their efforts to reduce their use of fiber obtained from endangered forests. For more information, go to www.greenpressinitiative.org.